Finding Success the First Year

A Survivor's Guide for New Teachers

Matthew Johnson

ROWMAN & LITTLEFIELD EDUCATON
A division of
ROWMAN & LITTLEFIELD PUBLISHERS, INC.
Lanham • New York • Toronto • Plymouth, UK

Published by Rowman & Littlefield Education
A division of Rowman & Littlefield Publishers, Inc.
A wholly owned subsidiary of The Rowman & Littlefield Publishing Group, Inc.
4501 Forbes Boulevard, Suite 200, Lanham, Maryland 20706
http://www.rowmaneducation.com

Estover Road, Plymouth PL6 7PY, United Kingdom

British Library Cataloguing in Publication Information Available

Library of Congress Cataloging-in-Publication Data
Johnson, Matthew, 1983–
  Finding success the first year : a survivor's guide for new teachers / Matthew Johnson.
     p. cm.
  ISBN 978-1-60709-732-7 (cloth : alk. paper) — ISBN 978-1-60709-733-4 (pbk. : alk. paper) — ISBN 978-1-60709-734-1 (electronic)
  1. First year teachers—Professional relationships. 2. First year teachers—In-service training. 3. Mentoring in education. 4. Teachers—Training of. I. Title.
  LB2844.1.N4J58 2010
  371.1—dc22   2010017970

Printed in the United States of America

CONTENTS

Introduction   I

UNIT I
THE SECRET WEAPONS   5

    CHAPTER I Enthusiasm   7

    CHAPTER 2 Setting the Right Tone   15

    CHAPTER 3 Respect   21

    CHAPTER 4 The Power of Positivity   29

UNIT 2
WHO ARE YOUR STUDENTS?   35

    CHAPTER 5 Teaching Common Sense   37

    CHAPTER 6 Students Are Fragile   43

    CHAPTER 7 Teaching Is a Game of Inches   48

UNIT 3
RELATING TO YOUR STUDENTS   55

    CHAPTER 8 Keeping Lessons Clear   57

    CHAPTER 9 How to Get the Most from Your Students   64

CONTENTS

CHAPTER 10 Student Accountability, or You Can Lead
a Horse to Water . . .   72

CHAPTER 11 How to Design a Foolproof Lesson   78

CHAPTER 12 How to Deliver a Foolproof Lesson   87

UNIT 4
MANAGING YOUR STUDENTS   95

CHAPTER 13 Idle Threats and Consequence Scales   97

CHAPTER 14 Using Your Voice and Body as
Teaching Tools   102

CHAPTER 15 How to Respond to Unwanted Behavior   107

CHAPTER 16 Trouble Is Complex   114

UNIT 5
BUILDING YOUR CLASSROOM FOUNDATION   121

CHAPTER 17 Setting the Ground Rules   123

CHAPTER 18 Physically Setting Up Your Classroom   133

CHAPTER 19 Classroom Rituals   141

UNIT 6
THE TOOLS OF THE TRADE   147

CHAPTER 20 Lectures   149

CHAPTER 21 Discussions   154

CHAPTER 22 Group Work   160

UNIT 7
CHEAT SHEETS   165

CHAPTER 23 How to Respond to a Question You
Don't Have an Answer For   167

CHAPTER 24 A Student Cheats   173

CHAPTER 25 When Bad Things Happen in
Good Classrooms 179

CHAPTER 26 Pressing the Reset Button on
the Classroom 187

UNIT 8
THE TASKS 193

CHAPTER 27 Dealing with Parents 195

CHAPTER 28 Teaching to Everyone 203

UNIT 9
THE TRAPS 211

CHAPTER 29 Just Say No: The Pitches 213

CHAPTER 30 The Urge to Be Groovy 217

CHAPTER 31 Friendly Fire 221

UNIT 10
THE TRICKS 227

CHAPTER 32 The Advantages of Being a New Teacher 229

CHAPTER 33 The Role of Emotion in the Classroom 235

CHAPTER 34 The Use of Technology 241

CHAPTER 35 Becoming an Organizational Champion 251

A Final Word 257

About the Author 259

INTRODUCTION

I have never experienced anything as terrifying as trading in the comfortable world of college for the highly uncomfortable position of standing alone every day in front of hundreds of adolescent eyes. Even after years in education classes, a semester of student teaching, countless hours of absorbing as much information as possible from senior teachers, and furiously reading every teaching book I could find, I still felt woefully underprepared for leading my own classroom.

And I was hardly alone. Every year around August a common refrain of new teachers from around the country strikes up as the school year rapidly approaches: "What do you do when . . . ?" "How am I supposed to . . . ?" "I wish I'd known . . ." Across grade, subject, and district lines, new teachers in every sort of situation generally repeat these same phrases over and over because they feel at least a little underinformed, ill-equipped, or (as a fellow new teacher from my education school cohort said) "like [they were] thrown into the deep end of a pool and asked to find the surface—and then got an elephant thrown on top just to make it more interesting." And they are desperate for any answers that can get them out of the pool.

That is where this book was born. This book came from that deep-down desire for answers that is so voracious during those first few months. It came from a sense that, although there are lots of good answers around, there could and should be even more. It came from a simple idea, based on frustration concerning the other materials available, of taking notes on all the good and the bad, successes and failures, and questions and answers that arise during a first year, and then seeing what happens.

What happened is that now those notes of a first year have evolved into a book full of answers to the I-wish-I-had-knowns, what-do-I-do-whens, and other questions that new teachers usually have. Helping it deliver these answers is the fact that, unlike most other works, it comes from a unique position that is far closer to the average new teacher. Instead of being written by someone fifteen, twenty, or twenty-five years removed from their first year, this book comes from a new teacher and is based on an actual first year of teaching and everything that comes with it. The result is something that takes on the questions and concerns of the first year of teaching in a different way.

Now a moment should be taken here to make it clear that this is not meant as a condemnation or rejection of the wisdom and insight of those who've been in the teaching profession for a long time. Veteran teachers contain a wealth of valuable information that is essential for properly training new teachers, and if not for several talented mentors this book wouldn't even exist. But that amazing wisdom that so many veteran teachers have does come at a price; as teachers grow in their experience and knowledge of the classroom, they begin to lose their understanding of what life was like when they were new to the classroom. Slowly the shifting sands of time work upon their minds and sweep away or alter many of the questions and concerns that were so pressing at one point. And soon, before they know it, they are further away from new teachers than they may even realize.

This distance opens up room and a need for another voice—that of the new teacher—in the training of new teachers. This "new" voice is not meant to replace veteran voices, but instead to work in tandem with them and fill in the perspective gaps created by time. And that is exactly what this book does.

The first of these gaps that this book takes on is all the questions that new teachers regularly have and regularly don't get satisfactory answers to. These are questions like "How do I get the students to respect me?" "How can I make sure what I'm saying is clear to students?" and "What do I do if I don't know the answer to a student's question?" Many new teachers, even those with great training and mentors, don't receive the answers they are looking for to questions like this because coming up with such answers can be deceptively hard for experienced teachers. A lot of veterans haven't had major concerns over getting respect or how to answer a question for a very long time, and so responses concerning them don't come easily to their tongues.

That is not the case with this book, where discussions of these nagging questions were the easiest parts to write because they were exactly what I was concerned with as I wrote it. That is also why this book has entire chapters on rarely mentioned things like "what happens if a lesson gets overly groovy" or "how to use body language effectively."

Beyond taking on answers to normally unaddressed questions, this book also plays the role of a tester and translator for suggestions regularly given to new teachers by filtering them through the experiences of a real teacher in a real classroom. By testing common advice concerning things like classroom management, lesson planning, and organization in an actual first-year classroom environment, the bad advice is exposed and eliminated, dated advice is given an upgrade, and good advice is presented in a way that is most useful for the new teacher.

This book also goes beyond the suggestions it prescribes and explains the whys and hows for each point made. Far too often when new teachers look for advice they receive only overly simplified suggestions without a clear explanation of the logic behind them. ("That is great that I should be student-centered, but how do you do that, why is that important, and what does that even mean?") For anyone who has encountered this (and also for the lucky ones who haven't), this book strives to make the reasons for everything as clear as the suggestions themselves. This means instead of just telling teachers to establish a set of rituals, use a lot of group work, or incorporate movement, it explains why those things are important and exactly how they can be implemented. It also warns of the potential pitfalls and missteps that new teachers regularly take when trying to use such suggestions in their classroom.

In terms of organization, this book has three acts. The first act, which is composed of the first four units, is meant to provide a philosophical foundation for teaching. Included in it are subjects like how to become an authority figure, build a positive classroom environment, set the right tone, teach common sense to the students, get students interested and accountable in their own learning, and approach and execute behavior management. Within these chapters there are a lot of practical suggestions and specific ideas, but the main goal is to help new teachers establish a comfortable base of thinking to teach from.

The next act, covered over the next three units, is all about the nitty-gritty details. This includes topics like what a good computer or homework policy is, how exactly to structure a discussion or lecture (and when to use each), options for redirecting a class that is going astray, what kind of rituals work, and how to physically set up a classroom for success. As with the first act, there is still a lot of discussion of the ideas behind these policies, but this section's focus is on giving practical, on-the-ground suggestions that are ready for direct insertion into your classroom.

The final part of the book, the three units on tasks, traps, and tricks, is all about letting the reader in on the little time-savers that experienced teachers generally know. Included are crafty veteran tricks, warnings of possible hazards that often lurk around the classroom, and tips for making the necessary tasks of a teacher go as smoothly and quickly as possible.

So come along and explore the life of a new teacher with someone who has just lived it. Learn from my failures so you don't repeat them, find out what worked so you can make it work too, follow the map I outline to avoid common missteps, pick up whatever tips you can to claw back valuable seconds of your time, and discover the challenges and delights waiting for you inside those classroom doors!

THE SECRET WEAPONS

If you are heading into your first year, then there are likely a lot of people giving you a lot of advice right now. And though you probably want to hang on to most of that advice, if you are honest you know that the vast majority will slip through your short-term memory long before it finds a place in your mind. Sadly, that is the nature of our brains: they have a limited ability to soak up advice and store it in the working memory. These limitations mean that our brains have to be picky and aren't bashful about tossing away even good suggestions if there just isn't room for them.

When it comes to the subject matter discussed in this unit, it is very important that you tenaciously fight with your mind to retain it. This is not to say that the advice in the rest of the book is forgettable, but the topics discussed in the first four chapters are hands-down the most important things you can do as a new teacher to ensure success. They are the secret weapons that, if followed, will provide a steady foundation that is hard to fall off of. So whether you are reading this in the store or for a class, stay tuned and pay close attention to the next four chapters. Because these secret weapons are often the doormen standing between a tough but great first year and one filled with a lot of unnecessary pain.

CHAPTER ONE
ENTHUSIASM

P ut yourself in the position of a school administrator. You are talking
to a colleague about a new teacher you are really excited about. You
begin by saying, "I have a wonderful, young, and _____
new teacher." What word fits in the blank—*smart? capable? insightful? talented?* All of these words would certainly fit, but they probably aren't the
words that would roll off the tongue if the administrator were truly excited
about the new teacher. Instead, the word that most administrators (as well
as most other teachers, parents, and students) would use to fill in the blank
would probably be *enthusiastic.*

The reason *enthusiastic* fits so comfortably in that spot is that for young
teachers enthusiasm is widely considered to be the greatest asset they bring
to the table. To see this belief in action you have to go no further than the
popular representation of teachers in movies. Think about the major "teacher
movies" of recent memory: *Dead Poets Society, Dangerous Minds, Freedom
Writers.* The common thread that links all of these movies is that they
revolve around relatively young teachers whose unbridled enthusiasm over-
comes the prejudices, obstacles, and narrow minds surrounding them. These
teachers generally begin with limited knowledge and even fewer skills (except
Robin Williams in *Dead Poets*, though even he has weak spots), but their
enthusiasm is powerful enough to help them transcend their limitations.

And though enthusiasm on your part may not be enough to single-
handedly inspire covert late-night poetry sessions or the turnaround of an
entire inner-city school, this is one of the few areas where the Hollywood
portrayal of teachers is actually somewhat accurate. No trait is more essential
to new teacher success than enthusiasm, and it is hard to have much luck

without it. So with that in mind, let's take a closer look at what enthusiasm is, how it aids teaching, and how you can get more of it.

How Enthusiasm Helps

Enthusiasm is helpful all over the classroom, but here are a few areas where it can be especially beneficial.

Enthusiasm Is the Ultimate Antidote for Mistakes

Being a new teacher often ranks among the most humbling experiences of life. What makes it so humbling is that you will make mistakes—constant and very public mistakes. But if those mistakes are made with great enthusiasm, then the students, administration, and parents who witness them all become far more likely to forgive and forget. This could be because those observers recognize that even though you messed up, your approach was spot on—and they respect you for that.

Enthusiasm Demands Attention and Gives Your Words Weight

My college had two very different Shakespeare professors. The first professor was a truly talented scholar with incredible insights. He delivered the material in a fairly standard manner, but his class was generally considered to be both entertaining and eye-opening. The second professor was, for lack of a better term, a rock star, and he got the student body energized about Shakespeare in a way that hardly seemed possible.

In many ways this second professor was an unlikely choice for a superstar professor; he had an unusually long face, abnormally large hands, and a very odd delivery, and he was an eccentric in nearly every sense of the word. Also, he was not any more academic or insightful than many other professors at the school, including the other Shakespeare professor (in fact, many snobby English students went so far as to say he was less academic). But despite these limitations this professor was easily the most popular instructor on the entire campus.

So what was the reason for this professor's success? How was this oddball able to transform indifferent undergrads into Shakespeare addicts? The answer is a simple one: this man passionately loved his subject. It didn't matter whether he talked about *Macbeth*, *Hamlet*, or *Midsummer Night's Dream*, this professor delivered every lecture with the giddy excitement of someone presenting for the first time. Every time he talked about *The Tempest*, the hijinks of Stephano and Trinculo made him roar with laughter and the final soliloquy of Prospero brought him to the edge of tears. And this enthusiasm led to packed lecture halls, standing-room-only office hours, and a guaranteed invitation to speak at all major campus events.

Though gaining this level of affection and admiration cannot be accomplished by enthusiasm alone, there is no doubt that the professor's success was built on his passion and energy. It was these attributes that grabbed his students' attention and opened them up to his inspiration. And if you conduct your class with enough enthusiasm you will likely see some of the same positives, because in the end there is just something spellbinding, irresistible, and powerful about someone who loves and lives what he or she talks about (and if ever there was a group waiting to get swept up in such excitement, it is students).

Enthusiasm Is a Sign of Great Things to Come

One reason that enthusiasm is so highly coveted in new teachers is that they are all works in progress. Even if you are the most wildly talented new teacher with perfect instincts for conducting a classroom, you still will have much to learn before you reach your full potential. The message enthusiasm gives to administrators, parents, fellow teachers, and even students is that while you are imperfect now, you have the will and the energy to learn the lessons needed to become a great teacher. And that makes you seem like a sure bet.

What Enthusiasm Is

It isn't hard to recognize enthusiasm when you see it. But when it comes to defining enthusiasm, the task grows a bit more difficult. This is because enthusiasm can wear a thousand different faces. In one situation it can take the form of nervous energy and boisterous fast talking, and in another it can come out as intense quietness and unbreakable focus (even from the same person).

With so many manifestations, it is virtually impossible to nail down what enthusiasm looks like on the surface, but that doesn't mean that it defies explanation (for we can recognize it, and we must be looking for something). To find this elusive definition, it is important to focus on what enthusiasm comprises, as opposed to what behaviors come from it. Although the appearance varies wildly, the traits associated with enthusiasm are remarkably consistent. And if you want both staff and students to view you as enthusiastic, you need to learn what those traits are and what you can do to develop and demonstrate them. To help you with this process, here are the three most common enthusiasm traits and how you can cultivate them.

Enthusiasm Trait 1: Passion

Passion is like love to the third power. It is like all of the strongest parts of love boiled down into a reduction that sticks to your bones. In this world, there are some bubbly people who naturally produce this type of passion on a regular basis, and then there are the rest of us who are truly jealous of them. If you are someone who falls in the second category, fear not! There are ways to amplify, channel, and even develop passion, as odd as that sounds. And if you work on it enough it is possible to get to a point where you will be indistinguishable from the naturals.

Familiarity Breeds Passion

At first this statement may not look quite right. Passion isn't something normally associated with familiarity; more often it is used to describe something that is fresh, new, and exciting. It is a word that lends itself more easily to a budding relationship with hormones ablaze than a thirty-year marriage. But despite that, there are few things that have the ability to fill a teacher with passion faster than familiarity.

What makes familiarity such a potent catalyst for passion is the same thing that makes a die-hard sports fan yell even louder after fifty years of watching his or her team. It is the fact that true love comes from knowing something inside and out. Though finding out about something new is exciting, it is only when you dig down, explore the complexity, and develop a history with something that you can develop the type of passion exhibited by both college football fans and the most successful teachers.

In order to build your passion, make sure to carve out time to really get to know your subject (if you don't already). It doesn't matter if you teach English, math, or art, try your best to learn every little detail there is to know about your subject, and don't be afraid to dive in head first. So go to conferences, read books, see plays if you love English, go to science exhibitions if you love science, and make sure your subject is a regular part of your life. If you already do this, just keep feeding it, because true love requires constant meals to continue to burn as brightly.

Then once you have this passion, all you have to do is show up in the classroom. There is no need to advertise or otherwise draw attention to your love, for if you truly love your subject your passion will speak for itself. It will come out through how you speak and act, and it will be as clear as day to all those around you. And that will help your teaching in a multitude of ways.

Do What You Love

One of the most beautiful parts of teaching is that teachers have a lot more autonomy than most professionals. Even in the most scripted of districts, there is still a lot of room for teachers to put their own stamp and style upon what happens in class. With that autonomy in mind, try not only learning to love what you teach, but also slipping things you already love into your class.

When doing this, don't just focus on subject matter, either (though definitely try to slide subject matter you like into class, too). You can infuse things you are passionate about through delivery (for example, if you love movies, comedy, or bingo, use them in how you present material), activity choices (if you love rockets, have your students practice geometry with rocket design), and assessments (if *The Onion* is your favorite newspaper, have your final assessment of a chapter about the American Revolution be a satirical newspaper). Also, don't be afraid to go to your department chair with well-thought-out ideas for how to change the curriculum to match your interests. Many chairs will actually be quite open to this and commend you on your initiative.

Enthusiasm Trait 2: Hard Work

Because enthusiastic people care, they generally can't help but work hard. And though learning how to work hard may not seem like a topic that warrants discussion (OK, I just work hard), understanding how to effectively work hard is actually one of the most important skills a new teacher can learn. This is because burnout, a common result of working too hard, is possibly the number one hazard facing new teachers in the classroom. And anyone who has gone through a first year of teaching can definitely understand why. The work of a new teacher never stops, and at times it seems like there aren't enough minutes in the week to accomplish what you are asked to do in a day. And if that isn't enough, to do all of your tasks well takes even more work.

But for a new teacher it is essential that all the work be done and done well. Cutting corners and doing minimal work doesn't paint you as enthusiastic or a good teacher in the eyes of administration or your students, and that can cause problems with everything from gaining student respect to getting rehired. So what are you supposed to do in the face of such a predicament?

The first year has too much work to begin with, doing it right is important and takes even more work, and at the same time you need to watch out for working too hard because it may burn you out. If this feels like a fool's errand, have no fear. Though the first year is always going to be busy and require a dash of sleep deprivation from time to time, there are some tricks to alleviate your load and make it manageable, so you can stay sane and not burn out.

Work Smarter, Not Harder

If there are any other *Ducktales* fans out there, they will recognize this phrase as Scrooge McDuck's secret to success. Nearly once an episode he would repeat this mantra to those around him: "Work smarter, not harder." And though it is rarely phrased exactly in those terms, Scrooge isn't the only one pushing this advice. This simple mantra is commonly given by teaching veterans, and it can be an absolute lifesaver for new teachers.

The reason this recommendation is so popular and so useful is that once you spend more than a few weeks in the classroom, it becomes clear that the life of a teacher generally includes more work than time. With so much work required of them, most teachers constantly need to make some tough decisions on which tasks deserve time and which just need to be done. If (and more likely when) you find yourself in a position like this, it is smart to prioritize work and figure out what needs to be done well, what you would like done well, what just needs to be done, and (dare I say) what you can get away with not doing. With such tough choices likely looming for you, here are some suggestions for the areas where hard work is generally a smart investment with high returns and the areas where it is often more trouble than it's worth:

Areas where it's worth it:

- Doing something new and different every once in a while. Even the most dynamic lessons can get stale if they are repeated over and over again. Every few weeks it is worth sinking in a little extra time to throw the class a curveball and shake things up.

- Grading thoroughly from time to time. This will be discussed more in a later chapter, but grading is in many ways as personalized as it gets in school. Most of the time you are addressing the students as a group, but while you grade you are one-on-one with them. By grading thoroughly from time to time, you can open up a personal dialogue with the students that would be difficult to do otherwise.

- Getting to know your students (through talking with them and going to events). This one is also covered later, but when you get to know your students, a humanizing effect happens that is remarkable and well worth the time investment.

Areas where it might not be worth it:

- Grading every assignment. Though grading is a good way to have a personalized dialogue, if you try to thoroughly grade every element of every assignment you will likely exhaust yourself. There is nothing wrong with occasionally just checking in homework (or even not checking it at times), as long as you look at it closely on a frequent enough basis to keep your students honest.

- Doing something new and exciting every day. If you try to do something new and different every day, you will likely drain your inspiration dry. Every lesson doesn't need to blow the students' minds to be effective.

- Creating overly complex assignments. When you create assignments, it is important to keep in mind how much work the assignment will make for you. This is not to say that assignment design should be solely based on the work it creates for you, but don't forget about it, either. If you can create an assignment that accomplishes the same goals, but takes you three minutes less per student to grade, those three minutes will turn into hours of your life back.

Take Breaks

In a world where the work never ends, the key to completing everything as efficiently as possible is actually to step away from it from time to time. As a new teacher, you will find that it is often hard to turn away from the mountain of work hanging over your head, but it is actually well worth the time investment (or should it be divestment?).

Stepping away on a regular basis is so important, because without a break it is only natural to begin feeling uninspired, burned out, or unenthusiastic. These feelings, beyond being a drag, actually impede the speed and quality of your work, and if you aren't careful they can easily lead to more "wasted time" than if you just took a break in the first place. With this in mind, try scheduling a regular break into your schedule, no matter what is going on at school or in your life. Take Saturdays off, watch *Monday Night Football,* play basketball on Thursday nights, or just curl up with a good book on Sunday evenings. You and your students will be happy you did.

Enthusiasm Trait 3: An Urge to Innovate

When people get enthusiastic about something, they rarely love it passively; instead, they usually develop a relentless urge to do something new with it. This can best be seen in cooks and musicians, who are often notorious for never making a dish or playing a song the same way twice if they can help it—but it is also true for teachers. The most enthusiastic teachers constantly experiment, create, and generally consider their classrooms to be laboratories where more information is to be found than given. And if you want to be counted among them, you have to make a conscious effort to always strive for something new, too. These are some areas it can be fun and fruitful to experiment in:

- How you start class

- How you present the information

- How you assess student knowledge

- How you grade

- How you organize your classroom

No matter what types of experiments you try, the important thing is to do them with joy and giddy excitement. If you do, all of your ventures will likely stand as positive testaments to your enthusiastic nature, regardless of how successful they actually are.

Exit Slip

Enthusiasm is one of the most powerful forces on the planet. It wins hearts, captivates attention, and masks mistakes. It can also make your first year better than you ever thought possible. So regardless of the sometimes crushing workload and the inevitable negatives that pop up around you, fight hard to keep your fire burning bright and your classroom will likely follow suit.

SETTING THE RIGHT TONE

W hether a teacher is known as the tough teacher, the funny teacher, or the teacher who is easy to get off track, almost every teacher in school has a reputation with the students. The only teachers exempt from this are the new teachers, who usually walk in on the first day as a blank slate. They have no reputation, history, or rumors circulating about them, and the students have no idea whether to classify them as tough, easy, mean, nice, interesting, or dull.

Generally this lack of knowledge leads to a desperate curiosity in students for any information about these mysterious new teachers. So they watch new teachers very closely at the beginning of the year for any information that can help categorize them. After a few weeks, once enough information has been mined, the reputations of the new teachers begin to solidify, and before they've even settled in they have a reputation like everyone else.

The brief window to craft a reputation is important, because once students put you in a category it can be very hard to rebrand yourself. This tenacity of reputations within schools can be a blessing or a curse, depending on the type of reputation you gain. If you get a reputation for being a pushover, having no control of the class, or just generally not being a good teacher, this reputation could represent a major setback and will take a lot of extra work to repair (see chapter 26, "Pressing the Reset Button on the Classroom"). But, on the other hand, if you get a reputation for being interesting, firm, engaging, or an overall good teacher, you are already one very large step closer to having a successful first year.

With such stakes early, it is easy to get intimidated or nervous, but don't worry too much. Believe it or not, students generally want to like and respect the new teacher, and if you set the right tone early on they will likely embrace you. To get started, here are some tips for making sure that the tone you set is the right one.

Discuss the Guidelines

For most teachers, going over the classroom guidelines at the beginning of the year is a short, mandatory activity that doesn't take much thought. Generally teachers just get in front of the class, read their rules right off the syllabus, ask if there are any questions, and move on to more interesting activities. And for some this approach definitely works. But for new teachers, whose first impression with the students often comes as they provide the guidelines, a great opportunity for setting the tone is missed if they treat them as a minor administrative task. If, instead of rushing through, a new teacher takes time to examine and discuss each rule with the class, he or she can send some powerful messages about behavioral and performance expectations. This is commonly done in one of two ways, though as long you have a dialogue many different structures could work.

Behavior Contracts

The authoritative approach (though with a small bite of freedom) of behavior contracts means they are probably more applicable to middle-school students, though with the right tweaking they could certainly work for those in high school as well. The idea behind behavior contracts is that instead of coming in on the first day with a set of predetermined rules, you brainstorm with the students about what the rules should be. Once common rules are established, you make behavior contracts for the students (you can have one for the teacher as well) that outline the behavior expectations for the classroom.

Behavior contracts carry two significant advantages over just telling students what the rules are. First, they make the students feel involved in their learning process from the first moments of class. Even if you end up leading the conversation and nudging them toward the rules you want (though you would be amazed at how often the students come up with the same rules you desired), the students at least feel like their voices were heard. The second advantage is that by talking through each rule, students get a lot more insight into why the rules are necessary, and this could lead to significantly more willingness to follow them.

"What Do I Mean?"

One teacher in my school begins every year by telling students that the one principle he uses to govern his classroom is "No one can hurt anyone else in the room." He then asks the class what he means, and they begin what often becomes a whole-class conversation about the many ways people can be hurt (such as out-of-turn talking, put-downs, and even extending into how the teacher can be hurt by late work). After this he goes home and types up a sheet of policies based on the discussion, and with a few little alterations these become the mutually created classroom rules for both teacher and students.

This approach has similar advantages to the behavior contracts (the students feel listened to and see the logic behind the rules), but it is a more subtle method of discussion that plays well with older students. It also has the added advantage of taking a few logical steps, which gives a clear message to students that your class will be one of thinking deeply about the topics, not just regurgitating information.

Stand Tall When They Test You

Generally teachers give their major exams to students at the end of the year, but as a new teacher you will likely get your biggest tests from students very early. This is because no matter what messages you've sent and what tone you've established, the students will still need to test them for authenticity. So don't be surprised or overly offended when students, regardless of what you've told them or what threats you've made, try to take advantage of you early in the year. They are just investigating their limits, and if your responses to these common tests send clear messages, this behavior should drop off as rapidly as it arose.

They Will Test Your Rules and Policies

Students know that just because a teacher establishes rules, it doesn't mean that he or she will enforce them. They also generally learn through the grapevine which rules they can bend or break in an established teacher's class. But in your class they will have no idea, so they will probably assume that they can break all of your rules until you prove otherwise.

The way to show students that your rules are firm is simple—be firm with your rules. At the beginning of the year, after you have clearly articulated your policies, you must stay remarkably consistent in how you enforce them. For example, if your late-work policy is that students lose three points if it isn't there at the start of class, follow through on that. Don't only take off two points because the work wasn't very late, or let students talk their way out of it because they were away all weekend skiing. During the year there will be lots of times when leniency is a good policy, but the beginning of school isn't one of them (unless there is a very, very good reason). Being firm at the start gives you the credibility to be lenient later and still not appear like you are soft on your own rules.

They Will Try to Do Less Work

Similar to testing the limits of rules, students commonly test how a new teacher grades. Often this means they will do a less-than-stellar job on the first few assignments to see how little effort it will take to get the grades they want (so if your first few assignments are not of the quality you expect, don't freak out). Since students use these first few assignments to test the waters, these assignments are perfect spots to give clear messages about your expectations. If you want students to focus on details, be more creative, or generally work harder, grade accordingly on your first few assignments (and include more comments than normal so they can see your logic). You will be amazed by how quickly many of the students adapt to what you want.

They Will Try to Call You on Things

Students sometimes confuse lack of teaching experience with lack of knowledge, and especially at the beginning of the year this can lead to their trying to call out new teachers on information. At times students can be stunningly brash in trying to call out new teachers—I've had students interrupt me and say matter-of-factly, "That isn't right. You're wrong." When faced with having your competence called into question in front of the entire class, it is hard not to blow up at the student and outline exactly how little they know, but losing your cool won't help the situation. Instead, try following these simple steps:

1. If the student questioning you was even slightly rude and out of line, reprimand him or her, not for questioning the teacher, but for the manner in which the student did so.

2. Then lay down the academic law. If you know you were right, try to get a little overly technical in your explanation to show who the expert in the room is. If you know you were wrong (or think you might be wrong), use this as a moment to teach the class that anyone can make mistakes and then find a way to flex your academic muscles (by going in-depth) while correcting yourself.

Establish Yourself as a Pack Leader

Adolescents are definitely pack animals. To see this you have to look no further than the alpha students in your school and notice how far the other students are willing to follow them (sometimes it is truly frightening). With such strong grouping tendencies, it is important to make it clear that in your room you are the pack leader. This is not to say you shouldn't value, respect, or act kindly toward students, but if you don't establish yourself as the leader they will naturally look to someone else to follow, and it is unlikely that the student picked will lead the class as well as you.

One of the best ways to establish your position as a leader is to actively look for misbehavior to correct at the beginning of the year. The best types of behaviors to find are those that probably won't lead to arguments with the students. Look for things like students working on assignments for other classes, sitting with their head down on the desk, or not following the directions. Then once you find these behaviors correct them quietly. Tap the student with his or head down as you walk by, grab the paper from the student working on an assignment from another class and keep walking like nothing happened, and lightly chastise the student not following directions. Every time that you confront the students about these "minor" details and they don't dispute you back, you've done the same thing alphas do in dog packs. By challenging the students and not having them challenge you back, you've once again reminded them of your role as the undisputed leader.

This does not mean that you should go overboard and unnecessarily pick on students. Occasional checks on students send the message you are in charge; constant checks on them send the message that you are bad-mannered and unreasonable (which will undo any credibility you gain). Also, when checking students, try your best to do it in a subtle and nonverbal way. Quiet authority actually demonstrates more power than yelling at students, because it shows you don't need to get loud to get control.

Keep Some Distance

Old teaching doctrine states that teachers shouldn't smile until Thanksgiving (or is it Christmas?). Supposedly, not smiling shows your students that class is serious business and you are the instructor, not their buddy. Though this advice may not be applicable in a lot of situations today, there are some kernels of useful knowledge buried within it. One important lesson that can be taken from this old approach is the importance for new teachers (especially at the beginning of the year) of establishing some distance between themselves and their students. Having this distance reminds the students that you are still an authority, even if you smile every once and while.

Now in this situation, distance does not mean that you should be aloof, cold, or standoffish. There is nothing wrong with being engaged, warm, and caring. All it means is that you acknowledge and accept that you are the one in charge in the situation and you act accordingly. Depending on the situation, there are infinite ways to do this. Here are some common ways to get appropriate distance:

- Not always trying to make them happy or giving them the answer they want

- Knowing more about them than they know about you (a.k.a. withholding some information about yourself)

- Except in very rare situations, trying to remain objective, calm, and possibly even stoic on the outside, even if on the inside you are a hot mess.

Exit Slip

Setting the right tone early can make a huge difference and save you from a certain amount of hardship, but if the tone isn't exactly perfect in the first few weeks don't hang up your dry-erase marker yet. The fact is that the tone of the classroom evolves constantly, and these techniques can be just as effective two, three, or four months into the school year for giving your class the tone you want. This changeable nature of tone also means that even if you did a fantastic job at setting a good tone early on, you need to continue to cultivate it or it can very quickly get out of tune with what you want.

RESPECT

A good friend of mine spends his summers instructing and observing for Teach for America, and after years of working with brand-new teachers, he has come to the conclusion that the key to new teacher success is the level of respect the students have for the teacher. He claims those able to gain student respect early often flourish, and at times it seems like they can do little to derail the class. On the other side, teachers who lose student respect soon find it hard to do anything right in the eyes of the students.

Whether or not you agree with the idea that student respect is the strongest determinant of how a teacher will do, there is no doubt that it is a heavy weight on the scale of classroom success. When students have respect for a teacher, they often pay closer attention, are more willing to follow the teacher's advice, and become inclined to forgive even significant errors (because they know no one is perfect). But when students lack this respect, they often behave with little respect, dismiss what the teacher says more easily, and may begin looking to even the smallest errors as proof that the teacher is unqualified and their disrespect is justified.

To make sure you end up with students' respect, this chapter provides answers for how to build student respect in your classroom and how to do it fast.

Don't Waste Their Time

In general, there are few things human beings loathe more than having even a little of their time wasted. This is the reason that seemingly insignificant things, such as waiting for your computer to load or being put on hold by the phone company, tend to produce such disproportionately large amounts of anger and frustration. This is also one area where teachers and students can agree—because students don't like having their time wasted any more than anyone else does.

This human aversion to wasted time also means that teachers must be certain that their students don't feel like their time is being thrown away. And though this task seems simple and obvious (all right, I just won't waste their time), it is actually surprisingly difficult. To understand how difficult it is, all you have to do is think of the number of classes you've been in during your life that you would categorize as "a waste of time." None of these teachers probably saw their course as a waste of time, and they certainly didn't go into school each day with the goal of squandering an hour of your life, but in the end their classes came across as worthless and you probably came out with little respect for them.

To ensure you don't fall into the "waste of time" category, there are a few simple steps you can take.

Have a Reason That You Can Articulate for Everything

"Why?" is the most frequent question a new teacher is likely to hear, in large part because there are so many reasons to ask it. Students may ask why because they are testing the teacher, being obstinate, don't understand, need clarification, or are just plain curious. Whatever the reason, having an answer for this inevitable question generally benefits your teaching in several ways. First, through the process of coming up with an answer you will double-check your lesson for parts that have a vague or weak purpose, or no purpose at all. Furthermore, once you know the reasons, you will always be able to give students an authoritative reason for why their time isn't being wasted.

When figuring out the purpose for the things you do in class, make sure you also look deeper than just the information presented. It is important to look at why you present it the way you do (for example, why you have students write something on the board or work in groups), why the students' work helps them understand and retain information, and why the time allotment makes sense. By doing this you not only make sure everything has a reason, you also know that you are ready for any random "why?" the students can cook up.

Be the Expert (Even If You Aren't)

Students expect their teachers to be experts. They expect them to know more about their subject matter than they could even dream of. And though they won't admit it (and likely don't even know it), most students also feel that if they have to sit quietly in uncomfortable chairs and have even their most basic needs controlled by someone else, then they may as well be benefiting from the teacher's expertise.

With such high expectations there are few ways to rouse students' wrath and lose their respect faster than coming across as anything but an expert. If students view you as underqualified—or worse, incompetent—they will likely take out their frustration about being cooped up and getting little in return upon you. To ensure this doesn't happen, it is very important to come across as an expert at all times—especially if you are teaching something that you don't know very well. Here are some ways to do that.

Talk Like You Know It

No matter how well you know the subject, talk like you are an expert. This means talking with certainty, authority, and confidence. And remember, no matter what subject you are teaching, the odds are that you know it better than the students, which does make you the expert in the room.

Flex Your Academic Muscles Occasionally

At times during the year it is a good policy to show off your knowledge and enthusiasm a little bit. You have likely spent a lot of money on an education—and here is a spot where you can put it to good use! Ways to do this include throwing out random bits of information from time to time, occasionally going a bit too in-depth on an explanation or lesson, and going on intermittent tangents concerning your subject. Generally you want these occurrences to be rare enough that students don't see you as a rambler, but common enough that they notice the trend (generally around once every couple of weeks).

Don't Admit to Being New to the Subject or to Having Just Read the Subject Matter

Sometimes new teachers can be tempted to let students know they are new to a topic covered in class in order to relate to or connect with the students. Unfortunately, this approach rarely seems to work as scripted for teachers who use it. Instead, it can very easily lead to students feeling that they are learning from someone only one step ahead of them, and that isn't going to garner much respect.

Admitting Occasional Mistakes Is All Right

Even experts make mistakes, so admitting you made a mistake or still have more to learn (but not that you are new to a subject) is all right on rare occasions. But when doing this, it is very important that you maintain your status of being an expert. That means you must keep up your expert demeanor (don't lose your cool because you messed up) and make it clear that messing up doesn't mean you don't know your stuff. Also try to keep this to rare occasions, because to err occasionally is human, but to err consistently is sloppy.

Present Authority (Even If You Don't Feel Like It)

There are a multitude of reasons that presenting authority can be tough for new teachers: For our whole lives we've sat in the class and taken orders, not given them; it is the first time many of us have occupied the role of an authority figure (or been called Mr. or Ms.); and most of us are also firmly aware of how little we really know and how little power we actually have. On top of that, we may be reminded on a near-daily basis by both staff and students that we look a lot more like a student than a teacher. Despite all of these reasons (and also because of them), it is essential for new teachers to rise above these obstacles and become an authority if they want to have a chance to win the students' respect.

The way to become an authority figure when you aren't sure you believe it yourself is to channel your inner actor and treat it like a role that you have to play. Here are some character notes on how the authoritative teacher behaves.

They Give Respect

Not all authorities give respect. In fact, most authorities probably don't. As an authority, you may easily fall into the trap of not respecting those below you because you occupy a realm above them. But when authorities don't give respect, they often lose some of the power that comes with their position. To see examples of this, think about what happens to common authority figures when they act with disrespect: when police act with disrespect, the people they deal with often grow bolder and more combative; when politicians don't show respect, people rail against them in any media available; and when bosses don't respect their employees, the employees usually do less for them.

The reason that giving respect is so important to receiving authority is that authority is not a divine right. Even though authorities have power over people, that power is actually given by the people themselves. If this power is misused, people often can't help but begin to slowly take it back in small pieces. And nowhere is this truer than with students.

They Are Consistent

One of the traits that people generally look for in authority figures is consistency. If someone is going to lead any number of people, those people need to know that their leader has a clear plan, and consistency is the best way to show that. As a young teacher, though, you may find displaying this type of consistency difficult, because in some ways you don't have a clear plan. Your style and opinions are still forming, and if this doesn't make it tough enough, few situations in class are ever the same. Each seems to come with its own particular twists, which requires a slightly different response than all other situations before or after it.

What this combination of evolving style and forced improvisation means is that no new teacher is going to be 100 percent consistent. But it is very important that you strive for as much consistency as possible. The way to do that is to focus on staying consistent with as many little things as you can, so the moments of inconsistency don't seem so glaring. If you have established a ritual of starting class with correcting homework or you have told the class that all homework not in at the start of class is late, then you should follow those patterns as closely as you can. If it becomes clear that one of your policies or approaches isn't working, you should even be consistent about how you handle the change. This means that instead of changing on the fly you should announce the change to the class, for the class will probably still see you as consistent if your modifications to the class are well-thought-out and follow some sort of pattern, too.

They Are Comfortable with the Role

For a lot of new teachers, being an authority figure is not always comfortable. Whether it is administering punishment or telling students how they should change, some elements of the role just don't feel right. If you are like this, please know that you are not alone. For the first six months of my teaching, I was incapable of punishing students without instantly apologizing for getting upset (even when it was well deserved). But also know that being an authority figure is all right. When you punish students, tell them what to do, or otherwise exercise power over them, you are doing it as a service for them, not as a power trip for you.

It is also really important to your status as an authority that you feel somewhat comfortable with the role. Otherwise the students, who are generally far more perceptive than they are given credit for, will likely sense your reservations and not treat you with the same respect. So for those moments where you have doubt or feel like a charlatan, here are some reasons you are an authority:

- Regardless of the subject, you do know a lot more than they do.

- You likely have the highest confidence, intelligence (at least conventionally speaking), and sense of self in the room.

- You've had more life experience than you think.

- You know what is good for them better than they do.

They Don't Plead

Authorities don't plead. They may suggest, they may request, and they may demand, but they do not plead. And while addressing the class it is important to keep this in mind. So instead of pleading, ask nicely, ask sternly, suggest strongly, or say nothing at all (often when a class is being really bad, going silent shames them into behaving faster than any amount of begging could).

They Dress Like an Authority

Teachers are notoriously bad dressers. In the first year you will likely see your colleagues wear more ill-fitting slacks and eccentric sweaters than you knew existed. But despite that trend, don't be fooled into thinking that you can wear anything you want. Veteran teachers can get away with such fashion faux pas, but you cannot. For young teachers, it is very important that you come across as both professional and presentable. The professional side helps differentiate you from the students, and the presentable side helps students respect and look up to you more.

They Talk Like They Have the Answers

One of the keys to being an authority is to have a little dash of P. T. Barnum in your persona. Talk like you are the man or woman with the answers and your students would be fools not to listen up (because in fact you are). This usually means stating things clearly, confidently, and unequivocally. Whether you are asking them to get into groups or sing a song, give your directions like there is no doubt that they will do it and do it well. And if you can say it with a little sparkle in your eye and swagger in your speech (but not too much—there are few things students and administrators despise more than arrogance), all the better.

Be Yourself in a World Where Few Are

While first interviewing for jobs I always tried to ask a few carefully crafted questions of my interviewers to come across as inquisitive. Generally these questions were more for show than for learning, but at one school I received an answer to one question that I will never forget. The question was pretty standard: "What is the most important thing a teacher needs to be successful at [this school]?" And I expected the answer to be a standard quick response as well, but instead the interviewer stopped and gave the question real thought. Then after a few seconds she said resolutely, "The best teachers are themselves and don't try to be someone else."

This response had a sudden and profound impact on me, because up to that point I had been urged to be everything but myself (which is a common experience among new teachers). As a new teacher, you will find that everyone has a suggestion for you, and though these suggestions generally come from a good place and are quite useful, an unspoken pressure comes with them, too. The pressure is that you, as a new teacher, should listen and follow their advice, even if it doesn't fit your style, because they are the experts and you are the rookie.

To make matters worse, this pressure to take advice comes during a time when many new teachers also feel a personal pressure to suddenly grow up. The casual fun of college is winding down, and in its place stands the responsibility of a "real job" and "real life." And sometimes it can be hard not to feel like you should get a new you to match your new life.

The combined effect of these internal and external pressures often leads to new teachers' running a great risk of having their personality and style eroded by good intentions. This is not to say that teachers shouldn't make

27

some sensible changes (for example, going out five nights a week and doing your work the morning it is due should probably change), but it is essential to teachers that they remain true to themselves at the same time. The problem with not being yourself in the classroom comes from the fact that our society generally has a great love affair with people who are themselves and great distaste for those who aren't. And if anyone can smell insincerity from a mile off, it is students, who are often masters of it themselves.

But What If They Don't Like Who I Am?

Movies, TV, and books usually portray students as highly discriminatory and petty, but in reality students of all ages and backgrounds are generally far more accepting than most of the population. It is true that they often break into tight-knit and exclusive groups and can act really poorly toward each other, but this behavior is usually based more on their own insecurities than their prejudices. If you put those exclusively grouped students onto the same team, the odds are they would accept each other faster than a group of adults ever could.

Beyond being generally fairly accepting, students also probably want to like you and they want you to like them. They will never show or admit this to you, but they do. In the same way that most employees generally secretly long for their bosses to like them (even if the boss is a jerk), most students want your approval. And if you are young, that desire is instantly tripled. So be yourself in your classroom. Just make sure you are the expert, authoritative version of yourself, and no matter who you are you will have a good chance of gaining their respect.

Exit Slip

If you are looking for more advice on establishing yourself as an authority (not to mention how to set the right tone), think about looking into dog-training books like *The Dog Whisperer*. This may seem like a ridiculous suggestion and there are clearly some important differences between packs of dogs and teens, but there are also a lot of surprising similarities. And these books can have some great insights about leading packs of either species.

CHAPTER FOUR
THE POWER OF POSITIVITY

Think back to the last time someone criticized you. Maybe it was your boss or a significant other. Maybe it was a stranger or a close friend. Maybe it was deserved, expected, and constructive or unwarranted, surprising, and hurtful. Whatever type of criticism you received, there is a good chance that it stung a little.

Now think about going through a gauntlet of such criticisms hour after hour, day after day. Most of us would struggle to handle it and keep our composure, yet this is exactly what many students face in school on a daily basis. All except the best students often hear nothing but major and minor criticisms all day: don't put a comma there, your heading isn't correct, hurry up, slow down, be quiet, speak up, you should write your homework down, you should do your homework, you should care. The list goes on and on.

So why is it this way? It is doubtful that school administrators and teachers want their schools and classrooms to be negative places, so how come this is often how it ends up?

The answer may lie somewhere within the workload of teachers. The average teacher generally has hundreds of kids to keep track of, which gives the teacher only seconds per day to spend on each student. With new teachers, this time per student is even less because everything takes longer and they have other time-drains that soak up valuable minutes. With such limited time available to address each student, it is only natural that teachers—and especially new teachers—tend to focus on the areas where students need improvement. If a teacher has five minutes available to comment on a paper, is the teacher going to spend those scarce minutes giving kudos for things already working or use that time to try to fix a few errors? If the goal is student improvement, the answer seems obvious.

This tendency for most teachers to dwell upon the downside of student work can have a lot of negative effects on students, but it also opens up an opportunity for you to really make your classroom stand out (while also reversing the negative trend). The silver lining to this sometimes ugly side of schools is that even the smallest splash of positivity on your part can profoundly affect your class and students when contrasted with the negatives in the background. Because of this it is well worth trying to sneak positives into your class whenever possible.

Use the Fifty-Fifty Benchmark

Generally speaking, there are few more monotonous, please-get-this-over-as-soon-as-possible aspects of teaching than grading papers. Combine this tedious nature with the general time crunch of your average week, and you begin to see why grading is one of the areas where it is very easy to be nothing but critical and negative. You just want to go in, give them some advice, and get out as soon as possible.

But this sea of criticism, quickly scrawled on the paper (especially when it's in red ink), can have some negative repercussions. Instead of communicating the intended message of "these are the areas you need to work on," it can send a multitude of unintended messages. Depending on the student, it may tell the student that once again he or she didn't do anything right or that his or her gains weren't worth noting. It can also make students feel like nothing is good enough for you, so what is the point in trying?

Now, a second needs to be taken here to make clear that even though criticism can have negative consequences, this is not an argument for eliminating it. Students need to both see and address their errors or they will never improve in significant ways. Instead, the argument is that you shouldn't always rely on criticism as the sole form of communication. You should team your criticism with praise to make sure that it is not only palatable but also sends the right messages. Generally speaking, to accomplish this goal the best ratio of criticism to praise is about 1:1. Having half praise and half criticism lets the students know that they have both strengths and weaknesses, both areas to be proud of and areas to improve.

When sending positive messages, it is also important for you to give your praise the same care as your criticisms. Don't just slap "Good job" onto random spots, or the hollowness of your effort will likely show through. Instead, look for actual positives. If a student has made a significant improvement, point it out, because they likely are proud of it. If they haven't made a significant change, provide some legitimate encouragement to motivate them.

In the end, it is true that adding positive comments may mean less time to include suggestions, but it also increases the likelihood that the suggestions you do send will be better received than if no positives were included. It also increases the chances that the student will leave feeling good about himself or herself, about you, and about how work from both parties have made the student better overall.

Don't Limit Your Conversations to Negatives

When a teacher announces that he or she needs to talk to a student, the standard response from students around is an involuntary "Ohhhh." And generally speaking, they are right. Usually when a teacher pulls aside a student to talk, it is because the student did something wrong.

This tendency for teachers and students to talk only when trouble is in the air can at times make the classroom seem more like a one-sided dictatorship than the collaborative effort to learn that it really is. In order to reverse this feeling, teachers should approach their conversations with students like they would with any other collaborator. This means occasionally discussing negatives, but also touching upon positives and sometimes talking without any serious purpose at all. By talking to students like they are real people (instead of machines made for mischief), teachers can empower students and make them feel like real partners in learning. And this can make a huge difference in many ways.

Show Some Interest

Think about your favorite teacher. The odds are he or she didn't show up to all your events, know your family, or even talk with you personally on a daily or even weekly basis. What he or she probably did do was show some variety of positive interest in you, even if it was very small. To show this interest, maybe he or she stopped to chat in the hallway occasionally, commended you on your recent school play performance, or just remembered that you ran track.

When it comes to connecting with students, the fact is that you don't need grand gestures; all you need is a small amount of actual positive interest.

With students, a little bit of interest goes a long way toward making them feel connected and supported. This is because individual interest can be a rare commodity in schools. So many teachers are kept so busy with their classes that they don't remember or don't have time to show extra interest to their students. Set against that backdrop, standing out from the crowd can be surprisingly easy. Often all it takes is a small gesture or conversation to solidify your spot as a teacher the student feels close to.

It doesn't always even take interest to connect with students; sometimes all you need to do is just listen to them. It is not uncommon for students to attempt to chat with teachers (especially young ones) before or after class. It is also not uncommon for those teachers to be so wrapped up in their pre- or post-class work that they only halfheartedly converse with them (if at all). But when teachers brush off students like buzzing flies, a great opportunity is lost. These students, for the most part, just want to be heard, and if you give them a couple of minutes of actual conversation with eye contact, in response they will often feel a connection with you that inspires them to work significantly harder.

Celebrate the Positives (So They Keep Coming)

Though we may blush and say things like "It wasn't a big deal" or "Just doing my job," most people secretly love to get public accolades. With that in mind, try occasionally celebrating the good things students do in front of the entire class. If a student helps another, has made great strides in public speaking, or acts as a strong group leader, don't be afraid to thank or congratulate them in front of the class. If the entire class does a good job, applaud them for it, too. In general, as long as you keep your praise at a reasonable level (don't praise them for every little thing or for things, like high grades, that may make other students jealous or upset), it can improve the classroom in the following ways:

- Acknowledging positives gives them added value, and this added value means students will have incentive to do more positive things. When students receive something for good behavior (even if it is just a "Good job!"), they will be more likely to pursue good behavior in the future in the hopes of getting another accolade. To take this concept one step further, many teachers also develop some variety of system (whether with extra credit, "teacher bucks,"

or some other type of faux monetary instrument) to further reinforce good behavior.

- By pointing out the areas where students have grown, teachers
add value to their class and classwork. When students see their
areas of improvement, it shows them that the class not only has
a point, but is working—and this can be a powerful inspirational
tool.

- Adding positivity can help the students feel comfortable enough
to express themselves and take risks, because they know criticism
won't necessarily follow.

- Positive environments just feel better, and feeling is often vastly
underrated.

Exit Slip

Positivity is all well and good on paper, but there will likely be a lot of moments in your classroom where positives will be the last thing on your mind
(like when the class won't settle down, listen to you, or treat other human beings with decency). And that is all right. You don't have to focus on the positives at all moments to be an effective teacher. In fact, if you do nothing but
concentrate on the bright side, you make the same mistakes as teachers who
focus on negatives all the time—just on the other side of the spectrum.

Instead, what you want to do is have a classroom that includes both positives and negatives, areas to be proud of and areas to improve. You want a
classroom that isn't afraid to correct mistakes or celebrate successes, because
only in a balanced classroom will both your criticism and praise come across
as positives.

WHO ARE YOUR STUDENTS?

The famous educator Seymour Skinner once said after finding no children at any of his old hangout spots, "There are no children at the 4-H club, either. Am I so out of touch? No, it's the children who are wrong."

The great curse of getting older is that you never feel quite as old as you actually are. In the same way that people often don't notice physical changes in themselves until they look into a mirror, it is not uncommon for people to not realize how much they've personally changed until they encounter someone who hasn't. And nowhere is this experience truer than with young teachers coming back to school.

As a young teacher, it is easy to feel like the one thing you should have a great understanding of is the students, because you were in their position not too many years ago. But as soon as young teachers encounter the students, it often becomes painfully clear how many twists, turns, and lessons of life lie between them. It is not uncommon for new teachers to walk away from their first few weeks in school feeling that their students, who can sometimes be similar in both age and appearance, hail from a completely different species.

If you are one of these new teachers who are at a loss concerning a lot of student behavior, don't worry. You are far from alone, and this unit is here to help. In the next few chapters this book will reacquaint you with what it's like to be an adolescent by providing snapshots of the student brain and how it works. It also aims not only to define who students are, but also to help you connect and educate individuals so far removed from where you are now.

CHAPTER FIVE
TEACHING COMMON SENSE

On only the second weekend of my first year of teaching, I spent over ten hours grading a stack of essays. I wish I could say that what made this experience notable was that it was preventable and could have been avoided if I had known more, but unfortunately the reason it receives mention is because this type of experience is usually the rule, not the exception. Most teachers, whether they are English or history teachers grading a stack of essays, science teachers grading lab reports, or math teachers grading a ten-page test, need marathon grading sessions on occasion to get through all the papers they have.

Going through a stack of papers often takes this long because teachers are required to do more than just notify students about whether they are right or wrong (at least on the major assignments). They can't just slap a grade on the paper and move on; teachers must also let students know why they received the grade they did and offer suggestions for improvement. When you take into account that doing this usually requires teachers to read, judge, justify, offer suggestions, and motivate, ten minutes to grade a five-page essay suddenly doesn't seem so unreasonable. And if you multiply that ten minutes by sixty papers, the time required to grade them stands at ten hours—which for many teachers is only half or even a third of their course load.

Despite the massive time commitment and the obvious monotony, there is a strange satisfaction that comes with grading papers. The hectic school day offers little time to work individually with the students, but when you grade a student's paper you can focus purely on the student's needs. This opportunity to provide each student with personalized messages and suggestions for improvement makes the time spent grading a worthwhile investment, even if it doesn't feel like it after grading all day on a Sunday.

Though these benefits of teacher comments are obvious to most instructors (for we are the ones giving them), they are not always clear to the students. This could be why so many students barely glance (or don't glance at all) at the comments when they get an assignment back. Instead, they hurriedly search for the grade, and once it's found they toss the paper into their backpacks or binders in a way that clearly indicates they have no further use for it. Some may even throw theirs straight into the recycle bin or crumple them into balls right in front of the teacher's nose.

As a new teacher it pained me to watch students disregard the comments that I put so much effort into, but I have to admit that I followed the same find-the-grade-and-move-on approach in high school. In my defense, it has been a long time since I thought that way, but that is exactly the problem—we as teachers are not mentally in the same place as the students. Something as commonsensical to most adults as reading comments from an instructor may not even register in a student's mind. And that isn't the only commonsense thing that students seem to routinely overlook. Things as simple as asking questions when you don't know something, writing down homework assignments, and even reading test directions may never cross a student's mind either.

As a teacher you really only have two options with students concerning these commonsense issues: You can get upset at students every time they don't use the common sense they don't have, or you can teach them common sense so you aren't continually getting angry about the same things. In terms of teaching them, each student has his or her own commonsense gaps, but there are some holes that students commonly have.

They Don't Read Teacher Comments

It is important to remember that the majority of kids probably don't take your class because they love the subject. Generally they are there because it fulfills a requirement and they want a good grade. And when you consider that perspective, it makes sense that the majority of students ignore the comments in the margins of their papers. Most students aren't concerned with improving their writing, their knowledge of history, or their trigonometry skills beyond what is needed to get the grade they want. And with such modest goals in mind, reading through five pages of comments is definitely overkill—especially if their grade is already pretty good.

So what can teachers do to get students interested in their comments if they don't seem to care about improvement? The answer is simple: make them care. Teachers can do this by tying the comments to something students do care about, like grades. Instead of just giving major assignments back to students and hoping they will read the comments, teachers can make sure they read them by turning the corrections into a graded assignment. And depending on how far they want to take it, they can go further with this concept by having students complete assignments that require them to reflect on their problem areas or even teach lessons to others on one of the topics they struggled with.

They Don't Stay Organized

Adolescents, outside of a rare few, are not naturally organized. In fact, if left to nature, the majority of adolescents will let their binders, backpacks, and lockers turn into disheveled squirrel's nests in less than a week. This is why teachers, especially those of middle-school students, must step in and mandate organization if they wish their students to have any semblance of organization. Because otherwise it isn't going to happen.

Just like with reading teachers' comments, you can inform students of the merits of organization as much as you want, but if you really want them to stay organized you need to turn organization into an assignment. There are numerous ways to assign organization, but the most commonplace and efficient way to do it is to set certain standards and then have occasional binder checks for points to keep them honest. These standards don't need to be complicated; just make sure students have all their notes in one place (computer or notebook), a planner, appropriate materials for class, and a system of storing papers that have come back to them. Beyond that, give your system whatever personality fits your class. As long as you follow through on them, a lot of different styles can work because organization will gain value—when, for many students, it had no value before.

In terms of the level of organization to mandate, it seems to work well to require a lot for middle schoolers and less for high schoolers. The reason for this split is that high-school students generally view high levels of organizational oversight as insulting to their increased maturity (at least, in their minds they are mature). Middle-school students, on the other hand, will be the first to admit they are highly unorganized, and thus they are often very willing to accept help with organization. For both groups, there is value in requiring a certain level of organization (needing binders, materials, and a place for notes), but middle-school students often stay organized better if the teacher is more hands-on with the details.

The last thing that needs to be said about organization is a warning: All sorts of organizational systems can easily work, but all sorts can easily fail, too. And they almost all fail for the same reason—lack of oversight. If you don't commit to monitoring your system, its success is in jeopardy because, like the universe, students tend to drift toward disorder. And as soon as the oversight that holds the students' preference for chaos at bay disappears, so does any semblance of organization from most students.

They Don't Write Down Their Homework Assignments

Most adults seem to like making to-do lists. This could have something to do with the fact that there is something supremely comforting about having everything required of you written down where it can be easily seen and remembered. But unfortunately many students don't share this outlook. Instead, most seem to see writing down the things they need to do (like homework) as a waste of their precious time. When asked why they find it a waste, students commonly question why it is worth writing something down when all you have to do is remember it. Even more amazing is that this view is often shared by students whose minds regularly don't remember what they need to do.

When faced with such seemingly irrational resistance, the only response is to make not writing down assignments a bigger pain than just writing it down. To do that, give students set time at the end of class where they must write their homework in their planners. During that time walk around and prod those students who don't have planners or write the homework down in their notebooks. Then combine this with occasional planner checks (both before class and on the way out) and light chastisement of those students whose assignment isn't written down. The whole purpose of this minor cajoling and prodding of non–planner users is to make the option of refusing to use a planner more trouble than it is worth. And often this pushes even the most resistant planner users toward the easier option—writing everything down.

They Don't Always Treat Each Other Decently

The vast majority of kids are decent, but this doesn't mean their behavior always is. Students often interrupt, put down, talk back, and treat people in other disrespectful ways. To most adults these behaviors seem obviously wrong, but the same may not be true for students. If you watch students, talking back, putting down, and interrupting are all common behaviors when they interact with each other. In fact, a student's ability to dig at a classmate or sarcastically talk back may even increase their standing within some groups. With such a gulf between how many students interact with each other and how teachers expect them to interact, it is no wonder that even the nicest kids can sometimes act in shockingly rude ways.

Because students are often accustomed to interacting in a way that adults in their future will find disrespectful, it is worth trying to instruct them on how to interact "properly." To do that generally takes two simple steps: first, you need to lay down clear rules of interaction in the classroom (no interrupting, no poor treatment of others, no put-downs); then you need to enforce them vigorously and without exception. Generally these "decency" rules are some of the most common rules to have their limits tested by students, which is why it is so important to remain firm with them. Once students realize you are resolute in those rules, they generally improve their behavior significantly and have few problems behaving "decently."

They Don't Read Test Directions

This one is amazing. It is easy to predict that students will struggle at times with organization and behavior, but the number of students who don't read the directions on homework, tests, and quizzes is truly shocking. A perfect example of this came on my first seventh-grade test, where over half my class either misread or disregarded the following prompt: "State which character said each of the following quotes and then explain why each quote is important." Some of the students answered this by writing why it was important without saying who said it, others just put the name of the character and nothing else, and a few even inexplicably wrote answers that didn't address either requirement.

After grading these tests it was clear why so many teachers review even the simplest directions with their classes. For some reason, possibly because they assume what the directions will be, an amazingly large percentage of students won't read them otherwise. To remedy this problem of student disregard for directions, teachers can do more than read questions aloud, though. They can discuss with their class why reading directions is important and possibly even make up some assignments to reinforce this idea. Or if teachers wish to really bring home the idea, they can take even more unorthodox approaches such as beginning every single class with an unusual practice set of directions or putting somewhat unexpected directions into assignments and quizzes to keep the students on their toes.

However far you go with it, overall it is generally a good idea to make it as clear as possible to students that reading directions closely is one of the easiest ways to ensure yourself a good grade.

Exit Slip

At end of the day, even after being schooled in numerous aspects of common sense, students are not going to be rational human beings. Developmentally, their brains just aren't there yet (and won't be there for many years—recent research has found full rationality doesn't develop until well into the twenties). So keep this in mind when you deal with them. Irrationality is not necessarily a sign of trouble or that students are on the wrong track; normally it just means they are teenagers.

STUDENTS ARE FRAGILE

One day I was sitting in my classroom preparing for the upcoming lesson. A few minutes remained in the passing period; students milled around just outside of the classroom doors, but none were ready to come in yet. As the first student walked in, I was so focused on figuring out how to start the lesson that I didn't look up right away. When I did look up, I noticed that the lone student wore a pained look. Unsure of what else to do, I asked the student from my desk if everything was all right. As I said this the student's face tightened up and she struggled for a moment to fight back tears. Then she broke down and drove her head into her arms.

I quickly made my way over to her desk to provide some comfort. I asked what happened, and between sobs she was finally able to explain that there was a mix-up in her last class. As she choked on attempts to further explain I couldn't help but wonder what kind of mix-up might lead to such distress. Was she wrongly accused of something? Did she get into an argument with a friend? Was she sent to the office? Caught skipping? Found to have a controlled substance? As she sobbed, a myriad of hypotheses went through my mind and I braced for the worst.

Finally the student composed herself somewhat, and between sniffles she explained the issue. The problem was that she was originally told that she got an A on a quiz, but there was a mistake with the addition of the score and instead she got a B+. Because it was the beginning of a new semester, this quiz comprised a sizable percentage of her grade for the moment (by the end of the semester it would have almost no impact upon the grade), and that meant for the time being her grade dropped from an A to an A−.

This answer was so far removed from all of the horrible expectations I had built up in my mind that now it was my turn to freeze up. Finally, I collected myself and tried my best to both sympathize and remind her that by the end of the semester the small quiz wouldn't weigh so heavily upon her grade. At first my words seemed to do little good, but by degrees she began to settle down and within just a few minutes she was back to her normal cheerful self.

This experience reminded me of a lesson that I learned again and again last year—that though students' exteriors may often portray toughness or indifference, underneath they are often startlingly fragile. This chapter examines the ways in which students are commonly fragile and what this fragility means for teaching, while also providing tips for not inadvertently trampling on particularly fragile students.

All Concerns Big and Small

The striking thing about the example above is the size of the gulf between student and teacher. The student reacted with such severity that it is fairly safe to say she viewed this experience, at least momentarily, as a significant setback and a major obstacle to her future goals, whereas from my perspective the trivial loss of points was of such little significance that calling it inconsequential would be overstating its importance. Even more remarkable is how easily these tables can be turned; in another situation it would not be unusual for that same student to completely dismiss the significance of something as important to me as learning how to write an effective essay.

This profound difference in priorities means that staying mindful of how differently student brains are wired is essential whenever grading, planning, or teaching. This is important because any seemingly "little detail" can be magnified in the minds of the students. Proof of this can be seen when talking to people about their memories of school. Get most people talking for long enough and you will hear multiple stories of how little things like a poor grade, an embarrassing moment, or a random comment shifted the course of their schooling forever.

One of the scariest things about being a teacher is that you can never be sure of how students will react to even the smallest of your actions. It is very doubtful that most teachers want to chase students from their subject, but it happens anyway, often without the teacher ever realizing it. To give yourself the best protection against inadvertent negative effects, try to treat students like you would a package with "FRAGILE" labels plastered all over it. If there is even the slightest chance that one of your actions, big or small, could cause damage, then proceed with the greatest of care.

This does not mean that you should refrain from everything that may upset students, though. Bs, Cs, Ds, and Fs need to be in the classroom alongside As. Sometimes students need to be corrected, reprimanded, or punished. And sometimes their feelings will probably be hurt. What it does mean is that when you do hand out a D or a punishment, do it in the least hurtful way possible. For example, if a student gets a low grade on a test, don't just hand it back and move on; instead, talk to the student, explain the grade, and point him or her to the bright side or provide some encouragement for the future. Also, don't limit this behavior to the events that only seem major for you. For some students (and you will generally be able to figure out who they are), being told to stop talking during class or getting B+ is a terrible and discouraging fate, and it is just as important to handle these situations with care, too.

Common Fragile Spots

Most students share one thing in common—just when you think you have them figured out, they defy your expectations once again. What that means is that the following list is by no means comprehensive or the same for each student. But that being said, these are the areas where the average student tends to be particularly fragile, so it is worth giving them some extra attention:

- *Grades.* Much of student identity, for good or bad, often gets associated with grades. Though most adults recognize how small a tenth-grade math quiz score or a quarter grade in eighth-grade English is in the long run, to many students those small marks along the way represent nothing less than how successful their life is at the moment (and possibly will be in the future).

- *Poking fun.* Many adolescents do little but poke fun at each other. And to witnesses of this behavior it may seem that if kids are equipped to do anything, it is to take a joke. But with many students it is the exact opposite. They are so worn down by the constant jokes from their peers that even small and harmless digs can compound their insecurities. This doesn't mean that you can't poke fun at students in a light-hearted manner; it just means be careful, because some can be surprisingly sensitive.

- *Effort.* When teachers receive assignments that seem like they were done with little effort, they commonly let their students know (verbally or in writing) that they need to try harder. Though this is fine response in many situations, it is very important that the teacher know that the student didn't put in much effort if they take this route. The reason for this is that few things are more offensive or discouraging to a student than to be accused of not putting in effort when they did try hard (or thought they tried hard). One way to get around these potential hurt feelings while still letting the student know that more effort is needed is to tell them that the assignment "looks like" not enough effort was put in, and then give them the reasons why it appears that way. By doing this the message is clear, but at the same time there is no accusation.

Take the Claws Out of Your Criticism

Every discipline has its added burdens. For English teachers, one of the major responsibilities is to be incredibly precise with your language in anything sent to parents. English teachers are supposed to be masters of language, and even the slightest grammatical or rhetorical slip-up could lead to unwanted questions about your competency.

Because of this added pressure, I asked a senior English teacher to look over some student narratives I wrote for the first report card (a school policy). She, true to her nature, agreed with a smile, but when I went to pick up the narratives the next day her mood had changed. And when I saw the paper I understood why. My narratives, pristine white when delivered to her, now bled with red pen like a thousand small paper cuts.

Looking at my bloody paper I was instantly thrust back into school. I was no longer the teacher; I was the student who had much to learn. And not only that, I was the student who had underperformed, rushed the assignment, and done a sloppy job. Instantly I grasped in my mind for reasons to justify why the work wasn't done properly. Overworked. Done late at night. Burned out. Just a draft. As the teacher explained the corrections, all I could think about was why things needed to be corrected in the first place. Each red mark represented an affront to my already battered ego, and all I wanted was to find reasons to make my mistakes all right.

This embarrassing episode with a colleague I admire (which included convincing her I did in fact know simple grammatical rules) was horrific in many ways, but in other respects it was very lucky. The reason that such an experience could ever be construed as lucky was because it gave me a new perspective on how students might experience criticism from their teachers. As a teacher it is easy to fall into the mindset that students will just take our criticisms for what they are: suggestions for improvement. But they can also take it other ways. They can just as easily grow defensive or ashamed and start reacting the way I did—with feelings of worthlessness and excuses for why they messed up—and completely overlook the lessons that need to be learned.

For most teachers, eliminating constructive criticism—even with its potential dangers—isn't an option (nor should it be). So to make sure students take criticism in the way intended (as a tool to help them improve), teachers need to preemptively strike against the students' feeling worthless, defensive, or ashamed. The best way to do this is to make it clear both ahead of time and in the comments that the student errors are understandable, correctable, and not an indication of personal defects. To further lessen the blow, it also works to circle the criticisms with comments focused on student gains and victories (as was discussed in the chapter 4). Then once the distractions of shame and defensiveness are eliminated, you can be a lot more confident that the lessons will get through.

Exit Slip

With the fragility of even the toughest students, it can be very easy for new teachers to feel guilty about giving poor grades or reprimanding students. We don't want to see them hurt and when they are, and by something we did, it can pull quite hard on the heartstrings. But in the face of these guilty feelings it is important for new teachers to stand firm and not withdraw the punishments or bad grades they've administered (at least not right at the moment while they are emotional). Students may be fragile, but so long as you tread carefully with your grading and reprimanding, a little correction or punishment from time to time should strengthen, not damage them.

TEACHING IS A GAME OF INCHES

The morning after first-semester finals I went to school to grade the last pieces of student work I would see until after winter break. My spirit soared for several reasons on this day. First, only a thin stack of paper stood between me and three weeks of freedom. Second, these papers weren't just any random papers—only optional essay revisions remained.

Optional revisions may seem like a strange thing to get excited about, but I always look forward to them because although I give all my students the opportunity to revise their papers, only the most motivated students generally take me up on it. (This could be a good policy for you. The idea is that they can get extra points, but they have to earn the points through improving their writing.) This round of essays was no different, and I found it fitting that my first semester would end with my spending time with a handful of thoughtful revisions from some of my favorite students.

There were a lot of reasons why I expected these essays to be exceptionally well done. The essays all came from my most conscientious students— the type of kids who revise essays not because they have to or it will improve their grades (every single student in this group already had a grade in the A range for the semester), but because they know it will help them learn. I had also gone out of my way to make sure that every student possessed all the tools needed to do it right. They all received a copy of their essay with copious comments in the margins, a short letter detailing their strengths and weaknesses, and a five-minute one-on-one conference with me to discuss the revisions. Everything seemed foolproof—but sadly, that was a foolish notion to have.

As soon as I started grading the papers it quickly became clear that my lofty expectations were not being met. Paper after paper still contained the same glaring errors that plagued them the first time, and my comments stood largely ignored. As I shuffled through the stack I grew irritated at the students for wasting my time with such effortless revisions. I wondered why they would even use the paper to print the same errors over again. But then, as my original wave of resentment diminished, I began to realize that nothing added up. These weren't the type of students who turned in work without a strong effort. And even if one or two gave a half-hearted attempt, it hardly seemed likely that all the students would give such lazy efforts.

After I accepted that the students probably did give some effort, I encountered a whole new set of worries. Was the problem that my feedback wasn't effective or the students weren't getting the instruction they needed? Was the subject matter too advanced for a fifteen-year-old brain to comprehend? Or maybe they just weren't strong students. As these concerns swirled around my head, I couldn't accept any of them. I had certainly made mistakes, and at times the students struggled, but there were no previous indications that the class and I were in over our heads. So where did such a profound gap between expectation and performance come from?

I didn't receive an answer to my question until the staff holiday party several days later. During the party, teachers inevitably spent much of their time comparing notes about the first half of the school year. During these discussions a wide range of topics came up, but the themes of little victories and the (at times) almost glacial pace of learning came up again and again. Hearing how these seasoned teachers celebrated the small gains of their students helped me realize that my students' revisions were completely normal. It wasn't that my students were dumb, didn't try, or suffered from poor teaching—it was just that teaching is a game of inches.

I use the old and overused cliché that "football is a game of inches" to describe teaching because the two actually share some similarities. Football is called a game of inches because it generally takes a series of small gains to accomplish the goal of scoring a touchdown. The same is true with teaching. Occasionally the students will have epiphanies or learn in wide swaths (just like in football a deep pass will occasionally work), but more often it takes a series of small steps for students to learn successfully. To truly get something they may need to spend some time with it, work with it, process it, reflect on it, have it repeated, forget it, and find it again. These small steps, though unimpressive on their own, should not be scoffed at. When it comes to both football and teaching, the line between success and failure is measured by fractions of an inch more often than one would expect.

Rinse and Repeat

One day I gave the students a quick grammar lesson during the last five minutes of class. The next class the students had a short vocabulary quiz and, needing one more question to finish the quiz, I decided to throw in a question on the grammar I had gone over the day before. Since I had said it, it seemed like fair game.

When the results of the quiz came back, it became obvious it wasn't fair game. Out of twenty students, only one got the question right; over half the class later admitted they didn't even remember talking about it.

The reason for this bout of class amnesia? Students, like adults, don't re-member everything told to them. The assumption on my part was that once the information was passed to the students they knew it and could use it. But that is not the way the human brain works. People don't absorb anywhere near all of the information that comes their way. The figures on this differ slightly, but the consensus seems to be that oral retention of information for students in a classroom setting is somewhere in the neighborhood of 5–10 percent (which seems very informally corroborated by my 5 percent success rate on the quiz).

This retention rate goes up dramatically as home, class, and group work are mixed in, but even these approaches come nowhere near yielding perfect retention. In the end, the only way to ensure students will get and retain information is to mimic the marketing strategy behind the FreeCreditReport .com song—say it again and again and again and again until your message is thoroughly entrenched in the neurons of your students' brains.

Repetition is one of the hidden stars of education, because not only does it give the students multiple chances to grab the information, it also signals to students that it is important. The average school day tosses a lot of infor-mation at students, and repeating the important points helps them stand out from the crowd and become memorable. Because of this, making repetition a foundational element of the classroom is rarely a bad choice.

Repetition Reminders

- Repetition isn't doing and saying the exact same thing over and over. Information and ideas can and should be packaged in many different ways. Keeping the same message, while changing its delivery, allows the lesson to remain fresh even if the facts are not.

- Young teachers may be surprised by how many times they need to repeat something before it takes hold. A good rule of thumb is that when new teachers think something has been said enough, they should say it five or ten more times—just for good measure.

- Put up visual reminders around your classroom of the most important points. This will continue the reinforcement even when they are spacing out and gazing at the walls.

Sometimes Students Need to Struggle Their Way to Success

When a matador waves the red flag at a bull, the bull probably recognizes at some level that charging in and taking care of business themselves isn't the best approach—it just can't help itself. Teachers are often faced with a similar dilemma when they see their students struggle. For many teachers, watching a student struggle is like watching that bright red flag dance back and forth. It captivates their attention, plays upon their best intentions, and is painful to ignore. And they want nothing less than for their students to learn. But like the bull, if they charge in without thinking, the chance of victory is slim.

The problem with providing a ready answer to every problem (or being a wiki-teacher) is that answers aren't always what students need in order to learn. Sometimes students need to learn how to come up with their own answers. This process can often be long, arduous, and excruciating to watch, but ultimately, lessons the students figure out themselves stick far better than those spoon-fed to them.

It should be mentioned that this section doesn't advocate teachers ignoring their students' requests for help. It merely warns teachers to tread carefully with that help. If teachers begin making the connections for students and coaxing responses that have more to do with their coaxing than student learning, the students no longer benefit (even if they appear to initially). Because if the students don't form the necessary pathways and connections in their own brains, they likely won't be equipped to walk through the exact same concepts the next day.

Don't Try to Turn Students into Hemingway or Einstein with One Onslaught of Your Pen

Everyone has had a teacher who makes papers bleed like they were graded on a butcher's counter. Generally, these teachers are technically correct in the errors they mark, but that doesn't mean they are necessarily correct in their approach. The problem with marking every single error is that one lesson is hard to learn, which makes one hundred lessons the academic equivalent of an alpine expedition. And for anyone who has spent time in secondary schools, one hundred errors over a five-page paper is not unusual.

There are a variety of reasons why young teachers are at greater risk of becoming paper bleeders. They are just emerging from the world of college, where every little error is generally noted. They also may want to flex their academic muscles to make up for the anemic feeling they have about their teaching skills. But most likely, they will get caught up in a desire to help their students as much as they can. (If one correction helps a little, think how much a hundred corrections will help!)

With this predisposition for giving overwhelming amounts of corrections, it is important for teachers to think carefully about how many errors they point out and focus on. Remember, teaching is a game of inches; don't try to gain all the yards in one play. Noting each of a student's eighty-seven errors may seem like a favor, but more than likely the sheer quantity of red pen will scare a student away from even looking at the paper. If a student is brave enough to look at all the errors, the amount of information could overwhelm him or her to such an extent that, despite the best intentions on both sides, the student could leave the paper with no lasting lessons.

This means that whether you are a science, history, English, or drama teacher, there are probably going to be times when it will be more productive to ignore some mistakes in order to focus attention on the major problems. For while the prospect of fixing eighty-seven little errors will likely overwhelm a student, fixing two or three major errors is far more reasonable and manageable. (To pick the errors, focus on the most glaring ones or errors that connect to what has been discussed in class recently.) And though leaving some errors left unchecked is often a painful experience, having them all get ignored is far worse. Besides, it is not like you will ignore those mistakes forever; you are just focusing on giving your students some basic skills now that will put them in a perfect position to tackle those unchecked errors next time.

Exit Slip

Remember that as a teacher you don't need to teach students everything in one year. The year you spend with them is just one among thirteen (seventeen with undergrad and closing in on twenty with a master's), and though you no doubt want to teach them everything, if they can come out with a couple of important lessons and a brightened interest in learning, your year was likely a success. So celebrate the little victories and keep working in the trenches to gain every inch you can, because soon those inches will add up to some pretty impressive stuff.

RELATING TO YOUR STUDENTS

I f men are from Mars and women are from Venus, then students are from somewhere in the vicinity of Alpha Centauri. That is to say, while the logic of the opposite gender is often quite confusing, the logic of adolescents is regularly incomprehensible. Students regularly do and say things that demonstrate a thought process that couldn't be any further from what is normally defined as rational thought. But contrary to how it feels in the moment, this behavior is natural and a by-product of the fact that adolescent brains operate in markedly different ways than those of adults.

With such different brains, successfully passing knowledge between teacher and student is often like passing information between Macs and PCs: if it is not done with care and through the right steps, data has a very difficult time jumping between such drastically different operating systems. To help you with this gap, this unit lays out all the steps it normally takes to transfer information from your head to the heads of your students. It also aims to continue adding to your understanding of students so you can connect with, vaguely understand, and educate them to the best of your ability.

KEEPING LESSONS CLEAR

 One of the toughest things about teaching is that you are expected to study hard, immerse yourself in a certain discipline, become a master, and then step into a classroom and relay your subject to someone who generally knows nearly nothing about it (or possibly even knows the wrong thing). This means that to be effective, you must both retain your expert status and simultaneously take enough steps backward in time to relate to your students. And if this isn't hard enough, your memories of what life was like before you knew about integrals, dangling modifiers, or ribosomes (depending on your subject) can be pretty fuzzy.

Knowledge is not the only large gap that teachers must hurdle to relate to their students either. Even if you are only a handful of years removed from high school, the difference in perspective between you and your students will likely be immense. Because of these knowledge and perspective gaps, you must always guard against becoming unclear to your students. No matter how clear something seems to you, whether it is clear to your students is another matter. Often the simplest things—things that seem impossible for anyone to miss—will somehow go right over their heads. To help you avoid landing in this position, here are some areas where communication between teachers and students commonly becomes cloudy, and some tips on how to make sure it doesn't happen to you.

Directions

One day I broke my class into groups, gave them five questions, told them they had fifteen minutes, and left the rest up to them. Within five minutes it became painfully clear that the students were not giving the assignment much effort. As I walked by each group they discussed the questions on a token and surface level, but this façade of interest only lasted as long as my eyes were upon them. Once they were free from the examination of my eyes I could hear their conversation shift to the upcoming dance, the parties of the weekend, and a multitude of other topics very far removed from the assignment.

After another five minutes, I came to one group whose conversation didn't shift when I approached. As I levied my best teacher look at the group, my eyes fell upon a boy who was at that moment telling the other students about a new band he liked. Feeling my displeasure, he gazed up at me and responded to my unasked question. "We're done," he said matter-of-factly, motioning to a sheet of paper on the desk next to him. On the desk stood a paper that had five simple sentences scrawled in doctor-like handwriting.

Upon hearing this, my lip curled slightly in irritation. I couldn't believe this group of students would even pretend they'd completed the assignment when in over ten minutes all they had accomplished was a couple of hurried and illegible sentences. As I glanced around the room, it was clear they weren't the only ones, either. Most of the other groups had equally sloppy sheets in front of them, and their conversations seemed to be about everything but the task assigned.

So what happened during this activity that led to such behavior on the part of my students? It took a while, but I eventually realized that despite their actions the students weren't trying to be overly obstinate or rude; in a strange, twisted, and diluted way they actually thought they were doing something that fell within the range of what I wanted. I had asked each group to answer five questions, and each group did answer five questions. However, since I was very vague about the level and length of answers, the students gravitated toward doing the least they could possibly get away with.

I am also not the only new teacher who has found himself or herself in this type of situation. New teachers often have to deal with students who aren't doing the quality or amount of work they want on assignments, and in a lot of these situations overly vague directions are the culprit.

How to Avoid Overly Vague Directions

Directions are overly vague when they don't make the whole picture clear to students. For example, if you give students a list of questions to answer in groups and tell them merely "Answer these," the students can't be sure how long their answers should be, how much time they need to spend on each question, or what level of quality is required in their answers. Without this knowledge, many will generally err on the side of doing too little work instead of too much—because since they are not adults, this often seems the more sensible of the two options.

To correct this behavior, the key is to not give them the option. Don't leave anything up to interpretation. Let the students know exactly how long and how hard they need to work, what type of involvement you expect from each member of the group, and exactly what you want the final product to look like. What makes this approach so effective is that when you fill in all the details, the right path is made crystal clear, and if students want to avoid a scolding they no longer have the option to take any path but the right one.

In many situations the chances of students misunderstanding directions can be reduced even further by modeling. Showing the students exactly what you want takes away even more guesswork on the part of the students. Even with exceptionally thorough and clear directions, you can never be sure how students view an assignment, but if you show them the result you expect or the process you want, then they really have no excuse to stand upon if they don't deliver.

Directions 2: It's Complicated

If being vague is the best way to guarantee that students will misunderstand directions, getting overly complicated has to be a close second. Overcomplication is also a common mistake of new teachers, who in their exuberance and desire to do something different can sometimes ask too much of students. Here is an example of an assignment that asks too much:

Each semester you will be required to read at least three outside reading books. One of the three books has to be from the outside reading list. If there is nothing on the list for you, please meet with me and we will figure out a book we can agree on. The other two books you read each semester are your choice.

Each semester you will be required to do several things with your outside reading books. The first thing you must do is to make a chart of all the books you read over the semester. This chart should include the title (underlined, of course), author, number of pages, a rating of how good the book is, and three sentences explaining why someone should or shouldn't read this book.

You must also do a small activity for three of the books you read. For two of the books you must pick a writing activity from the list below, and for the third book you must give a one-minute speech describing why others should read the book or how it changed your outlook in some way.

This set of directions is overly complicated because it has too many working parts, and that can be a way of courting disaster. Many students have trouble following even simple directions, so if an assignment includes multiple options, various due dates, or several steps you will need to be prepared to spend time guiding students through it and answering questions. If your assignment includes all three like this one, you might want to rethink it, unless you are ready to field more questions than you probably want.

Now this is not to say all lessons should offer no choices, avoid multiple steps, or be otherwise simplified or dumbed down. Giving students choices is often a good thing (more on this later), and many of the best assignments will contain a series of directions. But at the same time, it is important to be cognizant of how many balls you ask students to juggle. Here is a good rule of thumb for knowing if you've asked too much: if your explanation of an assignment or activity needs over a minute or two, if you get lost or otherwise struggle while explaining it, or if the students' questions about it persist longer than normal, there is a good chance it has wandered into overly complicated territory.

How to Make Complicated Assignments Clearer

If you do have a fairly complicated assignment, try using layout in your printed assignment to make it easier to follow. Use numbers and bullets to make each step and its requirements separate and clear. Also, use white space to add to the clarity. This means surrounding your main points with blank spaces so they stand out. A giant block of directions like the one above will always lead to more confusion than one which contains more thoughtful spacing.

The Information Transfer

The essence of teaching is taking something that you know and transferring it to someone who doesn't know it. And though this process seems straightforward and easy, as you've already probably figured out, it is often the furthest thing from it. There are a thousand different areas where information can be lost in translation. The following are a few of the most common.

Talking Shop

In the same way that sixteen-year-olds a week after receiving their driver's license have a difficult time remembering life without a car, as teachers we can have a difficult time remembering life before we knew the terms regularly thrown around in our disciplines. We've heard terms like *preposition*, *hypothesis*, or *staccato* so many times that using them often becomes as natural as eating or breathing.

It is this level of comfort that makes accidentally "talking shop" or using lots of specific technical terms so dangerous. To us there may not be anything confusing about these words, but to some of your students there is a good chance they might as well be Greek. And often the average student ability to understand technical terms is a lot less than teachers expect. The odds are that if you say a term as basic as "adjective" in an advanced senior English class at a great school, there will be at least one student who can't quite remember what that means.

The way to avoid the confusion that can come from talking shop is not to shy away from it, though; many technical terms are important and the students should get familiar with them. Just be mindful that whenever you begin talking shop, make sure the students are clear on what each word means. Doing this can be as simple as stopping after mentioning a term like *adjective* and saying something to the entire class like "Who knows what that means?" With a prompt like that, at least one student will inevitably say, "It means a word that modifies a noun," and then you can be sure that anyone who didn't remember before knows now.

The Wrong Information at the Wrong Time

The amount and level of information covered can be one of the biggest determinants of lesson success. If a lesson covers topics that the students already know or if it moves too slowly, your students will likely react in the same way most adults do when they think they're above something: they will check out. If a lesson covers topics that fly well over the students' heads or if it moves too fast, students will likely check out as well—though this time it will be because they are confused, discouraged, or otherwise intimidated. Either way, if you want the students' full attention, you need to make sure the information covered is right for them.

Knowing how much or what information to cover is not an easy task either, especially for new teachers with little familiarity with what the students can handle in the classroom. If you count yourself among this group (or even if you don't), try these quick tips to help you with this process:

- Before you begin, ask them what they know. Students love to talk about themselves, so before you start a new unit have students tell you what already know about it. You can do this verbally, through writing, or even with small projects. Just by the act of asking, you will make a lot of students feel more involved in what they learn, and their answers will often point you in the direction of what they know and need to know.

- Aim high. When given the choice between information going a little above the students' level or a little below, it isn't a bad idea to err on the side of going above with the information. When you go above the students' level, at least they feel like you have high standards and something to teach them; if you go below you run the risk of their feeling above the level of the class, and generally this only comes with negatives. This is not to say that you should constantly aim at going over students' abilities, but if you miss the mark, that is the better side to land on.

- Assess regularly and assess right. New teachers generally know about assessing student knowledge, but they rarely know about how important it is. Assessing student knowledge is one of the most important things a young teacher can do, because every time it's done effectively the teacher gets a glimpse into what the students know. Since this information can't be known any other way, it is worth trying to squeeze in as many assessments as you can throughout your lessons (not just at the end of the lesson like most teachers). Common assessments include everything from informal discussions to exercises and activities to little student presentations. It is also worth trying to regularly mix up the types and formalities of assessments, so you have an accurate reading on whether all varieties of learners comprehend the information equally.

Information Overload

It is not unusual for new teachers to find themselves in the following position: They glance at the clock and realize that they have ten minutes to do something that they budgeted half an hour for. And even worse, they need to cover all of the information or the homework won't make any sense. Unsure of what else to do, they channel their inner auctioneers and blow through the information as quickly as is humanly possible.

Unfortunately, when assaulted with such an overwhelming wave of information, students generally remember even less than the exceptionally low amount they normally do. To understand why this is, think back to grade school and the game of dodgeball; in dodgeball, when one ball is thrown, you have a decent chance to catch it if you focus. But when the other team unleashes all of their balls at once, something in your brain short-circuits and the balls ricochet off your face, leaving you with no balls and a slight headache. The same is also true when it comes to information: a few "balls" (or pieces) of information thrown at staggered times give the students an opportunity to grab onto them, while a barrage generally leaves students with nothing beyond a disoriented head.

This "dodgeball effect" means that the best way to get across the most information is to actually limit the amount of information students receive and how quickly you throw it at them. If you do find yourself in a position where you need the students to learn a lot in a short amount of time (for homework, an upcoming test, or for any other reason), think about altering the assignment or pushing the test back instead of cramming information into them. Because if you plow ahead too fast they won't perform well on the assignment or test anyway.

Exit Slip

When people learn how to ride motorcycles they are often told to drive like every car on the road is out to kill them. Of course, every car on the road is not out to kill motorcyclists, but by thinking that they are, the motorcyclists can better see the cars that could represent hazards and be ready when dangerous situations do arise. This same approach also works when it comes to students and clarity. When teachers assume that every student doesn't understand them clearly, they will likely watch more vigilantly for those students who aren't following them and be better prepared when a "lost in translation" moment arises.

HOW TO GET THE MOST
FROM YOUR STUDENTS

Many schools have regular meetings when the staff gets together to discuss struggling students. One of the most striking things about these meetings is that they often showcase the drastically different sides various teachers can see in one student. It is not uncommon for one teacher to see a student as lazy, withdrawn, and rude, and the next teacher to see the same student as enthusiastic, engaged, and warm. It is also not unusual for a student to do a lot of work for some teachers and very little for others.

This variation in student attitude, effort, and performance has countless causes, and often it comes down to things you have little control over, such as your subject, personality, or the collection of students in your class. (As a new teacher, you also need to know that no matter how you run your classroom some students will likely respond to it and some likely won't.) But that doesn't mean that all approaches are equal; some approaches and techniques are more likely to bring out the good side of students or at least suppress the bad. If you can master those, there is a good chance that you will be the one at the meeting who is getting the most from students.

How to Get the Most Attention

Attention span is one of the most fickle attributes of students. Generally it is thought that students have very short attention spans—and in some situations this is definitely the case. It is not uncommon for students' attention to jump so quickly that they make a housefly look like the Buddha in comparison. But at other times, students can actually stay focused far longer than most adults ever could. Think about video games: few adults could play anything for eight hours, yet it is not uncommon for kids to spend that long on a video-game session.

What dictates students' attention span is a combination of factors. First, students have different natural levels of attention. Often they are broken down into ADHD or normal, but in reality students are on much more of a continuum. In your class you will likely have a few students who can't focus for more than a minute on anything, a few who will listen carefully to even the driest material for as long as needed, and the rest, who occupy some area in between.

The outside factors of the day also weigh heavily upon the attention span of students. Their ability to pay attention can grow or shrink based on how much sleep they got, the time of day, their level of hunger, what is going on at home, their proximity to the boy/girl they like, and a million other things. This changing level of attention is a large part of the reason that students and even entire classes will perform very differently on a day-by-day basis.

These first two factors—natural attentiveness and outside factors—are largely beyond the control of teachers. They also vary so significantly between students, classes, and days that to know what attention span to expect from your students on any given day is impossible. But as a teacher this doesn't mean you have to be held captive by the attention span that your students bring in the door. Though you can't change your students' natural attentiveness or the outside factors playing upon them, there are some approaches you can take in the classroom that will strongly improve the students' attention span and make sure that those with short ones still get the information.

Keep Them Active

If I had to come up with a list of the three types of activities during which students frequently stop paying attention, it would go as follows:

1. Whole-class discussions

2. Student presentations

3. Reading aloud during class

(This is not a condemnation of discussions, presentations, or reading aloud. All three are useful exercises, and I use them extensively. Instead, this is a warning about not structuring them correctly.)

What do these three activities have in common? During all three the majority of students are inactive at any given moment.

The reason students tend to lose focus during inactive moments is the same reason that we all have a tendency to zone out when we aren't doing something—when given the chance the human brain tends to drift toward other, more interesting topics that happen to be floating around it.

Luckily, guarding against attention slippage during the inactive moments of the lesson is simple—keep the students active! For example, instead of a straightforward, sit-down discussion you can have them move around the room according to their opinions, organize into teams and debate, or jot down the five best points their classmates make. When it comes to student presentations, instead of having students just listen they can grade them or write a response to them. In the end, there are lots of areas where a little bit of creativity can turn an inactive exercise into something that deserves the title "Activity," and this will help keep even the most distractible students with you.

Keep Up the Pace and Enthusiasm When It Is Inactive

It is a worthy goal to try and get students active during every second of your class, but in reality this probably isn't possible. Inevitably there will be times when students will just have to listen to you or their peers without being active—which actually isn't such a bad thing. Learning to listen quietly is an important skill. During those times it is not a bad idea to try to keep up the energy and enthusiasm of the class so that it can compete with the distracting thoughts of the brain. If you can make what is happening in class more intriguing than the other thoughts bouncing around the students' heads, they will probably stick with you.

Take Breaks

Just like teachers need to take breaks to remain fresh, students sometimes need breaks during class to keep their attention span up. Like all of us, students have certain thresholds for how much information they can absorb and how much class they can endure before their brains quit on them. The amount of information required to reach this level generally depends on the material being covered; if the class is covering something the students enjoy, they will likely have a much longer attention span than if the class is covering something they deem boring. So keep this fact in mind when you are planning your lessons. If you are doing something that you think the students will enjoy (like building model rockets) you may not need a break, but if you are doing something the students will likely find boring (like learning about trigonometry, so they can build rockets later) then it might be a good idea to build in a break or at least a moment to stretch, so the students can get refreshed.

Plan Like They Will Zone Out for Some of It

There aren't many situations where an audience will stay totally engaged the whole time. Even when people are at their favorite band's concert, their favorite team's game, or their favorite Broadway play, there will likely be moments when their minds drift somewhere else. Good playwrights and musicians know this, and they write their works accordingly. To see this you have to go no farther than Shakespeare. Shakespeare's plays always include cues to reclaim the attention of the audience members who have drifted before he introduces important pieces of information and major plot twists (common cues of his include sudden rhyming, something exciting like a fight or argument, or the unusual staging of a scene).

As a teacher, remember that if even Shakespeare's plays, great concerts, and sporting events lose the audience's attention at times, then no matter how active or engaging your class is you will still likely lose students at points. To make sure that this lost attention doesn't turn into missing information, it is important to take a cue from Shakespeare and learn to insert signals into lessons that warn your students that something important is coming up. These signals can be as simple as saying "This is important" or "This will be on the test," as subtle as raising your voice or changing your body position, or as fun and creative as you can imagine. In the end, just make sure that you do whatever you can to point to important information in the lesson, so students don't daydream through it.

How to Get Them to Retain the Most Information

Whether a school is private or public, urban or rural, successful or underperforming, most teachers are expected to impart a lot of information to students in a relatively short amount of time. This expectation is made even more difficult by the fact that students have brains like the rest of us, which means there is a finite amount of information they can absorb in a given span of time. But there are ways to get around these biological constraints and sneak in extra knowledge if the teachers are wise in their delivery. Though brains can only absorb so many different units of information over a set period of time, if that information is packaged in the right ways you can often slip in a lot more.

Cluster Information

There is a very good chance that if you've ever taken Psych 101 you've done some variation of the following experiment. But whether you have or not, give it a try:

Look at the following list of numbers for ten seconds, internalize them, and then look away. Once you are no longer looking, try to remember as many numbers as you can.

95   17   69   36   9   75   80   53   24

All right, how many did you remember? There is a decent chance that you didn't remember all or even most of them. Now here is another list that includes the exact same digits. Do the same thing and see how many you can remember this time.

1995   8675309   365   24/7

How many did you remember this time? The odds are you remembered a lot more, and here is why: Though both lists included the exact same numbers, the second list had one important difference: the numbers were grouped into fewer, more meaningful clusters. Whereas the first list had a lot of numbers that likely had little meaning for you, the second had fewer numbers that probably meant significantly more to you. (The first number is a year that most people are familiar with, the second is a telephone number from a hit 1980s song, the third is the number of days in a year, and the fourth is a common phrase.) By clustering the numbers into meaningful units, the job of remembering it is made significantly easier because you only have to remember a few memorable details instead of a lot of random ones. (Do you remember them still?)

This simple experiment may not be innovative by today's standards, but it has some very important applications when it comes to giving students information. If you want students to remember as much information as they can, try clustering it into meaningful groups whenever possible. Depending on what discipline you teach, this may mean sorting topics into meaningful units (in English, clustering all literary terms into one unit instead of sprinkling them throughout the year), occasionally jumping out of chronological order to find similar pieces of information (in history, you could go over all the great Native American leaders throughout history in one lesson instead of tacking them onto lessons about particular time periods), or introducing the information in unorthodox but sensible ways (in science, combining lessons about the stars and the elements, which fit logically together but rarely share the same lesson because one is chemistry and one is astronomy).

Embed Information into Stories

There is a reason that everything from dandruff commercials to bottles of milk on the supermarket shelf has a story that comes with it—and the reason is that stories are possibly the most efficient memory-storing devices in history. I had a history teacher in high school who did something that would make many education researchers shudder—she did nothing but lecture all day. And though pure lecturing is generally looked at today as a surefire way to help your students not remember the information, this teacher was actually wildly effective and her students regularly scored exceptionally high on AP history exams.

So what was her secret? How did she introduce material with a style of teaching that is considered to have minimal retention, do nothing to reinforce the ideas (as this book suggests), and come out with students who knew everything? The answer is that she had an unbelievable knack for creating stories. Her lectures weren't just lectures; they were grand tales of the blood, sweat, and tears behind our country, complete with twists and turns, good guys and bad guys. And we students loved them so much that we refused to ever forget them.

To see how efficient stories are, you have to go no further than the human trend toward passing on information through myths. For thousands of years, myths were the primary mode for passing on information because they were far easier to remember than a list of rules, beliefs, and ideas. And when my history teacher or marketers tells a story, he or she is using this same tactic.

As a teacher, turning your information into stories doesn't mean that you need to create tales full of gods and heroes (though it couldn't hurt); it just means you should strive to present your information as an intertwined story instead of as a series of disconnected facts. There are some disciplines, such as English or history, in which this is easier than others, but whether you are teaching math, science, or art your information will almost always have connections, and connections can very easily become a story if you line them up in the right order. So have some fun with it; when you talk about chemistry, turn it into a narrative of the inner workings of the universe, not a dull list of facts; when you talk about Thomas Jefferson, talk about him as a character in a great tale, not as a random name you should remember; and when discussing classical music, talk about the evolution of music as a coming-of-age story, not a series of trends.

Use Their Prior Knowledge to Create New Knowledge

If your education school experience was like mine, there is a good chance that "prior knowledge" is up there with "multiple literacies" and "pedagogy" on the list of buzz words and phrases you never want to see again. And it would be hard to blame you. But unlike some of the educational jargon, "prior knowledge" is worth another look. Often prior knowledge is only mentioned in the context of trying to figure out where to start a lesson (and indeed that is very important), but prior knowledge can be very useful during the lesson, too. Few approaches can make information more accessible and memorable than using prior knowledge.

The best practitioner I've seen of using prior knowledge to teach information is another history teacher who luckily shares a wall with my room (where I overhear his lessons). This teacher uses prior knowledge constantly and to greater effect than any teacher I've ever come across—and when he does his students always seem to learn on fast-forward. A good example of how he uses prior knowledge is a lesson he taught about Christianity, Islam, and Judaism. To start this lesson he had the students write a column on the board that included details about their religious background (like their holy day, their holy cities, and what their spiritual leader was called). Then he simply made new columns next to that one and filled them in with the same details from other religions.

This lesson may seem straightforward and simple, but the effect it had on the students was profound. As soon as they realized that Muhammad was a prophet like Moses, Mecca was a holy city like Jerusalem, and a mosque, church, and synagogue were the exact same thing, it was clear from the buzz that they weren't going to forget.

Using prior knowledge is powerful for the same reason that a metaphor is powerful. Metaphors take something the reader already knows and compare it to something he or she doesn't know. (For example, in the expression "sea of troubles," it is assumed that people who know how big a sea is will instantly get a much better picture of how many troubles there are.) Prior knowledge does the same thing, just with information. By taking facts the students already know and comparing them to new ones, you give them context and a starting point, which make facts easier to understand and more memorable. And that will help you get the most information into your students.

Exit Slip

When it gets boiled down, teachers are essentially in the marketing business. The basic premise of our job is to get information from our discipline and make it both engaging and memorable, so our students will remember and buy into it. As members of the marketing community, we shouldn't shy away from the wealth of knowledge that already exists concerning how to persuade people and make our ideas stick. There are numerous books (including a great one by Chip Heath and Dan Heath called *Made to Stick: Why Some Ideas Survive and Others Die*) about how to make information more appealing. By reaching outside of the teaching community to other related fields, you can find many great lessons that will be perfectly at home in the classroom.

STUDENT ACCOUNTABILITY, OR YOU CAN LEAD A HORSE TO WATER . . .

A t the end of the year, the teacher I shared my room with had a unit that I had to stand in awe of. The unit's premise was simple: The class read the novel *Hiroshima* and looked at it through the lens of whether we should have dropped the bomb or not. Then at the end of the unit the class broke up into two sides and debated whether nuclear weapons should have been used on Japan.

The striking part about this unit wasn't its originality, its execution, or the information covered; instead, it was how committed the students became to their side of the debate. Within a couple of days, the students became so engrossed in arguing their side that they began to meet voluntarily outside of school to discuss their position; during class the teacher was able to send them away without any fear that they would get sidetracked.

At first this teacher's ability to rouse such passion and commitment with such a seemingly simple premise was a mystery, but as the unit progressed it became clear that much of her success was due to one motivational skill used exceptionally well: student accountability. This teacher had succeeded in getting the students to be accountable for their own learning, and once she did they became self-sufficient learning machines that she couldn't have stopped if she had wanted to.

Often teaching is viewed as a one-sided affair of information-slinging on the part of the teacher, with the students responsible only for showing up and giving a solid effort. And when accountability is mentioned in teaching circles, it generally is in reference to teachers, schools, and administrators. But student accountability matters too—just for different reasons. Student accountability is so important because to have learning at the levels present in these "Hiroshima Debates," students need to embrace their role in the process. Then and only then can learning be truly maximized.

Give Them Real Responsibility

Using responsibility in the classroom generally goes in two directions: Dr. Jekyll or Mr. Hyde. This is because most people (including students) are more than willing to step up and take on important responsibilities—but at the same time, few things are more offensive to the average person than being responsible for tasks that they consider menial or below their capabilities.

To see this principle at work you have to go no further than the teachers at my school. Many of these teachers work day and night to make sure every student has all the tools needed to succeed because they view it as important; but when asked to do little tasks that they view as pointless (such as lunch duty at our school, which consists of walking around during lunch one day a week to police the kids) it is amazing how consistently these normally conscientious teachers will come late, goof off, avoid what duties they can, or even not show up at all.

So while planning your lessons, keep this dual nature of responsibility in mind. Giving students real responsibilities can inspire them to become passionate and accountable for their learning, but pointless responsibilities may inspire the exact opposite feelings. A good litmus test for determining if a responsibility is real or pointless is to look at the outcome. When someone doesn't do a real responsibility, people normally feel the effect, but when someone doesn't do a pointless responsibility, the odds are that no one will notice or be significantly impacted.

To further help you see the difference between real and pointless responsibilities, here are two examples of common classroom activities—student presentations and group work—and for each activity there are two examples of responsibilities a teacher might give, one pointless and one real.

Student Presentations

Pointless Responsibility

Have students in the class rate every presentation on a sheet of paper and do nothing with the rating. This responsibility is pointless because the ratings have no meaning. If their ratings don't actually mean anything, students will likely use them as props for jokes by making them overly high or low and then showing them off to anyone who will look.

Real Responsibility

Tell students that you will collect their ratings and take them into account on the final grade, or even better, that they will comprise a quarter of the grade. You will be amazed at how seriously the students take the exercise.

Group Work

Pointless Responsibility

Break the students into groups and tell them to come up with answers to five questions that the class will discuss as a whole. This task could seem fairly pointless to students because if everyone is coming up with the same answers, it isn't such a big deal if they don't do some of them because somebody else will.

Real Responsibility

When you break students into groups, give each group one of five questions and tell them that they will lead the class in a discussion of that question. This is a real responsibility because if they don't do it, everyone in the class (you included) will recognize that they didn't do the work; the discussion afterward will also suffer.

Tie Schoolwork to Grades or to Something Else They Care About

A lot of students loathe the idea of participation grades. And in a way they may have a point. If they do the work correctly, a case can be made that it isn't fair for the teacher to knock down their grade just because they didn't feel like sharing or showing enough effort.

When looking at it from the teacher's point of view, a good counterargument can also be made for having them, though. In the same way that tying points to organization can motivate students to stay organized, teachers can use the associative property to make students care about all sorts of different things they didn't care about before (like giving a strong effort during discussions or group work) by linking them with something they may care about (like grades).

This principle doesn't need to end with points, either; teachers can also tie other things that students care about to their work and behavior. For example, a teacher could tell a class that if they do a fantastic job on something they can leave a minute early for lunch or choose their own seats. They could also have the students present work in front of the class (which will tie in the students' desire to look good in front of their peers) or promise some sort of prize (like a movie day or food) if a class accomplishes certain goals. In the end, there are hundreds of different ways teachers can make things more interesting by connecting student desires to work or to activities that students might otherwise be indifferent about.

However, just because tying student work to things they care about often succeeds doesn't mean it is always the right way to go. In the end, every behavior shouldn't have a treat tied to it, because that can send the wrong message and come across as manipulative. As a teacher, you need to pick your moments. For example, I still don't include participation grades in my class because I worry about the effect it will have on students who are adamantly opposed to it, but I do assign points to how well students take notes, work in groups, or present in front of the class. I also occasionally promise other desirables like early dismissal, small blocks of free time, or even a slice of key lime pie to encourage students. (Important lesson: never underestimate the power of food.)

Effort Begets Effort

One of the worst parts of being a writer is the lingering fear that no one will read your work and that the fruits of your labor will rot on the vine. But this condition is not just limited to authors; we humans do not like to have our work, no matter how trivial, go to waste. So as a teacher, use this to your advantage. When you have major projects in class, make sure your students invest significant amounts of time and effort in them. You can do this by having them get started in class or show you steps along the way. For many students, with every bit of energy they expend on the project their desire to see it do well will increase exponentially.

The self-perpetuating nature of effort is the reason that ambitious projects like having a class memorize and act out all of *Romeo and Juliet*, produce a full-length newspaper, or complete intense competition math questions are often the most successful of all assignments. This was also one of the major reasons that the Hiroshima debates grew so lively. At first the students were no more interested in the debates than in any other unit, but as they got more and more involved their desire to do well exploded and created a cycle of effort that perpetuated itself.

Inspire Them

There is no group, short of Oprah's Book Club, more programmed to receive inspiration than teenagers. Though they often appear apathetic on the surface, on the inside many middle-school and high-school students are anxiously waiting for something to get excited about, even if they don't realize it themselves. As a teacher, you should take full advantage of this desire by trying to inspire your students whenever the opportunity arises—because if you are able to tap into their inspiration, they will do inspired work for you.

In one short year I witnessed inspired students do a number of jaw-dropping things. I saw a seventh grader write a fifty-page story for a five-page assignment, a freshman work tirelessly for months to complete a graduate-level math problem for a couple of extra-credit points, and an eleventh grader create a whole graphic novel of *The Scarlet Letter* for no reason at all. In all of these situations the students didn't do this level of work because they wanted an A (for they could have gotten an A with a fraction of the work); they did it because they were inspired to do something great.

When it comes to evoking this level of inspiration in students, the key for teachers is to elevate their subject in the eyes of the students. If students feel like they are doing work because they have to, they will likely just do what is required. If students feel like they are doing work for a grade, they will likely just do what is needed to reach the grade they want. But if students feel like they are doing work for a greater purpose, who knows how far they will take it?

To elevate your subject, the most important thing you need to do is to give students an understanding of why there is more to your class than just getting a good grade. For math and science, show students that these subjects are about looking into the secrets of life, tapping into universal truths, and understanding how our world works. Across the hall in English and history, let students know that they are in a conversation with the greatest thinkers the world has ever known and that they can feel free to add their small slice to the pie. Then once you've given reasons to care, repeat them from time to time while adding regular doses of enthusiasm and positivity (remember chapters 1 and 4), and you will hopefully be on the road to inspiration.

Exit Slip

One of the best lessons students can receive at school is, in the end, that the person who is most responsible for their own learning is themselves. While students are young, their teachers and parents certainly share in this responsibility too, but ultimately they are the most important part. To help students understand this, make it clear to everyone in your class that each student holds the starring role in his or her own learning, and the show will only succeed if they each give their best performance.

HOW TO DESIGN A FOOLPROOF LESSON

There is nothing more elemental to teaching than creating a lesson, and yet when I entered my first year I could count on one hand what I knew about it. I knew the parts of a lesson (objective, materials, activities, and assessment), that objectives should be phrased "Students will be able to . . . ," and that it is wise to put approximate times next to each activity. That's about it.

I don't blame anyone for my lack of lesson-writing knowledge—not college, not the books I read, and not myself. The fact is that writing and delivering lessons is deceptively difficult. On the surface it seems like a simple endeavor: Put down what you are going to do and then do it. And for veteran teachers, so practiced in the art of creating lessons that they no longer notice the subtle complexities, it may appear this simple. But designing a lesson is anything but simple. This is because a truly great lesson generally requires you to do more than just figure out the information you want to transmit; for maximum success, a lesson often must contain varied activities, appeals to different learners, smooth transitions, efficient timing, and a dash of flexibility—all woven together in a seamless fashion.

This chapter dissects the lesson into its nitty-gritty parts and shines light upon its secrets in an effort to help you with the deceptively difficult but infinitely important art of designing perfect lessons.

Good Lessons Should Be . . .
Precise

There is an English teacher at my school who comes as close as humanly possible to having no behavior problems in her class (and with eighth graders, no less). The reason for her disciplinary magic? Her lessons are like Swiss watches, with every part well crafted and working in flawless rhythm with the others—and the result is near disciplinary perfection. The students in her class don't have the opportunity to misbehave because each activity, transition, and set of directions in every lesson has been refined over nearly thirty years. In that period the troublesome spots have been aged out, leaving only the parts that work.

This type of precision is so effective at eliminating bad behavior because students generally go with the flow. When they have clear directions and a purpose, their natural response is often to trot along like lemmings—even if they don't particularly enjoy what they are doing. But when they don't have a clear task or set of directions, something needs to fill that void, and that something is often mischief. This is why preemptively identifying and eliminating soft spots in lessons is so important. Each hole filled might be one less chance for students to misbehave and one less time you may have to make tough decisions concerning how to punish them.

To find these holes in your lessons, look for any areas where the students might not know what to do, even if only for a few seconds (for it only takes a few seconds to start trouble). Though these moments of uncertainty can appear in any part of the lesson, here are a few common areas where lessons often get a little loose.

Transitions

It is easy not to give transitions much thought. If students need to get into groups, take out their vocabulary books, switch papers, or transition in any other way, the logical approach would be to simply ask them to do it. Unfortunately, you are dealing with students, which means the logical approach often may not be the best approach. The main problem with transitioning by simply asking students to do something is that students move at different speeds. When asked to do something, some students will generally be done by the time the teacher finishes asking, while for others even finding and taking out a piece of paper is a five-minute production. This means that while you wait for all the students to finish, the faster students have nothing to do—and that free space is usually filled very quickly with chatting, goofing around, or possibly even worse behavior.

To make sure that the seeds of trouble aren't planted during your transitions, try tightening them up by giving students more specific directions. Instead of just telling them to get into groups, say something like "You have one minute to get into groups and decide which role each person is going to have." The reason that the second set of directions is more effective than the first is that it both inspires students to go quickly (because if they don't get into groups fast they won't have time to pick their roles) and it gives everyone something to do (because students will inevitably argue about what roles they should have until someone stops them). When it comes to smooth transitions these two elements—inspiration to go quickly and everyone having enough to do—are often the secret to keeping students on task and out of trouble.

When There Isn't Enough Work

You rarely hear students say they misbehaved in class because they had too much to do. But "I didn't have anything to do" is easily one of the most common excuses for student misbehavior. Keep this in mind when planning your class: When students don't have anything to do—even if the absence of work is due to their working hard and finishing early—trouble normally follows. Because of this it often helps to have a second, third, and possibly even a fourth thing students can do if they finish the work assigned. For example, instead of just letting students sit around after a quiz, you can give them the choice to read from the bookshelf, get started on homework, write in their journals (having a running journal can be an incredibly handy thing for a class), or even help you set up for the next assignment. In the end, it doesn't necessarily matter what students do, just so long as they have something to do. Because if you don't give them something to do they will find something to do, and it will most likely end with you saying, "Hey, stop that!"

While You Do Things

The final area where lessons often get a bit loose is when the teacher needs to do something. Whether it is taking attendance, collecting homework, writing on the board, or handing back papers, these moments when your attention needs to be on something other than the class pop up all over lessons. In order to discourage students from playing while the cat's attention is away, try giving them little assignments or tasks. Again, whether it is a free-write while collecting homework or asking them to make corrections as their papers are passed back, these tasks are all about getting the students doing something. As long as they have something to do, they will be less inclined toward trouble.

Good Lessons Should Be . . .
Interesting

The odds are that your students will not be intrinsically interested in what you are talking about. They are probably more interested in who might go to the next dance with them, the new video game they just bought, or whether they are starting in the basketball game tonight. Compared to those concerns, topics like vocabulary and isosceles triangles just aren't that fascinating.

This lack of student interest is a problem because interest is an incredibly powerful suppressant of poor behavior. Think about a movie theater. During a good movie, hundreds of adults and children sit perfectly still and quiet for hours. If anyone in the audience so much as breathes too loud, a hundred angry stares shame the offender into behaving.

The movie theater experience illustrates the power that interest can have. If people are interested in something, they will put their natural urges to talk and move, their previous concerns, and even the need to go to the bathroom aside. This power is also why we as teachers must strive to make our lessons (which students normally have little interest in) interesting—because there is no better way to preemptively scratch out bad behavior.

Add Interest through Presentation

This year our school had a speaker named Louis Mangione, who gave a presentation called "Indelible Instruction." This presentation had a lot of highlights, but one activity that really stood out was a geography lesson he gave about Spain. The geography of Spain is not necessarily the most interesting topic in the world, but through his presentation Mangione made it both interesting and memorable. The way he inspired interest was to give the entire presentation without an actual map. Instead of using a map, Mangione outlined where all the geographic features were on an invisible map in front of him. To further add to the illusion, he also had sound effects and an invisible controller for the map and he regularly moved the invisible map around so everyone could see it. When this presentation was over, the entire roomful of teachers was not only still with him, they were anxious to see the real map so they could compare it to the maps in their minds.

All of us may not have the showmanship to pull off an invisible map, but Mangione's point is well taken. By presenting information in an unusual, unorthodox, or just generally different or interesting way, you can breathe interest into even the most mundane information. But how you do that is up to you.

Use Multimedia, or at Least Multiple Senses, As Often As Possible

Students are often used to having their sense of sight, hearing, and (if they have a Wii) touch engaged at the same time. With this in mind, try to get multiple senses involved in the classroom whenever you can. Instead of just saying information, write it down so they can see it, and maybe have them write it, too. Instead of telling students about a science experiment, show them—or better yet, have them do it during a lab. If you are talking about Genghis Khan or about how hurricanes form, have them close their eyes and envision the sights, sounds, and feelings of the moment. And when talking about right triangles or graphing 3-D shapes, give them the shapes (or have them make them) to see how they physically feel. In the end, more than one sense can be brought to any topic if you have enough imagination, and added learning will probably follow.

Vary How You Present It

One of the most successful and popular lessons of my first semester was a debate where the class argued who the greatest hero in Greek mythology was. This lesson worked perfectly—the kids were engaged and enjoying themselves, they demonstrated and reinforced the information, and they secretly practiced their essay skills. I was so happy with the outcome of the lesson that I held another debate less than a month after, with the expectation that it would be just as successful. But instead this debate, though organized and approached in the same manner, flopped badly, and multiple students questioned why we were debating again.

The problem with the second debate wasn't that it wasn't a strong lesson; it was that it was a lesson that had already been done. In the same way that even the best food can taste worse if eaten too often or the best song can grow stale if overplayed, a lesson can definitely suffer if it is done too much.

So in your class it is worth changing your style, activities, and lessons often enough that they don't wear out their welcome.

Give Them a Reason to Care

As a teacher it can be easy to fall into the trap of believing that just because you love the inner workings of your subject, your students will, too. In reality this isn't normally the case, though; instead of loving your subject, most students just endure it because their grades or their family's and friends' approval depends on it. Beyond getting a good grade to impress those around, they tend not to have a lot of interest in it.

But it doesn't have to be this way. In the same way that you can teach students about George Washington or plate tectonics, you can also teach them to care about more about George Washington or plate tectonics. The first, and biggest, step toward teaching this added interest is to prove to students that information they receive in class will directly improve their lives outside of school. Generally even the most advanced students may not be aware of how trigonometry, adverbs, or Newton's laws will help them in the long run, and thus they aren't too worried about really learning about them.

But as teachers, we do generally know the reasons for learning these things or else we wouldn't be teaching them. So we should tell and show students whenever possible why the subject manner is essential to their life. To do this, we can create activities and assessments that reflect the real world (if you are teaching the students how a bill goes through Congress, walk through the process with a real bill), bring in real-world applications of the information (show them articles about the information or examples of how it is used in the world), have them do projects that actually have an impact upon the world (one math teacher I know enlisted her class to help me mathematically measure out and actually build a two-hundred-meter track for the track team to run workouts on), or just take a moment to explain how knowing the information will make their lives better.

Most things in school can probably be connected to the world outside of the classroom, and by taking a moment to find the connections you can show your students the value of the course beyond a grade on a transcript. For once students see the point of learning a specific piece of information, even if they never come to cherish it as you do, they will still often grow far more willing to learn it and learn it well.

Good Lessons Should Be . . .
Ready for Time Anomalies

For new teachers, one of the most unsettling parts about designing a lesson can be that you really have no idea how long your activities will take. Sometimes an activity scheduled for thirty minutes will take two full class periods, while other times a whole period of activities will only take half the class. The reason for this insanely large window is that time, by some perversion of physics, does not move evenly in the classroom. One day it will move at breakneck speeds, with minutes melting off like seconds, and the next day a whole class period can feel like a lifetime. Because of this, it is essential that your lessons be prepared for the unexpected. If you expect a lesson to take sixty minutes, be ready for it to take thirty or ninety, because sometimes it will.

Out of these two situations the scarier (yet far less common) scenario is for a lesson to run short. I remember one of my chief fears before my first year was running out of material before the class ended and having to turn to the expectant faces of the students with nothing to do. Luckily for me and for anyone else who shares this fear, lessons almost always run long, and if they do run short there are a few simple tricks you can use to cover up the planning error.

The first thing you can do to protect yourself against activities running faster than anticipated is to keep a short exercise or two in your drawer just for the rare occasions that you run out of material. The exercise should be fun and interesting enough that students won't think to question why you are doing it (because it probably won't go with the rest of your lesson). The second, and more widely used, option is that you can almost always give the students extra homework time or a study period. Students are often nearly as overwhelmed as you are, and in general they welcome any extra time to make a small dent in their work; that makes study time a perfect cover for timing errors.

Whereas lessons going too fast is a fairly rare occurrence, running out of time before everything is done is incredibly common. This could be because in many ways lesson plans are best-case scenarios—they are what will happen if everything goes according to plan. But in the world of teaching, having things go as scripted is much more the exception than the rule, so it is worth keeping in mind that during a lot of class periods you won't cover all the material you intended to.

The major problem with time running short is that it forces teachers into the often messy business of ad-libbing. For most veteran teachers, these on-the-spot decisions are just another part of the job, but for new teachers they can be truly terrifying. In a few moments, you need to make all the decisions about whether to rush through, trim, or cut out the remaining activities. If you decide to trim or cut activities, you may also need to quickly figure out what is going and what is staying and then reformulate it into a coherent lesson.

If you find yourself in this position, there aren't many hard-and-fast rules for how to make quick fixes on the go, but that doesn't mean there is nothing you can do. The best way to improve your ability to improvise lesson changes is to think about possible alterations before you even start. By figuring out beforehand what parts can be cut or amended if time runs short, the need for quick thinking is taken away and replaced with just following through on a ready-made plan.

Good Lessons Should Be . . . Ready to Move

I am always somewhat miffed when education speakers and authors tell teachers that movement in their classes is important, give one or two random examples of movement helping students, and then move on. What makes this approach irritating is that few teachers dispute the notion that getting students to move is a good thing. Anyone who has spent more than ten minutes around adolescents knows that for many kids constant movement is as natural as breathing.

The reason for a lack of movement in many classrooms is not that teachers are ignorant of its advantages; it's that for most lessons it is not a comfortable fit. Movement doesn't exactly connect easily with topics like adjectives or factoring, so most of the time, despite its advantages, it is left out. Here are some tips to help make movement a more natural fit for any lesson you teach. Even with these you will still have to use your imagination to constantly incorporate movement, but they should form a good jumping-off point.

- Getting students into groups is a great way to incorporate movement. Even if there is no other movement built into the activity, at least students must move to get together. Having students in groups also makes it easier to build in other types of movement (such as having them go up to the board to write down their findings, act out answers, make small projects, or give short presentations).

- Take your class on the road by going to different locations around the school. A change of environment will automatically draw the attention of some students. Use this one sparingly though, and save it for locations that really help to bring the point home (so it doesn't lose its novelty).

- Most things can be acted out in one way or another (from how a cell works to going over the plot of a poem), so have the students act out what you are learning. This approach is always good to liven up the class and grab their attention.

- Have the students draw, close their eyes and imagine something, or do any other type of "movement" that we might not normally consider movement. Moving of hands, eyelids, or any other body part can meet their need for movement as well as jumping around.

- Be creative. In the end, movement can be found in most situations. If you are truly committed to adding movement, the key is to get creative, have fun, and don't worry too much if it doesn't work as you planned. At least you got them out of their seats.

Exit Slip

Sometimes what makes a lesson succeed is more magic than science. There are times that the best-planned lessons, chock-full of appeals to different learning styles and can't-miss activities, fail badly. And sometimes, even more inexplicably, lessons that enjoyed smashing success with one class will fall flat in another. Other times, lessons that are hurriedly or sloppily planned come together beautifully, and on rare occasions lessons will actually go as scripted.

All of this means that every time a lesson doesn't work out, don't pour all the blame on yourself. Lesson success depends upon much more than your personal preparation. The time of day, proximity to lunch, the weather, students' experience in the previous period, and the latest gossip about who broke up with whom are just a few of the outside factors that can either aid or thwart a lesson. This is not to say that you are powerless against such forces or should leave your class to the winds of fate, but don't be so hard on yourself if a lesson doesn't work out. Good lessons can go badly, too.

HOW TO DELIVER A FOOLPROOF LESSON

Y ou can have the tightest, most engaging lesson ever, but if you don't deliver it well, then all of its strengths probably won't mean a whole lot. On the other end of the spectrum, even a weak lesson, delivered by a talented performer, has the power to spellbind, inspire, and amaze students. This means that when it comes to your lessons, crafting them is only half the battle; for those lessons to have their full impact they also need to be delivered with great skill. As with enthusiasm, some people have a natural gift for presenting well and don't need any schooling for how to address a room. But for the rest of us, here are the lessons those naturals already know on how to go from being a transmitter of information to being a showperson.

Make Sure You Have Their Attention

A lot of new teachers regularly try to talk over their students instead of quieting them before speaking. The problem with this is that not only can information be lost when other voices compete with yours for attention, but it also shows a great deal of disrespect on the part of the students. By the time they hit middle school, students know that talking while someone else is speaking is very rude. And though most new teachers will reprimand students for talking over their peers, they often will let their students consistently talk over them.

As a new teacher it is essential that you have the students' attention and silence before you begin speaking. Waiting until they are quiet reinforces that you won't allow disrespect, and it creates a far more stable platform from which to start your lesson. Unfortunately, getting students quiet and listening is easier said than done, especially at the start of class when they've just come from the chaos of passing time. To help with this sometimes difficult process, try some of these tips for getting students quiet.

Get Conversational

In the beginning of class, instead of starting with a negative like "Quiet!" try something positive. Wish everyone a good morning, tell them it is good to see them, ask how they are, or just walk around for a second and say hi. Maybe even devote a couple of minutes to being conversational. Just by your standing and talking, most of the students will instinctively quiet down and possibly even offer you a muffled wish for a good day back. This approach carries many advantages over shushing them, including that it is positive and it doesn't take any teaching capital (because you aren't asking anything of them). And besides, who doesn't like starting out with a nice "Good morning"?

Stay Positive

Getting conversational may quiet the class sometimes, but it probably won't always work. When a greeting does little to dampen their conversation, it is important to still fight the urge to be negative (even if your feelings are shifting in that direction). Instead of getting somewhat hostile with your comments, like "Stop talking" or "Pay attention," try to ask for their attention in more positive ways like "Take a deep breath" or "Let's settle in." The advantage to this approach (besides being nicer) is that it isn't confrontational and thus has no chance of causing the students to get defensive or rebellious. If you tell students to stop talking and they don't, then you are in conflict with them whether you want to be or not. If you tell students to take a deep breath and they don't, then all that will happen is they will likely pass out.

Get Stern or Silent

Sometimes students need a firmer approach than a friendly greeting or positive suggestion; sometimes they need to be told to be quiet and listen. If you find yourself in this position, there are two approaches that generally work: You sternly order them to be quiet or you say nothing at all. When you sternly reprimand the students (as was discussed in chapter 3), what you say isn't as important as how you say it. At this point you want to make sure they understand that you aren't pleading or suggesting, you are telling and there will be consequences if they continue. This stern reprimand should also contain significantly more intensity than previous requests to be quiet, so the contrast in intensity adds to the overall power of the moment.

If you take the quiet route, the idea is that by your suddenly going quiet and staring at the students, they will be shocked into behaving. There is something profoundly unsettling to students about a silent teacher, and 99 out of 100 times the class will go dead silent within ten seconds of your going silent. The only issue with this approach is to avoid doing it too often, because in many ways the novelty of a teacher going silent is what makes it so potent.

Have Them Start with an Assignment

This will be discussed in chapter 19, but often giving students an assignment in the beginning of class will quiet them without your having to say anything. This works because a task gives the students something more important to do than chat with their friends.

Talk Normally

Once the class is silent it is time for you to start talking, and one of the surefire signs of a new teacher is how quickly they talk. While most veteran teachers are conversational in their tone and pace, new teachers often talk like they are stuck on fast-forward. And though students are used to rapid stimuli, even they can have trouble understanding a new teacher speaking at full speed.

As a new teacher, you will find it is worth spending some energy to slow the pace of your talking. By speaking slowly in a world of fast-talking newbies, you send the message that you are a capable and composed professional who may look inexperienced, but doesn't teach like it. Unfortunately, no tricks exist for doing this beyond just staying mindful of your speaking. Through recognizing and correcting the moments when you talk too fast, you will begin to train yourself for the future, and soon the speed of your speaking will be one less thing you need to worry about.

Channel Your Inner Thespian

It is probably fair to assume that most teachers were not heavily involved in theater in their youth, but whether they have a past with it or not, there is no doubt that they are heavily involved in theater now. The job of a teacher is nothing if not theater. You stand, you deliver lines, sometimes you need to change your persona (for instance, when a student makes a funny but inappropriate joke, you must reprimand the student instead of laughing like you might with your friends), and you have an audience judging your every move.

Since teaching is theater, and for my part I knew little about acting, I decided as a young teacher to turn to acting books and specifically to Ron Marasco's *Notes to an Actor* to get a crash course on performing to an audience. Here are a few acting notes I found along the way.

Use Who You Are

Again and again, acting resources discuss how in both acting and life, people are pulled toward those who are comfortable with themselves. Marasco claims that as people we have an intrinsic sense for whether those around us feel comfortable in their skin or not—and we gravitate toward those who do.

This insight may come as bad news to new teachers, whose confidence can get thrashed on a daily basis, but there is also a piece of good news buried in it. The good news is that one of the keys to being a good performer is to just be yourself (which you should be well practiced for) and to be proud of who you are. If the students get the sense that you are genuine and all right with who you are, they will gain an unconscious respect for you that will make up for some of the idiosyncrasies and faults you might have.

"Nontransition Transitions" Can Create Timing

Generally teachers have one goal for their transitions: do them as smoothly as possible. And in a lot of situations a smooth transition is exactly the right mark to shoot for. But sometimes you can use seemingly choppy transitions to give your lesson more theatrical timing. Marasco gives a great example of using unsmooth transitions for a positive effect when he mentions Wile E. Coyote from the Road Runner cartoons. When Coyote inevitably runs off a cliff, the fall is not done smoothly. First there is a cloud of dust, followed by a full second when Coyote doesn't realize he is in the air; then he looks down, looks at us, waits for a second, and suddenly falls for an abnormally long time before ending his tumble with a small, anticlimactic thump. This whole scene with Coyote has no smooth transitions, but it is exactly this lack of transitions that makes it so brilliant.

As teachers, we can use these unsmooth transitions or "nontransition transitions" to grab the attention of our audience or to prove a point. One way to do this is to use a noticeably awkward pause before an important point. This works in a similar way to Coyote's unnatural hovering above the cliff. Our audience, similar to his, knows that *something* has to come next, so they wait expectantly to see what it is.

Another way to do this is to use a puzzling transition, when you say something that has no meaning yet, like "If you start your essay with 'Since the dawn of time' I will ball it up and toss it in the garbage!" Once the students' brains have struggled for long enough and are thus invested in the answer, you give it to them: "'Since the dawn of time' is a cliché; essays need to start with something actually interesting, not with a cliché!"

A final way to use nontransitions to add theatrics is to have occasional shocking transitions, when you say something so far from what students expect that they are dumbstruck for a moment until you continue. Try using a wild quote, fact, or idea and you will find that from there you often have the students' full attention. I once taught students about why it's important to learn about structuring an argument by telling them they had an extra five-page paper due by the end of the week. When they protested, I told them they could only get out of it by arguing effectively, and followed that shocking startup by explaining that you need the ability to argue to get out of situations you see as unreasonable. I have never had more attention during an essay lesson.

Great [Teachers] Have a Feel for Story

Marasco claims that all great people in our society—be they actors, politicians, or teachers—have the ability to turn seemingly anything into a story. And this is not just because a story can make information easy to remember (see chapter 9). Stories are central to being a good performer because they can captivate our attention as few things can by manipulating our biological need to have our questions answered. Effective stories always have loads of unanswered questions, and as readers we often become willing to wait as long as it takes to find out what the answers are.

While planning your lessons, you too can impart this feeling for story by remembering the power of questions. If you can fill the minds of the students with questions, and they are even vaguely interested, the vast majority will mentally stick around to find the answers. And don't just think about questions in the traditional sense (like "Who was the first Holy Roman

Emperor?"); try inspiring questions in your students' minds through your delivery and organization (for example, you could start an activity without giving them the full story of what they are doing, or organize the facts so they don't quite make sense at first). Also, it is important to remember that they probably don't love your subject as much as you, so you should strive for questions that the students will find truly interesting, too.

How to Remember It

Unless they have a teleprompter, most performers not only have to worry about delivering lines, they also need to remember them, too. And few performers have to remember more lines per day than teachers. What other profession is required to internalize hours of script per day, while also having to occasionally take a break to reprimand the crowd for talking? With so much to remember, in minds that are already overextended, it is essential that new teachers cut as many corners and use as many tricks as possible to make the task of remembering their lessons more manageable. Here are some ways to lighten the load.

Keep an Agenda on the Board

Most students probably think the daily agenda on the board is for meant purely for them; little do they know that the agenda is often more for the teacher than the students. Daily agendas can be great friends for teachers for the same reason that they are useful for students—with one glance you can see where the lesson is going. This is good for students because they know what to prepare for, and it takes away the "What are we doing?" whine—but as a teacher it gives you an easy cue card that is always just a glance away. When the outline of your lesson plan is on the board, it is nearly impossible to forget a section of the lesson or get accidentally sidetracked for too long.

When Giving a Lecture, Use Aids That Don't Look like Aids

When you give a long talk in front of the class, it is often a good idea to pair it with a PowerPoint presentation, a set of notes, or a worksheet. Not only do these accompaniments make the information more accessible to visual learners, but if you use them you don't have to memorize an entire lecture.

Make Lesson Plans That Are Glance-Friendly

In college you probably were graded on whether your lesson plan contained the following (or similar) categories: objectives, materials, refresher, classroom procedure, assessment, and reflection. Now that you are on your own, keep all of these categories in mind when making a lesson, but toss most of them off your final lesson plan for class. Instead, try using a slimmed-down and streamlined lesson plan form for one reason—it makes a better in-class reminder. During class, teachers generally have just seconds to steal glances at their written lesson plans. If your lesson plan is full of objectives and assessment goals, it often means more searching to find the reminder you need. But if your lesson plan holds only a simple list of the activities, a quick peek is generally all you need to jog your memory about what comes next.

Exit Slip

For most new teachers, few things are scarier than changing their very well-thought-out plans. When they are off the cuff, it can feel like anything can happen, and that leaves too many possibilities to be comfortable. But to be truly good performers, teachers need to grow somewhat comfortable with the off-the-cuff region. One of the keys of performing is to play to your audience, and sometimes to truly connect with them takes a slight change of plan. So don't be afraid to follow where the lesson takes you (at least to an extent), because those unexpected areas are where some of the best learning can take place.

MANAGING YOUR STUDENTS

W hen I look back at my daily notes from the beginning of my first year, several themes stand out surrounding classroom management. Entries concerning student misbehavior, the best way to discipline students, when to discipline students, and general talking and disrespect come up again and again. What do all these topics have in common? They are all negative, and they are all reactive. And as a new teacher, this is how I looked at classroom management. Classroom management was a negative business where the teacher set the boundaries and waited for students to break them. Then when students misbehaved, it was the teacher's job to crack the whip and restore order.

I spent much of my first year with this viewpoint, until I joined a group of teachers charged with thinking about ways to improve the school's disciplinary policy for the upcoming year. To my surprise, these meetings did not focus on punishment of bad behavior as I expected; instead, they focused on preventing bad behavior and increasing the amount of good behavior. As I listened to these conversations about prevention and positives, I began to realize that the most important part of every teacher's behavior management system is how it eliminates poor behavior before it starts.

This realization is why the unit on behavior management comes in the middle of the book, not at the beginning. Everything you've read about so far, from planning lessons to gaining respect to making students accountable, is a form of proactive behavior management. It is meant to help you keep order in your classroom by preemptively striking at bad behavior before it starts.

But unfortunately, despite all of the best preparation, some negative behavior is unavoidable—and that is where this unit comes in. This unit covers the motivations behind poor behavior and lets you know about all the ways, from nonverbal communication to detention, to deal with it. It also doesn't forget about the importance of prevention, and it continues to give as many pieces of advice as possible for how to get positive and preemptively strike against all forms of unwanted behavior.

IDLE THREATS AND CONSEQUENCE SCALES

When it comes to their course load, many teachers have one section that becomes "The Class." What makes a period "The Class" is that it simply doesn't run as well as the others. Lessons may not go as smoothly, students might not progress as quickly, or behavior might be consistently worse. Whatever the reason, this section gets the designation as "The Class" because it stands out for the wrong reasons.

For me, my "Class" was one of my sections in the middle of the day. What made this section so difficult wasn't a lack of talent, motivation, or potential. The problem was their talking. Every single action in this class, whether it was a quip from a classmate or a direction from me, seemed to trigger a cascade of comments from the students. To make matters worse, controlling these outbursts proved difficult because, unlike in most classes, there weren't one or two students at the epicenter of trouble. Close to half the class fell into the category of "talkers," and any one of them had the ability to set off those nearby, which would ultimately start a chain reaction ending with the class consumed in talking and my yelling above them to quiet down.

Throughout much of the year my issues with this class built, until one day in February they reached a crescendo. On this day the students chattered incessantly from the moment they walked through the door. They couldn't seem to do anything without talking, and I couldn't seem to even slow them down. By the end of the period I had given at least six or seven students a "final warning" and reprimanded double that number at least once. Yet amazingly, despite all of the trouble caused and warnings issued, not a single student walked away with any sort of punishment.

The reason that students walked away without punishment on easily the worst behavior day of the year? It was because they didn't deserve it—or at least, according to the criteria set by my behavioral system they didn't deserve it. At the time my system consisted of students receiving an undefined number of warnings, followed by detention if they were really bad. Unfortunately, this system provided little defense against a day like the one I'd just had, because although the class as a whole was unbearable, each individual student committed only minor infractions. Even those given "final warnings" never built a body of bad behavior to justify the major penalty of detention.

So with these insufficiencies in mind I decided to build another behavioral policy that was ready for any type of day. Not knowing where to begin, I turned to the teachers around me and came away with three quotes that guide my behavioral policy to this day.

"Never Threaten Something That You Aren't Willing to Do at the Exact Moment You Say You Will"

When students misbehave, many teachers (especially new teachers) make idle threats to try to scare students into behaving. This approach can be quite appealing because making an idle threat is very easy and they usually quell bad behavior. Generally students will stop their bad behavior when threatened with consequences, even if deep down the teacher knows that the consequences aren't real.

The problem with idle threats isn't that they are wholly ineffective—it's that they are a gamble. When an idle threat works, it gets the students to behave. But when a student continues to act up despite the threat, the idle threat turns from ally to enemy. At this point the threat puts the teacher in a tough situation: you can either follow through on the threat, despite the fact that you didn't mean it, or you can not follow through and lose a sliver of your credibility.

If you don't follow through on enough threats, very slowly and subtly a message is sent that your threats aren't credible. This is the reason that it often takes a few months for new teachers to have their most significant behavioral problems. This was also the reason that in February, five months into the school year, my class behavior was at its worst. I didn't realize it, but throughout the whole year each time I uttered an idle threat (like "last warning") and I didn't punish them for the next slip-up, no matter how small, my credibility chipped a bit until my students eventually no longer feared the consequences I threatened.

"The Punishment Should Fit the Crime"

The notion that even wrongdoers deserve a fair punishment is a theme that runs along the very foundation of our society. Our most popular movie heroes dole out fair justice to the unfair evildoers of the world, our court system prides itself on its "fair and impartial" verdicts, and the Constitution, the basis of our society, sides with fairness when it condemns "cruel and unusual punishments." Despite this societal emphasis on fair penalties, many new teachers can be anything but fair when they punish their students. This disciplinary inequality on their part rarely stems from a desire to be unfair, though; rather, it usually comes from their lack of tools for controlling the classroom.

Many new teachers have very limited behavior management systems that often consist of little more than warnings and major consequences (like detention). The problem with a system like this is that there is no middle ground—and that is exactly where the majority of student misbehaviors fall. Whenever students commit misdemeanors like occasional talking or mildly inappropriate behavior, a teacher with this type of system has only two options: warn them or throw the book at them. With such a limited range of punishments, teachers are often forced to administer punishments that don't fit the crime. Sometimes this means that they need to come down too hard on offenses that don't warrant it, while other times it means students don't get the punishment they deserve, which is equally unfair (especially since some students are overpunished).

To avoid the handcuffing that comes with a system of warnings and severe punishments, it is worth coming up with consequences with varying levels of severity for your class. In doing this, there is no set type of consequences that you need to include. Some teachers use fairly standard punishments (like lost points or privileges; mini-detentions during break or lunch; having students clean parts of the room, complete other small tasks, or call home to explain what they did), while others go more alternative routes (like having monetary systems where students gain and lose class "bucks" for their behavior). In the end, it doesn't matter what type of consequences you have, so long as you have consequences for most types of misbehavior.

After figuring out consequences that you feel comfortable with, the last steps are to match your consequences with the types of behaviors that might warrant them and then make sure they are clear to the students. This way when the students inevitably test their limits, you and they will know what consequence is ready and waiting for them.

"Whatever Your Last Line of Defense Is, Keep It in Your Pocket"

One of the greatest lines in literary history is from *The Wizard of Oz*: "Pay no attention to the man behind the curtain." This line is wonderful for many reasons, but one of the unexpectedly great things about it is that it perfectly describes the power dynamic between teachers and students. To most students, teachers are big, bad, all-powerful beings—much like the wizard was to Dorothy when she first met him. But if the students were to peer behind the curtain they would see someone with substantially less power. Teachers have the power to tell parents and administrators about bad behavior and to suggest that students undergo some type of punishment. Beyond that they can't *force* a student to do anything. They can't ground a student, they can't kick him or her out of school, and they can't even lower a student's grade for poor behavior.

Because teachers have such limited power, it is important for them to reserve their greatest punishments for the times when they are truly needed. This is because after levying their strongest punishments, teachers are ironically left powerless. At this point, there is nothing more they can do to penalize students, which means the students are free to do and say what they want without fear of further retribution. Also, once a student returns to class after suffering the teacher's worst (and thus seeing behind the curtain), they are often far less worried about causing trouble because they know the limits of the teacher's power.

The dangers associated with punishing a student severely are important to keep in mind, but they don't mean that teachers should never use the full extent of their power (whether it is detention, a trip to the principal's office, or a call home); they merely mean that teachers should keep their most potent punishments in their pocket for the moments that truly call for it. If you hand out your worst on a regular basis, you may not only desensitize the students to the effects, you also run the risk of appearing in the eyes of the students as a man or woman with limited power, instead of as a great wizard.

Exit Slip

The key to behavior management (and to so much else in the school) comes down to consistency. Having a system of classroom management is a great first step, but if you aren't consistent with its enforcement then your whole system probably won't do a lot of good. Of course, 100 percent consistency is impossible in a world as varied and fluid as the school, but every percentage of consistency you are able to add will likely make your disciplinary system that much stronger.

USING YOUR VOICE AND BODY AS TEACHING TOOLS

Before my first official student teaching critique, I had a lot to worry about. My handling of student talking, timing of lessons, and speed of speaking were just a few of the many faults on my teaching résumé, and I expected to hear all about them. But instead my mentor teacher ignored all of those issues and focused the entire session on my body language, which he claimed was the number one thing for me to work on.

At first this choice of topic came as quite a shock; compared to my other concerns body language seemed laughably trivial. But after this I started to pay attention to it, and I quickly found out it was anything but. Body language may not get the press that a lot of other teaching topics get or be the first thing on new teachers' minds, but few things are more effective at helping manage a classroom. In the same way that a picture is worth a thousand words, one piece of clear body language can send an unmistakable message that cannot be achieved through speaking alone.

Classroom Positioning

For new teachers it is common to feel incredibly intimidated by the students. Even if you are significantly bigger than they are, it isn't hard to feel like the smallest person in the room while in front of their gazing eyes. Because of this, many new teachers, often unconsciously, teach their lessons from afar. Like a newborn cub staying close to its mother, they refuse to stray from the part of the room that they deem comfortable (such as their desk or the front board) for longer than a few seconds. When they do venture out they often limit their movement so they can get back to their comfort blanket as quickly as possible.

When teachers instruct from a stationary and still position, they lose out on a very potent behavior management tool—their location in the classroom. It may seem ridiculous, but something as small as a shift of a couple of feet toward a student will nine times out of ten drastically improve the student's behavior. This happens for the same reason that people always drive more conscientiously when near a police car, even when there is no possible way the police car can clock or even see them. They know The Law is close enough to get them in trouble, so they want to look like model citizens until the danger of being caught subsides (at which point they generally go back to breaking laws right away).

The quiet power that your presence possesses makes it one of the best weapons against student misbehavior. It is far less disruptive than verbally reprimanding students and it expends far less teaching capital. It also sends a message that is equally clear—especially if you make it clear in your movement that your presence there is not a coincidence. Because of these strengths, using your body positioning as the first warning to misbehaving students is rarely a bad idea. That doesn't mean it is always the right choice or superior to verbal reprimands, but generally speaking it is the least invasive way to tell students to get in line, and that makes it a good first option.

Body positioning can be used for far more than just a disciplinary tool, though; it can send a plethora of different messages if used right. For example, students generally look at the teacher while giving presentations, so if you want a student to speak louder, back up. It is amazing how often students raise their decibel level when the teacher backs to the farthest corner of the room. You can also sit down on the same level as the students during discussions to give the conversation a more informal tone, remain standing with an attentive pose during group activities to remind students they are being watched, move quickly throughout the room during lectures to add extra energy, or sit quietly while the students write so they don't feel like someone is looking over their shoulder. In the end, there is no limit to the number of messages you can send through your positioning, so don't be afraid to play with your positioning and see what messages it passes along to your students.

The Teacher Look

Have you ever gotten in front of a mirror to practice your "teacher look"? Be honest. If you have found yourself in this somewhat ridiculous situation (as many of us have), it is probably because you remember a teacher from your schooling who had the ability to clear a room with one stern stare—and you desperately want that ability.

Unfortunately for those mirror lookers out there, the secret to the teacher look has nothing to do with how you can contort the muscles in your face. Rather, it is all about the emotions behind the look and messages they send. If you too want to produce a room-clearing look, there are three essential messages you must write upon your face:

1. I am confident.

2. I am angry.

3. My anger is restrained *for the moment.*

Confidence is the starting point for any teacher look, because without it students likely won't take any messages you attempt to send very seriously. For many students, a lack of confidence in your look means you aren't comfortable with the feelings you are trying to express, and thus would also not be comfortable with doling out the possible punishment they suggest. So they disregard your look as harmless and continue with their day. But when they see from your look that you are confident and mean business they usually listen up.

After you have confidence, the next emotion you want to display in your teacher look is anger. Anger tells students that their behavior is unacceptable and you won't stand for it. Don't take this anger too far, though. When a lot of new teachers try this, they make the mistake of blowing their lid at students and wondering afterward why the students seemed relatively unmoved or possibly even amused by it. The reason an explosion of anger often doesn't work is that while it is somewhat intimidating, it is also often a pretty entertaining spectacle for a thirteen-year-old. And for some of the students, it is exactly what they are secretly hoping for. (Who doesn't love getting the teacher riled up?)

On the other hand, if you restrain your anger an odd thing happens: Instead of getting less scary because the intensity is toned down, your anger actually grows infinitely more menacing. To understand why this is, think about an active volcano. While an erupting volcano, throwing lava and ash into the sky, is certainly scary, if you are not too close it is more of a spectacle worth watching than a hazard. But a volcano that is threatening to erupt, but so far has only released small puffs of smoke and a couple of moderate rumbles, is nerve-racking to watch from any distance because you don't know how big it will be when it explodes. The same is true with your anger. If all of your anger is unleashed, students know whether they are in the blast zone or not; but when they know you are capable of more, they will all have the slight worry that when you do detonate, they could catch some of your wrath. And that is what silences a room.

The term "teacher look" often describes a disapproving gaze used to curb bad behavior, but there are other teacher looks that are just as important. The look on a teacher's face is often where students go for cues on their behavior, so give them something to work with! For example, you can instill courage in a struggling student by softening your face, prod an off-topic student back on track by pursing your lips, or validate a hardworking student's effort by looking attentive. So don't forget about what is written on your face and don't limit your looks to negatives; cultivate a wide range of conscious looks, and you can give a wide range of useful messages.

Voice

Your voice probably isn't the first thing you think of when you think of body language; generally that is under the umbrella of regular language. But there is one side to the voice that actually does fit better with body language than verbal language—its intonation. Vocal intonation is much more of a part of body language because the messages it sends don't come through the words, but through how you say them.

Some intonations will likely come naturally to you. In times of anger or happiness, your tone of voice will probably reflect those emotions without any conscious effort on your part. But there are other intonations, ones probably more useful to the classroom, that may not come as naturally. You can also use the tone of your voice to soothe, offer empathy, prod, show irritation, express sadness, and give a thousand other messages. Learning how to speak so all these intonations are clear is one more subtle skill that veteran teachers often use (generally in concert with other types of nonverbal communication) to make sure their students understand what they want and how they feel.

Exit Slip

The most important lesson from this chapter is that body language matters. New teachers regularly forget all about their body language, and when they do they probably aren't sending out the signals they would want. But the second they do give body language just a little bit of thought, it can turn instantly from a liability to a real asset. Few things are more effective at communicating such a wide range of messages to students (from "I'm confident or excited" to "You need to try harder [or stop talking]"), so take advantage and don't let your mouth do all the talking for you.

HOW TO RESPOND
TO UNWANTED BEHAVIOR

I f you were to poll new teachers about their biggest worry coming into their first year, the runaway number one answer would likely be "What do I do when students misbehave?" Whether it is misbehaving through talking out of turn or talking back, it is hard for many new teachers to avoid letting worries about students behaving badly consume large swaths of their brains. These thoughts are nearly impossible to escape for many new teachers, because they know there will be a fair amount of bad student behavior on a daily basis, but they have no idea what form it will take. During some classes, misbehavior could be minor or even nonexistent, while in others it could be severe and rampant. One day the unwanted behavior could materialize in the form of tardies or interruptions, and the next as inappropriate comments or attitude. And as the students file in every day, as a teacher you don't know what is walking in and how bad it will be.

With the potential for trouble present in every period of every day it is hard to not dwell at times on what could happen and how you will respond when it does. And that is not necessarily a bad thing; though new teachers often take their worries a bit too far, thinking about possible trouble and how to react to it does help prepare for when it inevitably comes.

But you need to be smart about how you do this. There aren't enough seconds in a day, month, or year to think about all that could go wrong, nor should you be worried about everything. Instead, focus your thinking on the most frequent misbehaviors. By figuring out how to respond to common misbehaviors, you will begin to create patterns of reaction that can be extended and modified to fit the unusual ones. To get you started on this path, here are some of the most widespread misbehaviors and useful responses for dealing with them.

How to Respond to Talking

Unwanted talking might be the most frequent type of bad behavior that teachers must deal with. It is therefore one of the most useful to have a plan for dealing with. Here are some ideas for responding to unwanted talking.

Using Body Language and Presence

A good first line of defense (as discussed in chapter 14) is to use your body language and presence. This approach is often not disruptive, doesn't make a scene, and, most importantly, works really well. The only downsides are that for some situations it is not a strong enough response, and sometimes, a student who isn't very perceptive may not realize that he or she has been reprimanded at all (and thus gets away with it).

Reprimands

There is nothing wrong with reacting to unwanted student talking by simply telling them to be quiet. Every response to students doesn't have to be complex or psychological; sometimes there is something to be said for being straightforward. One distinct advantage to just saying "Be quiet" is that it is uncomplicated. It doesn't require any on-the-spot calculations, it doesn't take long to do, and it provides the second least amount of interruption to the lesson (after body presence).

The only downside to reprimanding students is that if you do it too often you will appear weak. Though asking individuals or the class to quiet down once or twice doesn't send any messages except that you want quiet, constantly asking them to quiet down sends the message that you don't have control. A good rule of thumb for knowing when you've crossed this line is that when you begin to realize you're asking a student to quiet down too much, the other students have probably just started to notice the frequency of your requests as well. At this point, give the misbehaving student one more firm warning and the next time he or she misbehaves, use something more than chastisement.

Punishments

When you punish a student, it is important to do so quickly. A punishment is far more likely to lead to a student protest than a simple reprimand, and it is very important to avoid arguments with students in front of the class whenever possible (for reasons discussed below). By giving the punishment swiftly and then getting back to the lesson, you don't give the student time to challenge you because before he or she has formulated an argument, you're onto something new.

After levying a punishment, it also often works to give the student who received the punishment an opportunity to get a lesser punishment if he or she improves the behavior for the rest of class or the week. This will give the student a incentive to do positive things and will limit any acting out because the student is angry at you. As with all of these approaches, don't offer this option too often, or your original punishments will lose their power.

Avoiding a Showdown in Front of the Class

When reprimanding or punishing a student, the last thing you want to do is to get drawn into an argument with the student in front of the class. Students usually behave very differently with an audience. When students feel the eyes of their classmates upon them, they feel great pressure not to fold and thus lose face in front of their friends. This pressure often leads them to stubbornly stick to even the most irrational points, and it can make even level-headed and meek students downright obstinate and combative.

If you do find yourself in an argument in front of the class, it is important to get out of the dispute as fast as possible while also remaining strong and firm. One good way to do this is to tell the student in a resolute manner that you will talk with him or her about it later. This approach often works because it doesn't force either side to back down from the disagreement (and lose credibility in the eyes of the spectators); instead, it just moves the discussion to a time and place that will take the pressure off both (and if the student agrees to move the argument you've subtly ended the dispute with the student agreeing to one of your terms!).

Talk to the Student One-on-One

While students often grow defensive, combative, and closed when addressed in front of their peers, when spoken to one-on-one the opposite reaction generally occurs. When students know no other eyes are watching, they usually become far more open, reasonable, and agreeable. Even really upset students often have a difficult time maintaining the anger that comes so easily with an audience when they are one-on-one with you. This ability to increase openness and lessen hostility makes talking to students individually one of the most effective behavior management tools you have.

Because of the many benefits of talking to students individually, there is almost no situation that one-on-one conversations can't help. Whether a student has been talking too much, comes late every day, seems distracted, or just can't seem to keep his or her head up, there is a good chance that a two-minute chat can go a long way toward helping the situation. By speaking with the student, you will likely get a sense of the problem's root, and the student will get a sense of how you feel about it. You can also use the meeting as a clear starting point on the road to resolving the issue (or starting a dialogue about resolving it).

If you decide to have a one-on-one conversation, the best way to initiate it is quietly. Try pulling the student aside or grabbing the student as he or she enters or leaves the classroom. Setting up the conversation discreetly takes some pressure off, because then everyone doesn't know that the student is talking to the teacher (which is usually followed by lots of "Ooohhhhs").

Once you are ready to begin, try starting with something nonconfrontational ("I've noticed you've been doing _____ a lot") and ask a lot of questions ("What do you think we could do to improve _____?"). By avoiding unnecessary negativity and asking questions, you make it clear that the conversation is about finding a middle ground, you limit the risk of getting the student defensive, and you don't give the student the option to zone out. This does not mean you should hold back or not say what needs to be said; it just means you want to get the student involved and feeling comfortable enough to get somewhere. Try to end with a summation of both sides' points and a final thought about what the next step for the future should be (so the ending, which is the most memorable part, includes everything the student needs to know).

Other Unwanted Behaviors

Though student talking is the most common type of unwanted behavior that you will likely encounter, there is a whole host of other negative behaviors that regularly crop up in class. For the most part, you can respond to these behaviors in the same way that you respond to unwanted talking, but there are some that require a slightly different touch.

Attitude

When dealing with student attitude, directed either at you or at another classmate, the golden rule is to try to avoid giving any attitude yourself. Responding to attitude with attitude is like pouring water on a grease fire: It makes sense in the moment, but it nearly always ends with an explosion.

Instead of responding with attitude, try to keep your demeanor level, yet disapproving. (If you get riled up, try breathing deeply and counting to five.) It should be clear from your face and voice that that attitude won't be tolerated and will quickly land the student in hot water. The only exception to this is sarcasm, which can occasionally be used to successfully diffuse minor attitude—but please use it with caution. Students are stunningly bad at understanding sarcasm, and even the simplest sarcasm can vault right over the heads of your more concrete students. Also, even seemingly minor levels of sarcasm can hurt some students more than they will let on, so tread carefully with it.

Doing Work from Other Classes

When students do work from other classes, the best approach is to just go pick up the work and bring it back to your desk. Wait for the student to come get it at the end of class, and when the student sheepishly walks up, explain briefly about how insulting that behavior is before giving the work back. If a student attempts this multiple times, try giving the work to the teacher whose class it is from and let the student get it back from them.

Head Down on the Desk

Students putting their head down may seem like a little thing that doesn't harm anyone but themselves, but this couldn't be further from the truth. One student with his or her head down can quietly inflict a lot of damage on a lesson. When the teacher allows students to keep their heads down, it sends the message that the information being covered is both boring and optional, and that students only need to participate if they are in the mood.

The way to correct a head that is down is simple, though. Just walk by and tap the student or quietly whisper for the student to sit up or get his or her head up. The vast majority of times students will respond to this quickly, but if they resist for longer than a few seconds strongly advise them to go get a drink and a breath of fresh air to help them wake up. It also isn't bad to talk with the student about it afterward, for a lowered head, though sometimes born of obstinacy, can often be a sign of much bigger issues.

Not Paying Attention

The fact is that you can never know how much attention students are paying by looking at them. Even if they look distracted, that doesn't necessarily mean they are. And just because they look engaged doesn't mean they aren't a million miles away. Because being sure about a student's attentiveness is nearly impossible, it is important to find ways to reprimand students for not paying attention, aside from calling them out on it. If you accuse them of not paying attention and they dispute it, you will probably have very little evidence to back up your point, and students will likely take advantage of this fact and make a big deal about how you always pick on them.

Instead of slinging accusations, try to reprimand the students for their lack of attention in subtle ways. Ask them a question, walk over to them, or shoot them a stare if you don't think they are paying attention. These approaches send the same message as telling them "Pay attention!" but afterward there is almost no chance you will have to defend yourself.

A Poor Academic Performance

Responding to a student who did poorly on an assignment requires you to walk a tightrope between negatives and positives. You want to make sure the student understands that the work was unacceptable, but at the same time you want to give him or her encouragement and inspiration to do better the next time. In the end, exactly how tough or motivational you get depends on the student and the situation, but there are some basic rules that should generally be followed regardless of the outside circumstances.

- Don't put the student down. If you do, that is the part of the conversation the student will remember. It doesn't matter what else you say; there are few things more memorable to students than being put down by a teacher. This is not to say that you shouldn't criticize students (which is telling them what they did wrong), just don't put them down (which is telling them they are wrong).

- Break your prejudices. Whether it is giving students a grade, rating their conduct, or describing them to their own parents, as a teacher you are constantly asked to place students in categories. With so much time spent categorizing students, it is only natural that after a while teachers begin to automatically think of their prejudices when they hear or see a student (for example, seeing him as "that C-level student with lower than average conduct who could get an A but doesn't really care" instead of as "John"). When talking to students, one of the most important things you can do is try your best to forget about the categories you've placed them in. If a student gets even the slightest sense that you have pigeonholed him or her, the student probably won't listen to a word you say.

- Make the path to improvement clear. When addressing students who've done poorly, try to make the positive path to success as clear as possible. Talk through exactly how he or she can do better, even if it is painfully obvious. It might not be nearly as obvious to the student.

Exit Slip

One of the keys to responding to any type of negative student behavior is being very deliberate with your actions. Whether you are tapping a student who has his or her head down, telling a student to be quiet, or punishing a student, do it with purpose. If you are tentative with an action, students will likely see that even you aren't sure if the action is the right one; while if you are deliberate they will probably recognize that your mind is made up and that trying to change it will take a lot of effort.

TROUBLE IS COMPLEX

The life of a teacher would be so much easier if dealing with students were as simple as plugging situations into a formula. Unfortunately, the reasons students do what they do are far too complicated for any formula to solve (sorry, math teachers), and thus no set answer exists to tell you exactly how to handle a student who is talking for the third time in one day or not giving enough effort for the second assignment in a row. All of the topics discussed so far in this unit (like using body language, talking to students one-on-one, and avoiding idle threats) are great tools for managing all types of situations—but how, when, and to what extent you use them depends on your style, the class's personality, the exact behavior of the student(s) in question, and a myriad of other factors from the moment.

Ultimately, the complexity of the real world makes managing students essentially just a series of gray areas that require on-the-ground reconnaissance and on-your-feet thinking. And though no handbook can completely prepare you for what you will find in your classroom, if you combine the skills covered so far with a few basic principles to help you personalize your response, you will be in pretty good shape.

Figure Out the Root of the Trouble

The job of a teacher requires a lot more than just presenting information. You also have to control the crowds like a police officer, speak like an actor, advocate like a lawyer (for yourself, students, and the school), and advise like a counselor. And sometimes, to solve the major behavioral problems, you need to dig deep like a therapist.

Digging deep is often required because students are infinitely complicated creatures with infinitely varied motivations for committing the same infractions. Whereas one student may put his or her head down out of tiredness, another may do it out of protest. While some students talk because they want trouble, others may do it because they want another student in the class to like them.

Since there are many reasons for trouble, there is no one correct response for any given problem. An approach that works really well for one student may not work at all for another student doing exactly the same thing because their back stories to the behavior are completely different. This means that to know how to react to a behavior, you often need to get to its roots. And though there are as many motivators for poor behavior as there are students, some common reasons pop up again and again, and are well worth getting to know.

The Student Has No Impulse Control

The human body is impulsive; that is to say, at any given moment the body has multiple impulses coursing through the nervous system. Some students learn at a very young age how to control and delay these impulses, and these students often become the "naturals" in school. But there are other students—and nearly every class has a few of them—whose impulse control is either not very refined or even nonexistent. These students say nearly everything that comes to their brains and are often considered to be among the most troublesome of students.

The best way to deal with students with impulse control issues is often to open up a running dialogue with them about the difference between an acceptable and an unacceptable comment or question. You could also help them along this path by providing alternatives to yelling out or possibly even having your own set of rewards and consequences. For many of these students, the behavior of yelling things out is fairly ingrained, so getting them to change can be a long process. But if you keep up a dialogue, there is a very good chance that they will eventually begin to learn how to keep their impulses in check.

They Want Power or Attention

A desire for power or attention is one of the most common driving forces for misbehaving students, and with good reason. Through acting poorly, students can gain a significant amount of either. By talking back to the teacher, they prove they are strong enough to take on the most powerful person in the room; through disruption, they can hold thirty people's attention hostage whenever they feel like it; and if they get away with something, they've successfully beaten the system.

To discourage these power and attention grabs in your classroom, there are two things you can do: lessen how much attention or power can be gained through acting out and give the student an opportunity to gain it through positive avenues. How to do this depends on the situation. For example, if a student interrupts class for attention, don't give their interrupting much attention. Ignore the student, separate the student, or levy punishments and quickly move on. Then fill this urge for attention with some sort of positive way to get attention. For some students this may mean granting them a classroom role (like a group leader), while for others all it may take is for the student to know that they have a teacher who notices and listens to them, even if they don't cause trouble.

They Are Used to Getting Their Way at Home or Not Used to Having Boundaries

No matter what district you are in, your students are going to come from an expansive range of backgrounds. Whereas some students may not have any power or attention at home (these are often the ones who act out for power or attention in class), others may have all the attention in the world and no boundaries whatsoever. And since they are the center of attention in their own world and used to getting their way, it shouldn't come as a surprise when they have the same expectations for your classroom.

To respond to those with no boundaries, the most important thing you can do is put your foot down. At first they will likely resist this, but if you keep making it clear that they are no longer on their own turf and there is a new sheriff in town, these students will generally fall in line. Doing this means you should strive to be everything a good authority figure should be, while also possibly being sterner and more unwavering than you would be with a normal student.

Their Reputation Is That of the Cool Troublemaker

Some students have spent years cultivating the reputation of the cool troublemaker, and by the time they enter your class it is an ingrained part of their identity. These students need trouble in class to make them legit, and the more a teacher publicly rallies against them, the more they gain credibility with their classmates. So they actively seek trouble, and they are especially interested in finding varieties of trouble that have the possibility of eliciting explosive reactions from the teacher.

When students need trouble to sustain their reputation, it is important that you not give it to them. Don't let these students bait you into a fight or strong emotions, because as soon as that happens they've won, regardless of what punishment you throw at them. When you punish these students do it quietly, with a minimum of emotion, and as quickly as possible.

The other way to deal with these students is to make it so their trouble-making behavior actually endangers their standing with the other students. For example, if they are particularly unruly one day, tell the whole class that for the rest of the day poor behavior from anyone will negatively impact everyone by cutting into their lunch break. It is often amazing how quickly these students will snap into shape when their reputation is on the line.

They Want Others to See How Clever They Are

Who doesn't get a little ego spike from a clever comment? No matter what age you are, it feels really good to be the first one to a witty comment or joke. And for many students the good feeling of cracking a good joke overrides any worry about getting in trouble—so they fire away with as many jokes as they can.

There are two approaches that seem to work (especially together) to corral the look-at-how-clever-I-am students in your class. The first is to scare them straight. Often these clever students are also generally "good students," who want affirmation from their teachers and parents as well. By making it clear to them that such behavior will lead to punishment from both parties (through doing things like administering a punishment in class and notifying the parents about it afterward), these students can often be scared straight.

The second thing you can do for clever students is to give them outlets to be creative. This can be done by setting them up for jokes (or at least calling on them at times when jokes are acceptable) or by giving assignments where they can use and show off their creativity. By offering them an appropriate forum to crack a joke or show off their wit, you can often lessen the pressure they feel to be clever in front of their classmates, which means that it is less likely to explode out at other unwanted times.

Pick Your Battles

If you were to take a freeze-frame of any given classroom, you would likely find enough classroom rule infractions to keep you busy for days. Undoubtedly some of the students wouldn't have their books, USB drives, pens, notebooks, or other materials required. Several students would also probably be passing notes, talking quietly, misusing their computers, and doodling on their school-owned textbooks. At least nine or ten students would most likely have their phones accidentally (or so they claim) left on, and at least one would almost certainly be mid-text. And that would be just the tip of the iceberg.

With so many battles to choose from, you need to be very picky about which trouble you address and which you let go. There isn't nearly enough time to take on every little battle, so you want to take on only the ones that send messages worth the time spent. Here are some guidelines to help you decide which battles are worth it.

Which Talking to Address

Many new teachers see unwanted classroom talking as the great enemy to learning. And in certain circumstances, it definitely is. Unnecessary talking can slow the pace of class, drown out important information, or take members of the class (including the teacher) in the wrong direction. But unprompted talking isn't always such a clear negative; even though it can distract, some level of talking can actually be a sign of some very positive things. Among other things, it can show that students are awake, engaged, and following along with you.

The reason a somewhat talkative class can indicate that the students are actually on task is because a common involuntary consequence of interest is the accidental uttering of questions, comments, or thoughts. This is true for people of all ages, though students with their less defined impulse control (see above) react this way more than most. So when the students talk, don't necessarily assume they are off task (and when they aren't talking, don't assume they are on task), for during the times when they are most interested their mouths often follow.

Because all talking is not created equal, it is actually not a bad idea to let some of the "good" unprompted talking go unpunished. A useful rule is that if the talking comes from a place of interest and is said by someone who doesn't have a pattern of talking out of turn, it is worth letting go. By letting it go, you can actually demonstrate to students that being a bit overexuberant with your interest is all right at times. If, on the other hand, the talking is not even remotely tied to the topic, is done with any regularity, or the class is beginning to get out of control and you realize they need reigning in, then it might be worth reprimanding the student for their talking. But even when reprimanding a student, if the talking is on task, remind the student that the way he or she showed interest, not the interest itself, was wrong.

Behaviors That Should Always Be Addressed

Whereas talking is something that should be addressed on a situation-by-situation basis, some behaviors should always be challenged. Here are a few behaviors that pose a severe danger to the class or to your goals and should never be overlooked:

- Any comment or behavior that has a chance of hurting anyone else in the school. This means you must always address something that is derogatory toward other students or teachers, no matter how playful and regardless of whether the subject is present. Students love to talk and write about people in the school, and even if this is done with the lightest of hearts these comments can cause heavy pain. So to eliminate the threat of students talking about others, try introducing a rule at the beginning of the year that outlaws comments about members of the school community that are anything but overwhelmingly positive. Then when students try to talk about their classmates, you can simply remind them of the rule (instead of having to explain yourself over and over) and move on.

- Cutting corners. The little things in life matter, especially because they always have a way of turning into big problems. In the classroom when students are allowed to cut little corners, major repercussions generally follow. This is especially true in regard to any variety of academic dishonesty or students not being prepared. If students ever figure out that they can lie, cheat, or just be generally unprepared, then expect a plague of these behaviors to descend upon your classroom. So hold this plague back and make sure to keep your students honest by not letting them cut any corners.

- Any challenge to you or your classroom. In chapter 2, there was a discussion about the pack mentality of students and the importance of establishing yourself as their leader. With this role in mind, it is very important to address any behavior that could be construed as a challenge to your authority—because with packs, when the leader backs down, that means the status of the top dog is in question. Some behaviors that fall into this range include inappropriate comments that you are meant to hear, any accusation that something in your class is stupid or worthless, or any other direct challenge to you or your rules.

Talk to Them

Anyone in power runs the risk of getting isolated from those below, and teachers are no exception. With all of the work you have on your plate, it is easy to go months without having a real conversation with students. This lack of small talk may not seem like a big deal, but it can actually be a bigger loss than some teachers realize. There is a lot to be gained from short, seemingly meaningless conversations. Even the smallest of conversations can give you a window into what a kid is thinking and what is going on in his or her life.

This power of small talk also means that teachers should especially try to address students with a simple "What's going on?" any time a student develops an odd or unwanted pattern, breaks from his or her normal behavior, or starts going down other negative roads. If it is clear to students that you are genuinely interested in what is happening with them, they will more often than not open right up and tell you exactly what's wrong and why they are acting strange. And afterward, not only will you leave with valuable information, but the student will leave with a feeling of value and connection that can be one of the most powerful suppressants of bad behavior.

Exit Slip

When you boil the lessons from this entire unit down, most are discussing different faces of the same concept: the more communication you have with students, the better your shot is at keeping them under control. Whether it is having clear consequences, working on body language, talking to them one-on-one, or discussing impulse control with a student, it all comes down to communication. So don't let your worries or your tower of work keep you from a running dialogue with students, both individually and as a group. The more understanding each side has of the other, the easier it is to get along.

Unit Five
BUILDING YOUR
CLASSROOM FOUNDATION

Y ou don't normally find a unit about building your foundation halfway through a book, and in some senses the order is certainly a bit
unusual. But all of the chapters so far have been in a way laying the
foundation for this foundation. These chapters had specific topics and suggestions, but they also spent a lot of time discussing the thinking that goes
into teaching. Now, after having mentally set up the classroom in the first
half, the second half of the book is going to get on the ground with you and
discuss exactly how to set up every actual section that you teach.

This structure is meant to mimic what it is like to be a new teacher at
a school. First, you have nothing but a contract and maybe a basic idea of
the required curriculum, and so you mentally sort out what your class will be
like. Then one day you get a set of keys and suddenly your mental classroom
becomes very real. That "real" realization is where this unit (and much of the
second half of the book) steps in, to guide you through exactly how to turn
a set of keys and blank beige room into a well-oiled classroom that is full of
learning.

CHAPTER SEVENTEEN
SETTING THE GROUND RULES

O n my first day of student teaching, my mentor teacher did something that blew me away. He stood up in front of the class and told
them, "My one rule for the classroom is to be reasonable. As long as
you are reasonable with your behavior, whether it is in regard to late work or
to bathroom breaks, we will be fine." As a young, impressionable teacher, I
was amazed to see a seasoned teacher say something like this. It was the sort
of cool, unorthodox thing that teachers say in movies. It was the sort of thing
said by Robin Williams or Michelle Pfeiffer. It was not what real teachers
said in real classrooms, and for that I loved it.

When I finally got my own classroom I couldn't wait to come in on the
first day and simply tell students to be reasonable. What a wonderful way to
start a year and a teaching career! Instead of repeating the same boring set
of rules that every other class covered, I would offer something different that
challenged students to take responsibility for their actions. So that is exactly
what I did. The students came in, I gave a few general guidelines, I told them
my one rule was to be reasonable, they seemed genuinely impressed, and I
went home the first night feeling pretty good about my classroom management skills.

Unfortunately, these good feelings were short-lived. While the students
seemed on board at first, it only took about a week until some unreasonable
behavior began to slip into my classroom. Within another week, students
were consistently and openly abusing my "be reasonable" policies concerning
computer usage, bathroom breaks, and tardiness. After that they began to
break bigger rules, more and more work showed up late, and cheating started

to rear its ugly head. Soon there was no other choice but to acknowledge that my "Age of Reason" was going down in flames, fast.

Looking back, it is obvious to me now where my "be reasonable" rule went wrong—I didn't set up clear boundaries. And if there is one thing students need from a young teacher, it is clear boundaries. Boundaries are essential because they allow students to always know where they stand. Not knowing where you stand is, for most people, a truly unnerving feeling that we want fixed as soon as possible. The same is true for students, and when they don't know their standing, they will likely push, test, and prod until they figure it out. In my exceptionally ambiguous environment, many students never gained a solid impression of where they stood, and thus they continued to push upon the limits.

The reason the "be reasonable" policy worked for my mentor teacher was because, though I didn't notice it, he did establish boundaries in a very subtle way. After telling students that his sole policy was to be reasonable, he took the "What do I mean?" approach from chapter 2, where the class discussed the meaning of being reasonable in great detail. He then further brought home these expectations by making sure to be incredibly consistent with how he dealt with any issues that arose in class. Between his explanation, his consistency, and the reputation he already had, students had no trouble understanding what he meant or where they stood, and thus felt little need to explore their boundaries.

The lesson I learned from my failure is that having clear boundaries, no matter how you establish them, is essential for new teachers if you want your class to start on the right foot. It is especially important to make sure you have clear boundaries in the following areas.

The Little Details

For most new teachers, the majority of headaches come from the little things: students bringing the wrong binders, only half the students having the book for class, and printer excuse after printer excuse. These are the small details that can drive you crazy and waste hours of valuable class time over the course of a semester. Because of the impact these silly and small, but ultimately infuriating, problems can have on a class, establishing and enforcing rules about them should be one of the top priorities for new teachers. To help you devise your rules, here are a list of the most common "little issues" and some tips for dealing with them.

Printer Issues

If the number of printer errors that students regularly experience is accurate, then the printer industry is far less reliable than Congress, the airlines, and the post office combined. And though printers certainly do have their share of issues, it is hard to believe they are that erratic. Instead, these printer excuses, which can be so plentiful in many classrooms, more often result from some variety of human error. They come from students trying to print as they run out the door, waiting until school to print (where they find the computer lab is closed), or using it as a cover for missing work. Whatever the reason, almost all printer problems come from the poor execution and foresight of the human operator, not a mechanical malfunction.

Because these errors are preventable it is generally a good policy to take "My printer didn't work!" off the list of acceptable excuses for your class. If you allow this excuse, students will often abuse it; but if you don't allow it, 99 percent of the printers will miraculously fix themselves and you probably won't have to worry about it again.

When discussing printer excuses, it is also important to explain why excuses aren't allowed and to offer the students alternative paths to coming with excuses. A few possible suggestions for what to do instead of blaming the printer include the following:

- E-mailing the work to the teacher ahead of time

- Transferring the data to a USB stick and printing it somewhere else

- Coming into class early to print it on the teacher's computer

- At the very minimum, contacting the teacher ahead of time to let him or her know the issue

By going over these other options, it helps show students that your rule is less about being unnecessarily punitive (which is probably how they will see it if you don't explain the logic), than it is about using your head and thinking about the future. There is a good chance they will listen to that.

Students Not Bringing Materials to Class

If you were in school, you would bring your calculator to math class, a pencil to English, and your previous night's homework to science, right?

Most adults probably would. But this is not necessarily the way the adolescent brain operates. To a new teacher, it can be flabbergasting how many students don't bring simple items like pencils, papers, books, and, most shockingly, their completed homework (there will likely be several struggling students in your classes who actually complete most assignments, but regularly forget to turn them in).

One way to jolt the memory of these forgetful students concerning materials is to set up a policy that deducts points from the homework or participation grades of those not prepared (for example, when you ask them to take out a book or pen and they don't have one) and to have occasional material checks where you give additional points for preparedness. Recording and following up on these little errors may be a small pain for you, but by staying consistent with their enforcement you can avoid much larger pains in the future. This is because, much like with the printer excuses, as soon as students find that you won't accept their being unprepared, their memories concerning little things like pencils, paper, and books generally improve significantly.

Going to the Bathroom

Coming into school, what bathroom policy to have for your class may not be one of the details keeping you up at night. But, as mentioned above, in teaching the little, stupid, and unexpected things often become the biggest irritations. And few little issues can become a bigger pain than bathroom breaks.

The problem with bathroom breaks is that individually they are not a big issue, but when you cram a lot of bathroom requests into one class period, coupled with the rustling from students constantly leaving and re-entering the classroom, the cumulative damage to the lesson can be significant. But at the same time, outlawing or limiting bathroom breaks gives the class a totalitarian feel that can inspire students to argue with you over the morality and legality of limiting basic human needs.

With a subject as oddly thorny as bathroom breaks, the best approach is often to take it head on. Instead of either setting a quota or allowing a nonstop bathroom parade, it often works to admit to students that you know some students use the bathroom as an excuse to skip sections of class. Tell the students that this type of behavior isn't acceptable in class and if they abuse their bathroom rights they will lose them. Then just leave it at that.

The disclosure that you are looking out for misusing breaks followed by the threat of losing the privilege generally works to dissuade the vast majority of students from trying to take advantage of you. For those who still push their luck, pull them aside and warn them or cut off their privileges for a short period of time. By doing this, you will likely keep your bathroom policy from ever being something that disturbs your sleep.

Notes

As odd as it sounds, when a lot of students take notes they don't seem to truly understand what the notes are for. You can tell this by how haphazardly many students treat notes after taking them: the second they are done taking notes they jam them into their backpacks or binders in a way that says that they don't care if they ever see them again. If these students knew how much the notes would help on future tests, quizzes, or papers, you would think they would treat them with more care, but who knows?

Whether students understand the value of notes or not, it is certainly true that they disregard and consequently lose them constantly. To fight against this trend, try requiring your students to keep all their notes in one single notebook (instead of a loose-leaf binder). A notebook is much harder to misplace or crumple up in the bottom of a bag or locker. It also gives one easy and chronological place for their cumulative knowledge of the year, and it means you will hopefully no longer hear the all-too-common refrain of "I can't find my notes."

Late Work

As long as there are students, there will be missing assignments and late work. It is just a natural fact of life, and seemingly no matter how you run your classroom, nothing short of not having homework will completely eliminate it. When it comes to dealing with late work, teachers generally fall into two groups—those who accept late work and those who don't—and then their system for dealing with it builds off that. To help you decide which of these two roads you want to travel down, here are the pros and cons of both styles.

Those Who Accept Late Work

The main argument for accepting late work is that each assignment was created for a reason, and if students don't do them they miss out on important information and lessons. By keeping points attached to the work, it gives incentive and opportunity for the students to learn all of the lessons, even if they didn't do some on time. Teachers also often allow it because students are still learning, which means they will make mistakes. By accepting late work, the teacher gives students a chance to get up, dust themselves off, and make amends for their mistakes.

This system works for a lot of classrooms, but there are a couple of important things to keep in mind if you are planning on accepting late work. The first is to think about not accepting late work on an open-ended basis. If there is no deadline set for when students need to turn in the work, many of them will begin to mimic people with large balances on their credit cards. Like those with large credit-card debt, these students will continually defer work to the future despite the penalties associated (instead of interest the students suffer lost points), because to them the penalty is still preferable to the effort of getting it in right now. Allowing this behavior generally means you will spend most of your semester chasing down students for assignments and finally receive them at the end when you already have enough things to grade.

The second way to make accepting late work a smoother process is to have a sliding scale of points, in which depending on the point value of the assignment the students will receive a set level of deductions. For example, a late homework assignment of ten points could lose two points on the first day late and then an extra point for every late day after that. The advantage of this "meter running" approach to grading is it provides continuous pressure on the student to get the work in, which leaves less pressure that needs to be applied by you.

Those Who Don't Accept Late Work

While accepting late work is generally the most widely used approach, not accepting late work does come with a couple of distinct advantages. It means you will never need to chase down students for late work, and it serves as a giant incentive for students to get work in on time. Generally speaking, in classes with a no-tolerance policy there is less late work, and even when assignments aren't turned in they don't add extra work (via chasing students) to the teacher's day.

Not accepting late work does have its downside, though. The main problem is that students have no reason to do work once it is forgotten.

And though the number of missing assignments will probably be smaller, there will still be some that don't come in, and each missing assignment will represent a lesson left unlearned. Not accepting late work also means that if students mess up, they have fewer chances to redeem themselves, and especially with younger students this isn't always the best path to learning.

Because not accepting late work means students aren't given the opportunity to amend their mistakes, it is often best reserved for situations that truly call for it. For example, if your class needs (or you think will need) added motivation to get work in on time, a no-tolerance policy can be a great tool for making sure students don't get sloppy. Not accepting late work can also be a very effective temporary policy to send a strong message when a class's homework grows less consistent than it should be. But be thoughtful before you think about outlawing late work; not allowing late assignments can teach some good lessons, but many lessons are lost as well.

Make-Up Work

Make-up work is the quiet, but at times equally troublesome, sister of late work. Like its sister, make-up work is a variety of late work that you generally have to chase students for, but beyond that they are very different animals. Unlike late work, which can be hard to forget because the blanks in the grade book represent students not doing their jobs, make-up work is wildly easy to forget because the holes in the grade book are completely legitimate. Students with make-up work haven't missed an assignment in the traditional sense, so it is easy to put them out of your head until you run into trouble with their grades down the road.

It is this tendency to be forgotten that makes nailing down a hard-and-fast policy for make-up work so important, both for you and the class. The standard make-up work policy used by most teachers is that homework due on the day the student missed is due when the student gets back, homework assigned on the day the student missed is due the next class period, and if there are any bigger assignments the student needs to come see the teacher to figure out when they are due.

For the most part, students are good about taking the first steps after being absent (like talking to the teacher or turning in the original homework due the day they missed), but following the initial conscientiousness, they often can be quite poor with their follow-through. Even the best students will regularly forget to complete work from absences or show up for make-up tests and quizzes, and even the best teachers will regularly forget to remind them about it. Then before they know it a month has passed, the student still doesn't have a grade, and the teacher is left wondering whether to fail them, exempt them, give them the opportunity to redo what they missed, or just try to hide the whole business under the rug.

One reason that remembering make-up work is so difficult for all parties is that it lies outside of the routine. When students are absent the routine is broken. It is easy for them to remember to see you on their first day back. But after they are back in school for a few days they settle back into their routine and you continue ahead with yours. And the result is often a bout of localized amnesia surrounding the missing work.

The trick to making sure that you don't fall into this trap of constantly forgetting about make-up work is to ritualize it in some way. There are many ways to do this: You can highlight assignments in the grade book that need to be made up, initially give zeros for make-up work so the low grade reminds you and the student that something is up, or keep a list of students who owe you assignments. In the end it doesn't matter how you do it, so long as you have some sort of routine to catch the assignments that don't fit into the normal routine.

Computers

Facing a room full of students with laptops often feels like facing a room full of students with their backs turned toward you. The unsettling thing about laptops is that you can't see the screen and thus you don't know whether the students are taking notes or IMing. Despite this fairly significant drawback, laptops have a great upside to them as well. They can help organize students, speed up note taking, provide valuable services for students with dysgraphia and other learning differences, and they also just seem to come in handy when around the classroom.

Considering the laptop's ability to be a powerful teaching partner or equally strong tool of distraction, teachers must be very careful with the laptop usage rules in their classroom. Here are some tips on keeping laptop usage under control.

Have Computer and Noncomputer Times

Even though a lot of activities benefit from the presence of laptops, there are just as many activities where there is absolutely no reason why laptops would be required. Activities like discussions or demonstrations are in no way aided by individual student laptops, and that means the only impact laptops could have in those situations is a negative one. So for activities where no reason exists for computers to be open, simply ask students to close them. The easiest way to do this is to let students know early in the year that there are "computer times" and "noncomputer times," and when you say it is a "noncomputer time" they need to close their computers.

Keep an Eye on How Students Are Using Them

There are many times in the classroom where it just feels like students are misusing their laptops. Maybe they are typing when there isn't really a reason, their neighbors seem a little too interested in what is happening on the screen, or they are clearly more connected with the computer than the class. When you run across these moments, don't be afraid to discuss them with students later on. To do this, just tell them outright that their behavior seemed suspicious (but don't accuse them of anything) and remind them that computer abuse isn't tolerated. As long as they aren't accused of something, they generally won't grow defensive, and afterward they will at least know you have an eye on them.

Throw the Book at Offenders

Students are as aware as teachers that computer infractions are hard to enforce. And often this knowledge makes them bolder than they would be with other types of misbehavior. To counter this increased boldness, it is not a bad idea to have fairly severe consequences for computer misusage (or even suspected misusage) in your class. A lot of teachers even enact a one-and-done policy, where students lose privileges for the first offense. It also generally aids whatever computer policy you set up if you make it very clear at the beginning of the year that computer misusage will bring more trouble than it's worth. Because with something so slippery (all they have to do is close the window before you look), deterrence becomes even more essential.

Exit Slip

When introducing these ground rules to students, the easiest and best way to do it is with a course syllabus at the beginning of the year (possibly teamed with one of the activities from chapter 2). In this syllabus you definitely want to include all the topics discussed above, but you may also want to include some or all of the following information, too:

- A welcoming paragraph

- A list of required materials and/or texts

- Tardy policy

- How cheating is handled (much more on this later)

- The general structure of the class

- How you grade (whether there are certain percentages or if it is a straight point scale)

- The average amount of homework

- A concluding word

- Anything else that seems important

PHYSICALLY SETTING UP YOUR CLASSROOM

Physically setting up the classroom can seem like a burden that new teachers frankly don't have time for. With a load that already includes learning a new school, learning about new students, teaching new materials, and still finding time to eat, sleep, and breathe, the last thing many teachers want to worry about is what their classroom looks like. So they fudge it; they tack up a couple of random posters, bring in a box or two of tissues, and call it good.

But when teachers cut corners in their classroom setup, a strange bit of math happens that causes them to actually lose time in the long run, even if they gain it initially. This happens because giving some thought to setting up the classroom, which may seem like a waste of precious minutes at the time, is actually an investment. By taking time to get everything in order and well-thought-out, a teacher can save hours down the line.

Put Folders Everywhere to Absorb the Mess

In my first year I didn't receive a desk (because I shared a room), but I did get a slice of a small office that served essentially the same function. For the first few weeks of the year, the office worked out great, and there was more than enough room for all my papers, books, and other materials to fit in orderly piles in my little section. But as the amount of materials, and specifically papers, continued to grow, the office slowly became more and more crowded. By the beginning of October the neat piles had begun to congeal, by the middle of October the office was a bit cramped and cluttered, and by the end of October the room looked like an out-of-control squirrel's nest.

For the rest of the fall, I fought to restore order to the office, but the nest of papers could not be defeated. Every time the piles became even somewhat separated, it only took a matter of hours before they reverted back to an unruly mess. Soon I just gave up, and for the rest of the semester I spent much of my free periods digging for papers among the massive piles.

This tale of papers taking over is hardly a unique one in education. Walk into any classroom and there is a good chance you will see other teachers fighting the same seemingly unwinnable battle against clutter. It may reside on their desk or in their office, but nearly every teacher has a few disobedient mountains of paper somewhere in the school. So what is the reason for this widespread disorganization? Have teachers been hanging around students too long and gotten slovenly?

Though students do rub off a little on teachers (in the same way that pets and owners often start to look similar), a complete transferring of organizational habits probably isn't the answer to such rampant clutter. Instead, the disorganization usually has something to do with the number of papers teachers store and process each day. Between worksheets for class, homework, tests, quizzes, evaluation forms, and occasional bureaucratic nonsense, the average teacher encounters hundreds of papers a day. Add to this mountain of papers the fact that all the different varieties of paper need to be kept separate, and it begins to become clear how the job of a teacher can bring the disorganized teenager out of even the most orderly people.

In terms of conquering the papers, there is only one system that regularly seems to yield consistent results. Teachers who beat the mess seem to do so by using their classroom space as giant organizers. This makes sense too, because for most teachers the classroom is the biggest space they have (face it, a job in teaching rarely comes with a big office or house). With such a massive number of papers to deal with, teachers need all the space they can get, and the classroom has more than enough to go around.

The following is an example of a system that uses the space in the classroom to stay organized. This system isn't the only way to break it down, but it is probably the most common and one of the easiest to keep up with. The theory behind the system is to break all the materials that a teacher has into past, present, and future and then further divide them into smaller subgroups that are stashed around the classroom.

Past Papers

There are two types of assignments from the past guaranteed to be cluttering up your desk. One is graded work waiting to be handed back. In an ideal world, as soon as the work was graded it would find its way back to students immediately. But in the real world, graded work tends to linger. Sometimes it will sit there because you don't want to pass back a quiz or test until all the students have taken it, other times you will have a specific reason (like parent conferences or just waiting for the right moment) not to give it back right away, sometimes students will be absent when it is handed back, and most often you will probably just forget about it.

Whatever the reason, graded student work tends to always stick around and always seems to be in the way. So to get it out of your hair, try making a folder for every section you teach that is reserved purely for graded work. Then put these folders in stacking trays on the corner of your desk so they are visible enough to remind you and are always within easy reach to file away after grading.

The second type of "past paper" that inevitably floats around the desk is extra copies of handouts you've already passed out. Between absent students, teacher copies, and the fact that it is generally smart to print at least five extra copies (for reasons discussed in a moment), extra sheets usually remain after handing something out. In general these extra papers have 1,001 uses, from giving to students who lost the original copy to providing a copy for support staff, but they do have one downside, too: they can contribute to the messiness of the classroom if not dealt with.

To make sure that your extra papers don't add to your classroom clutter, try making a folder labeled "Extra Worksheets and Assignments" for each of your classes. Then stick these folders somewhere accessible to both you and the students, and toss all remaining copies of worksheets into the corresponding folder after it is handed out. By doing this you not only remove the papers from your desk and establish a single place for them to congregate, you also give the students a place to find any sheets they are missing (due to loss of the original or absence on the day it was handed out) without having to bother you about it.

Current Papers

When it comes to current work, or work that still needs grading, papers once again fall into two major categories: regular work and late work.

In terms of regular work, try making a folder for each class labeled "Needs Grading." Then put these folders in trays or dividers on the other side of your desk from the graded work. (For those who ask why you need both a folder and a tray or divider, it is because transporting folders for home grading is far easier than transporting trays, but trays keep things separate on a desk better than a stack of folders.) As you grade, you can just take work from the "needs grading" side of the desk and shift it straight to the "graded side" without having to worry about its cluttering up your desk.

Late work, though technically a type of paper that needs grading, deserves its own separate folder for one big reason—it almost always comes with a story. These stories range all the way from legitimate ("I had a doctor's appointment") to slightly suspect ("It was completed in my binder, I swear!") to outright admissions of guilt ("I just forgot"). But no matter what story is attached to it, putting late work in its own folder ensures that it doesn't accidentally get mixed in with the regular work until you've had time to process the story for each and assign reasonable penalties or pardons.

Future Papers

Copy machines are horribly fickle creatures. Despite that, and possibly also because of it, they are always mobbed with people. This combination of temperament and congestion means that doing copies in large numbers, thus limiting the number of journeys to the copy machine, is generally the best way to keep copy machine sanity.

The only downside of making large numbers of copies is that all those copied sheets for different classes need a place to reside until called into service. By having a separate file, accordion, or drawer somewhere in the room for these upcoming papers for each section (most likely labeled something like "Upcoming Papers"), you ensure that the time-saving technique of making large quantities of future copies doesn't subtract time in the end by adding to your disorganization.

Organize the Desks for Success

When new teachers get their classrooms, they commonly act as if the desks are bolted to the floor. Regardless of how the desks are set, they leave them exactly where the previous teacher or janitor put them, and the idea of moving the desks around doesn't even cross their minds. But not only are teachers generally allowed to move desks, in most situations they probably should. How the desks are set up can have a powerful effect on the class and can be one of the main contributors to or suppressors of bad behavior. And if teachers don't take advantage of that fact, they are letting a powerful tool go to waste.

The ways that desk configuration can affect a classroom are mostly common sense. If the desks are clustered together, the proximity combined with the fact that they are facing each other will likely encourage students to talk—which can be a good thing if you do a lot of group work (because no group member can hide) and not such a good thing if you are lecturing. When the desks are in rows or a U, the separation can discourage talking out of turn, but it will also discourage talking during discussions because at any given moment the speaker will either be talking to the backs of people's heads or won't be able to see everyone in the class. For students in a circle, discussion is greatly aided, but it can be awkward to lecture or use the board, because you will either have your back to some students or some will have their backs to you.

All of the pluses and minuses that come with each style of desk organization mean that there is no one style that is the right choice all the time. So just think about how you run your class and play with the desk set-up until you find one that meshes with you. Also don't be afraid to change up the desks for different activities; investing the five minutes to shift them can often make entire days of lessons significantly smoother.

Meet Your New Best Friend: The Grade Book

Though you usually don't note it when you enter, the grade book is possibly the most important physical part of the classroom. This is because it is like your sidekick. It is always there next to you, it backs you up, and there are times when most teachers need to lean on it.

All teachers are generally required to have grade books, but how useful they are depends on how they are used. Some teachers do fine with only minimal use of their grade books, but in the chaotic world of a first-year teacher the grade book can often be an oasis of calm, especially if you follow some of these recommendations:

1. Like when you do a crossword puzzle, you want to write everything in pencil. Grades change a lot, especially for new teachers

who aren't 100 percent confident in their grading scale yet. If you write in pen, be ready to make so many scratches in your book that it will look like a jar of ink became exceptionally ill on the page.

2. Have two copies, a hard and a digital, at all times. Make sure to keep them both updated as well. Hard copies have a way of wandering away and digital copies have a way of deleting things you've already input.

3. Use your grade book to note any time you give an extension, deduction, or otherwise change an assignment for a student. Students will often argue with teachers about incomplete or late assignments or accuse them of saying it was all right ("But you said I could turn it in late, remember?"). Often, these student claims seem ridiculous ("I wouldn't say that . . ."), but it is hard to be completely sure they are false (" . . . would I?"). This can lead to awkward and difficult-to-resolve conversations that are easily avoidable if you keep decent records. Generally the accusations of "But you said" disappear quickly once students realize you have comprehensive notes.

4. Write student notes about other topics besides grades as well. Any time a student does something noteworthy, good or bad, write it in the grade book. If a student goes to the bathroom too much, gives a flimsy excuse, or wants your help with his or her poetry, put it in there, too. The grade book is the perfect centralized place to put all student information because it is always with you. The combination of grades and personal information is exactly what you will need for writing blurbs about the students (for report cards, letters of recommendation, or anything else), conducting meetings with parents or administration about the student, or just generally staying on top of the student.

5. Skip lines if possible when putting student names in the grade book. The added space makes putting in comments and making grade changes that much easier.

Read the Writing on the Wall

When it comes to room decoration, the best teachers always have the most personalized rooms. Part of this probably has to do with the fact that these teachers' enthusiasm for their craft extends all the way to their walls. But there is more to it than that. An interesting and exciting room has the ability to send many messages to your students. It can tell them that you know and love your area of study, show them that you are willing to commit the time necessary to create a great class, or even humanize you by showing small slivers of your personality. Whatever the reason, having interesting decorations up in the room may not make you a great teacher, but it does seem to be something great teachers do. Here are some ways to liven up your walls:

- Get posters from a local teaching supply school. In nine out of ten schools, you can expense these items if you just ask your department chair (though definitely ask before you go).

- Put up student work. Have the students do a visually appealing project early that you can put up on the walls. They will be thrilled to see their work proudly presented and the only work it adds for you involves tacking it up.

- Add colors. Random bits of color are always a welcome addition to the beige that seems to come standard with every classroom in the world. Find places for color and it will add a little something to your class.

- Give the walls a personal flavor by bringing in something involving your personality or outside interests. This is not to say you should turn it into a personal museum, but if you feel strongly about skiing, cooking, or your alma mater, don't be afraid to bring in something to reflect that.

- Allow the students to personalize the walls as well. To do this you could give them a spot to post personal news or events, pictures, articles, or anything else they find interesting. You can also create student displays based on your discipline. For example, if you teach English or history, you could have each student bring in a quote and make a quote board, or if you teach music, you could have everyone bring in a song title to put under a recommendations list.

Exit Slip

The main point of this chapter is to shift the perception of the classroom from a room where learning happens to an interactive piece of the learning that can help you with everything from organization to inspiration. So give your classroom a few of those busy hours early in the year, and it will repay you with saved time plus interest in the future.

CHAPTER NINETEEN
CLASSROOM RITUALS

Early in my teaching career, I firmly resisted the idea of setting up classroom rituals. Of course, I'd been well versed in the many merits of rituals during education school, but to me they seemed overrated. I figured that as the weeks passed, students would figure out my tendencies and rituals would materialize on their own, so why worry about creating them?

It didn't take long for me to find out why rituals were worth worrying about. To illustrate the problems that arose without established rituals, here is a journal entry from a ritual-less class of mine from early in my first year:

> As I walked into the classroom today, several students instantly pounced on me with questions concerning a paper due the next meeting. After this crowd dispersed, two students raised their hands to ask if they could go to the computer lab to print their assignments due that day (and I addressed in a short speech why they need to have it before class). Once the students were off to the lab, another student reminded me that I'd asked him to take a make-up quiz, so I dug the quiz out of the drawer and sent him off. Next I gave a couple of short announcements, which brought the inevitable barrage of random questions, and then I finally took roll and collected the homework. By the time every piece of homework sat in my hands, twenty minutes had somehow slipped away and the lesson hadn't even started yet.

Looking at this entry now, it is clear how much this whole process could have been helped by rituals. If the procedures for student questions, make-up quizzes, collecting homework, and whether students could go to the computer lab had been ritualized, these silly little details wouldn't have eaten up nearly as much class time. This is one of the huge advantages to rituals: By organizing the little tasks of the classroom, you can save hours per marking period by making your students (and you) more efficient. It also means that you won't have to answer the same questions or make the same requests day after day, and that saves both sanity and time.

Another distinct advantage of rituals is the tone they set. If instead of having rituals, you run your class with little organization, the students will likely notice and it will likely cost you some of their respect. They may also get the impression that if you are disorganized it is all right for them to be disorganized, too. But if your class is orderly and ritualized, it helps students to understand that you are organized and prepared and expect the same from them.

These three reasons—saved time, added sanity, and improved tone—are three of the many strong arguments for why having rituals is one of the single biggest steps a new teacher can take to improve his or her teaching. To help you establish your own rituals, here are some of the most important things to keep in mind.

Opening Ceremonies

In the classrooms of many new teachers, the students are met with an explosion of minor tasks and announcements when they enter the door. Instead having a set order, everything that needs to be done in the beginning of class (like collecting homework, giving announcements, taking roll, reviewing the daily agenda, and answering questions) gets mashed together—and the result is as much pandemonium, wasted time, and confusion as you might imagine.

One of the major problems with this sort of disorganized beginning is that it usually makes both teachers and students more forgetful. For students, understanding simple things can be surprisingly difficult, so following along with such a random assortment of requests, announcements, and activities can be totally overwhelming. On the part of the teachers, even though they are leading the class, they too can easily get overwhelmed, and the sheer number of things to do on the average day can very easily lead to minor or major tasks getting lost in the shuffle.

When order gets bestowed upon the beginning of class, though, these issues with forgetfulness usually evaporate very quickly. After a few weeks of following the same rituals, both parties know exactly what to expect and exactly when to expect it, and soon they will do the entire dance flawlessly without even thinking. As they learn they will also build a speed and precision that allows the lesson to get moving as quickly as possible.

In terms of how to structure your opening ritual, there isn't really one best way. Depending on the class, the teacher, and the school, numerous approaches—if executed with care—could work with equal effectiveness. Just make sure that no matter what approach you decide on, it follows these two cardinal rules of opening rituals.

Cardinal Rule 1: It Must Be Orderly

As long as your beginning has a set order for everything, it doesn't really matter what the order is. Just by having a clear and consistent routine, students will never be at a loss for what is required of them during the first few minutes, and it will set the tone that you are organized and professional.

Cardinal Rule 2: It Must Have Student Engagement from the Opening Bell

Having students actively engaged in the first seconds of class is key, because students do not run better if they sit idle and warm up before getting to work. If students aren't involved with the class from the first few seconds, they will find other things to involve themselves in (such as chatting, drawing, or spacing out). These competing distractions will make it very difficult for your announcements or requests to fall upon anything but deaf ears, and permitting students to engage in them during the first few minutes also establishes a bad precedent that can be difficult to pull out of.

Other Tips for Establishing a Great Opening Ritual

- Some activities commonly used at the beginning of class include journals, correcting homework, warm-up problems, a review of the last class, a look at the daily agenda, and a quote of the day. All of these approaches can work well at getting students engaged and provide some order to the beginning of the class. They also are perfect little things for students to do while you take roll, collect homework, and do other minor administrative tasks that need doing.

- Getting students engaged from the beginning doesn't have to be complex. In fact, it can be accomplished by saying something as simple as "Listen to these announcements." Through the act of asking students to listen, you are requiring them to begin connecting with the classroom.

- To ensure students catch all the announcements and follow the agenda, put them on the board. This way even if students aren't listening to you, they still have a chance to see all the important information.

- You can further save time with your opening ritual by completing two, three, or four of the necessary tasks of the classroom simultaneously. For example, you could take roll while students pass their homework forward and answer a short opening question.

Ending Ceremonies

The beginning of the lesson normally receives the bulk of the attention in classroom ritual circles, and there certainly are a lot of good reasons for that. But it is not the only part of the lesson that can benefit greatly from set rituals. In fact, many teachers would argue that having a ritual for the end of class is equally important.

In the classrooms of some teachers, the end of the lesson consists of the teacher cramming all the remaining information into a couple of hurried minutes, while the students wait like expectant runners for the bell to let them go. The amount of retention in this scenario is about as low as you would expect from a situation where teachers throw massive amounts of varied information at students who aren't paying a lick of attention. And when retention is low from the part of class where homework is generally assigned and explained, you begin to see where many issues with homework are born.

This common combination of important information and student inattention at the end of lessons is why having a ritualized ending is so important. To create an ending ritual, you essentially need to do the same things you would do for an opening ritual (like having a set order of events and making sure the students are actively engaged with the class), but there are also a few added things to keep in mind to make sure the ending to your lesson is as smooth as possible.

Start Your Ending Before the End

If you start your ending seconds before, during, or after the bell, most students will be focused on getting out, not on what you have to say. So instead of fighting for their attention, start your ending ritual several minutes before the end of class, at a time when students don't yet feel the pressure of the clock weighing upon them. Also, because this pressure to escape class builds as the clock ticks toward the bell, try frontloading any important information to the very beginning of your end-of-class wrap-up, so that it meets as few distractions as possible.

Slow Down

By blowing through your ending at blazing speeds, you signal to the students that the end is very, very near. This type of approach can actually lessen student attention because it reminds them of how close they are to leaving class. What this means is that no matter how much information you have for the students, give it slowly and at a reasonable pace. The slow pace will both help students understand more of what you are saying and signal to them that class is still continuing and even if the bell rings, class is not over until all the information has been covered.

Don't Let Them Pack Up Until You Are Done

This one doesn't need too much elaboration. Students are notoriously bad multitaskers. If they are packing, they aren't listening. So don't let them put away a single object until your last syllable has been said.

General Classroom Rituals

The bookends of the lesson are essential areas of rituals, but there is no reason to stop there. Rituals can be valuable additions in all sorts of little corners of the classroom, such as the ones below.

Grade Printouts

Try to give your students grade printouts every two to three weeks. The reason killing the trees for this many printouts is necessary is because they come with so many advantages. Grade printouts keep the students notified of their standing and help avoid any negative surprises in terms of grades at the end of the marking period. They also force you to update your grades on a regular basis, and keep you aware of any students who are struggling. Finally, they are foolproof error detectors, because if you made a mistake on a student's grade he or she will let you know about it.

Regular Components

A lot of classes have regular components that they do week after week. These running themes come in many forms—from regular lists of terms to reading the back page of the *New York Times Magazine* on a weekly basis—and almost all of them can be aided significantly if they are ritualized. Ritualizing them is simple, too; all it means is that instead of picking random times to do them, you do each at the same time every week. What this standardization of regular components will do is significantly improve the students' ability to come prepared, because they will just get into the habit. The regularity should help students feel a little better, too, because it will give them an answer to the age-old question, "What are we doing today?"

Homework

If you want to eliminate all potential excuses in regard to homework, try establishing rituals all around it. If the place where students can find homework is always the same (for example, you could have it on a weekly assignment sheet, the upper left corner of the board, and the school website) then "I couldn't find/didn't know the assignment" ceases to be valid. And if students know exactly how you expect homework to be done (printed with a full heading) or where you want it turned in (in a box at the start of class), they have no defense when they don't meet your expectations.

Exit Slip

The best education you can get on rituals is to go around your school and watch how different teachers ritualize their classes. Rituals come in all sorts of shapes and sizes, and the odds are that if you see ten different teachers, you will see ten markedly different rituals. And not only will this diversity in rituals provide you with a wealth of possible ideas, the contrast also often sheds light upon the types of rituals that would work for you.

Unit Six

THE TOOLS OF THE TRADE

A t the start of the second semester, I felt freer than I had in a long time. No papers needed grading yet, thanks to winter break I was almost a month ahead on lesson planning, and over the previous three weeks I had slept for at least eight hours every single night. With my newfound and short-lived freedom, I decided to do something with my free periods that I'd wanted to do for a while: snoop into other rooms to see how different teachers ran their classes.

I knew from student gossip and discussions with colleagues that within the school resided a great variety of teaching styles, but nothing prepared me for the significant differences I saw. Every class I walked into was completely different than the one before. Some had informal airs about them, with students just hanging out at their desks, and others ran with complete precision, with even the smallest detail planned out. Some teachers spoke to their students with irreverence and sarcasm, while others were purely professional. Even classroom setups were drastically different; between wall decorations, placement of the desks, and the spot where the teacher stood during teaching, the physical states of each class were just as diverse as the teachers themselves.

Many of these differences I had guessed at or already knew, but there was one set of differences that truly gave me pause—the variety in how each teacher presented the material. For example, one math class I visited several times always seemed to work in groups. One door over sat a history class that was always involved in a lecture. A third classroom I visited belonged to another English teacher, who frequently had the students doing worksheets or individual work when I walked in. In fact, the only thing more remarkable than the differences in how each classroom ran was how effective each of these styles was in the hands of these senior teachers.

After seeing multiple teachers achieve success with very different practices, I am firmly convinced there is no right way to present material. In the hands of a capable teacher, nearly any style of teaching can and does have great success. With that in mind, this unit looks at the three most common types of instruction and doesn't take sides about which is better than the others. Instead, it tries to give the important information about each, including explanations, tips, and warnings of common pitfalls, so you can choose the tools that are best for your class.

CHAPTER TWENTY

LECTURES

I s there any part of school more vilified than the poor lecture? Unfortunately, probably not. For many teachers and students, lectures have come to represent all that is wrong with school. They represent the philosophy that school is nothing more than jamming information into students. They represent the teacher who is out of touch and inspiration and should have retired fifteen years ago. They represent boredom incarnate. But this reputation really isn't fair to the poor misunderstood lecture, which, if used effectively, can be so much more than a highly effective form of torture.

There is no doubt that if used wrong, lectures can be brutal marches through information. But a lecture in skilled hands can be just as wonderful as a bad lecture can be agonizing. Lectures also hold an important role in the modern classroom—they are where teachers teach. This is not to say that group work, discussions, and worksheets aren't part of the teaching process, too, but lectures are the purest form of information transmission. And for this and so many other reasons it is worth thinking about including them in your classroom. But when you do, keep the following points in mind.

Enthusiasm Is Key

Almost everyone has had a teacher whose lectures were the verbal equivalent of elephant tranquilizers. You know the one who talked at great length in a monotone voice about demonstrative pronouns or coefficients of linear expansion (an apology to the demonstrative pronoun and coefficient fans out there). But most people have probably also had a teacher whose dynamic lectures made you want to listen and learn more. Though the boring, dry lecture is the more prominent of the two, its alter ego, the exciting and engaging lecture, is out there as well. And to make sure your lecture falls into the exciting category, there is one major key—enthusiasm.

As was discussed in chapter 1, enthusiasm is one of the most powerful marketing tools on the planet. It's the reason infomercials and rambling television pundits are billion-dollar businesses. If politicians don't come across as enthusiastic, they will probably lose, and if marketers don't sell their products with excitement, the products generally aren't sold. Humans are wired for enthusiasm to have a powerful effect on us, and if something is exciting enough for people to get passionate about it, we can't help but have some interest about why.

Lectures are one of the best places for teachers to use this hypnotic power of enthusiasm. If you come across as excited about the information you present, the students will take notice. If you clearly don't care too much, they won't, either. This doesn't mean that you should slather excessive and artificial enthusiasm all over your lectures; instead, just get excited and use your youthful exuberance. If you aren't able to do that with any given topic, it is probably a good idea to find another way to introduce it.

Not Too Long

The best lectures are often a lot like commercials. They are fun, engaging, and over before you think to change the channel. The reason short lectures (or minilectures) of five to ten minutes are so effective is that they happen so fast that the students don't have time to get bored. Before they can say "Aw, not a lecture!" you've said what you need to say and you're on to the next activity. Minilectures also make it easy to keep the energy of both parties high, because there isn't enough time for the lecture to drag.

Another advantage to short lectures is that they help students process and remember the information. Absorbing, sorting through, and recalling all the important information from a class period full of notes is a daunting task, even for the most advanced students. By breaking the instruction into minilectures, you make the information significantly more manageable by giving it in installments. These bite-size pieces of information are far easier for the students to understand and recall, and they are easier for you to remember and deal with, too (for it means you don't have to memorize long lectures, either).

Just because minilectures are often the preferable way to introduce information, that doesn't mean you should never lecture for more than five or ten minutes. Sometimes longer lectures are needed, and that is perfectly fine as long as you keep one question in mind—are my students still engaged? As long as the students stay engaged, they are probably still learning and your lecture is likely still achieving most of its goals. If you are wondering how to know if they are engaged, just watch out for that unmistakable feeling that you are talking to yourself. When you feel that, the students probably have tuned out (which means you are indeed talking to yourself) and it is time to move on.

Combine Your Lecture with Other Things

The lecture, being pure information sharing, is great for passing on a lot of information in a short span of time. But because the information comes in such a condensed form, the lecture by itself is not a very effective tool for helping students remember that information. To help students retain and better understand the information, it is often useful to reinforce lectures with other types of activities. This is why most teachers have a discussion, set of questions, or some other form of related classwork tied in with the lecture. If you just move on after giving a lecture without giving the students' brains a chance to play with the new information, there is a good chance they will forget it by the time they walk out the door.

Beyond activities there are other things that can be added with lectures to take them to the next level.

Pictures

If you have the ability (or even if you don't), drawing pictures of the main points can add a lot to a lecture. Not only does this approach make the lecture friendlier to visual learners, it also adds a light-hearted variety that can make the information more approachable, and often the quickly (and, if you are like me, poorly) drawn pictures can add a dash of humor, too.

Movement

The best lecturers rarely stay still. And there is a good reason for that. When you stand still, your words follow suit and come across as stiff. This sort of formality is great for special occasions, but not so great for daily class. When you move, your tone naturally becomes more fluid to those listening, which can make the lecture feel more like a conversation than force-fed knowledge.

Note Taking

Even though they are literally old school, notes, like the lecture, should not be left in the twentieth century. Instead, they should be reinvented for the modern classroom. To do this, don't just make notes an unspoken duty of the students during lectures; discuss note taking with students, teach them how to take notes (you could see who can write the shortest shorthand and still have the important information), and have them change up their notes from time to time (you could have them fill in blank notes or add pictures, too). By treating notes as an important and interesting activity that deserves thought, you can often succeed in breathing some new life into this old technique.

Knowledge That the Lecture Material Matters

Students sometimes have a hard time understanding that a lecture given today will likely appear on a test tomorrow. By reminding them that they will be tested on the information, you can add a little boost of motivation.

How to Structure a Lecture

A good lecture isn't just a pile of information thrown at the students. It should have the same tension, structure, and engagement with the audience that comes with any good story. To help you do that, here are a few quick steps to planning the perfect lecture.

1. Start with an Attention Grabber

This "hook" can take nearly any form (from an odd fact to an intriguing question), so long as it gets the students' attention. This is important, because once you have the students' interest they are much more willing to follow you into the lecture.

2. Have a Coherent Path

The brain is a series of connections, so if your lecture is a bunch of disjointed points it doesn't stand a chance of sticking in the students' brains.

Instead it will probably just confuse and frustrate students into ignoring your lectures.

3. Wrap It Up with Important Points

People are generally able to recall the last things they heard significantly better than the things that came before. This means that you should always strive to wrap your lecture up with the points that you want the students to remember the most (and the repetition signals to the students that those points are important).

Exit Slip

Even though you now know better, lectures are considered boring by students until you prove otherwise. So use whatever tricks you can—from enthusiasm to pictures to PowerPoint—to show students that they aren't so bad after all. And if you do, you may be surprised by how fast the students not only begin to accept the lecture, but actually start to look forward to it!

CHAPTER TWENTY-ONE
DISCUSSIONS

For new teachers, the discussion can be a very appealing way to introduce material. Few things in school are more invigorating for teachers and students than a dynamic discussion, and a discussion in full force can also allow students to be heard, broaden and develop their understanding of the important topics in class, and learn to find their voice and themselves. Discussions are also often very comfortable for most new teachers, who are fresh from the discussion-heavy world of college, where in-depth conversations about everything from math theory to Faulkner are the norm.

While many teachers come to school with visions of discussions that resemble something from *The Breakfast Club*, the first discussions teachers actually have can sometimes look a little more like this: When the discussion starts, at least half the students zone out almost immediately. Common zoning-out activities include doodling, chatting quietly among themselves, or putting their heads down as a signal that they aren't even going to pretend to engage. Out of those who stay with the discussion, only a few are able to stay on the original topic and provide insightful answers. The rest either remain silent or more commonly sidetrack the conversation with random answers or by meeting the questions posed with far more random questions.

After a few discussions that proceed like this, it can be tempting to scrap the whole concept of having discussions in class—but when faced with this urge, don't give up. Discussions do have all the advantages listed above and more, but only if they are run right. That is why it's important to think about the following issues.

Including Mandatory Responses

Students love to talk, normally. But when it comes to discussions, far too often two or three students dominate the talking. Why is it that a roomful of people at the most social age of their lives has so few people willing to jump into the conversation? Some of the reluctance can be blamed on shyness or boredom, but surely those two alone aren't enough to explain such levels of silence.

Part of the explanation for this selective mutism could be that discussions aren't the best place to exchange ideas for everyone. For students who process information slowly, those with attention problems, and others who want to delve deeper into a question, the pace and depth of discussions can be irritating or intimidating. Many of these students may want to contribute ideas, but either the discussion is not happening at their level or it moves on before they can come up with an idea or develop their thoughts thoroughly enough.

One way to bring these students commonly left behind by discussions back into the fray is to use something called mandatory responses. Mandatory responses are where you have students write or think about a discussion question with free-writes or small problems before the discussion begins. Then once the discussion starts every student, regardless of how slowly he or she processes information, will have some answers ready and waiting. Forcing everyone to think of an answer beforehand may also bring students who are normally disengaged back into the discussion, because they may be curious about how the answers of others compare to theirs or feel compelled to defend their thinking if someone else has a different response.

Most mandatory responses come in the form of writing prompts because they can very easily be converted into discussion questions, but you can approach them any way you like. Examples of other types of mandatory responses include giving students strange questions or riddles to ponder, having them do something that connects to the upcoming discussion (science and math are full of great little tricks that you can have students do before talking about something), or having them search for something applicable, like a quote or fact. You can also structure your mandatory responses so that students have to answer different questions or find different things (like quotes or facts), and then use these varied answers/quotes/information as guideposts for the upcoming discussion.

By taking this mandatory response approach, every student is already somewhat invested in the discussion and has given thought to some of the key questions. This will hopefully bring all types of students back into the fray and increase the number of students actively engaged in the discussion from a few to a majority.

Think about the Types of Questions You Ask

All questions are not created equal. Some questions are simple and require just yes or no answers: "Is the sun a star?" Others still only have one answer, but you need more than one syllable to answer them: "How does the Electoral College work?" Next come the questions that have multiple, but still a finite number of, answers: "What are the different parts of the cell?" And finally there are questions with infinite (or at least an unknown number of) possible answers: "What was Shakespeare's viewpoint on love?"

When it comes to putting together a discussion there isn't just one type of question that you should shoot for. If all of your questions have only one answer, you probably won't have much of a dynamic discussion because there would be nothing to discuss. But the same principle is also true with more complex questions. If you were to start a discussion with a complicated question like "What was Shakespeare's viewpoint on love?" and you had never discussed the topic before, the class response would likely be nothing but blank stares. This is because a question like that takes a lot of different mental steps, and asking the students to make all those steps in one leap is a seriously tall order.

Instead of limiting your discussion to one type of question, you probably want to include all different types. This mixture of surface-level and deep questions will help it appeal to everyone and will give the discussion a varied rhythm that is natural in everyday conversation. You also probably want to build up to the big questions. For example, if instead of starting with "What was Shakespeare's viewpoint on love?" you start with individual questions about how love affected each character in a particular play and then ask the deeper question, you will have a much better chance of getting insightful answers for how Shakespeare viewed love.

Beware of Stepping Away Completely

Many new teachers approach discussions by compiling a list of thought-provoking questions for students and then stepping completely back so the students can come up with their own conclusions with only minor teacher interference. This hands-off approach, though nice in principle, will lead to discussions that are prone to taking bizarre tangents. This is not to say that it should be avoided; sometimes letting students explore their thoughts, no matter what direction the discussion takes, is a really good thing. But as a teacher you should be aware that if left to nature, student discussions will probably not go in any particular direction or make any set points.

Also Beware of Overcorrecting to the Lectoscussion

With the downsides that come with not enough guidance, many new teachers make the mistake of overcorrecting and steering discussions with an overly firm hand. The second they see students struggling or diverging from where they want them to go, the teacher steps in and nudges them in the right direction. And though this type of discussion often does lead to all the important topics being covered and usually has less tangents, in many ways it is no longer a discussion. Instead, it is what is often referred to as a lectoscussion, or a lecture masquerading as a discussion.

The key difference between a discussion and a lectoscussion is the intention at the core. Discussions are meant for students to discuss, sort out, and process their own ideas. Lectoscussions, like lectures, are based on getting out the information the teacher wants students to learn. During a lectoscussion the teacher may ask a lot of student questions, like a discussion, but their questions are generally fishing for specific answers. If the answer isn't found, the teacher provides it. If the answer is found, the teacher then moves on to the next point he or she wants to cover. When you look closer, this is not a classroom discussion where students are figuring out their own answers; it is just a lecture with ad-libs.

Because the lectoscussion isn't honest with itself about what it is, it often falls short of accomplishing the goals of a lecture or a discussion. Because the priority of a lectoscussion is to get the teacher's ideas out, students rarely have a chance during them to work with their own ideas. Lectoscussions also generally aren't as effective at transmitting information to students because the information comes in a more scattered order (because it comes from the students) than a lecture and with less control from the teacher about what is emphasized and included.

Providing Boundaries or Finding the Happy Medium

Just like with teachers, great discussions come in a variety of different forms. But if there is one overarching characteristic to all successful discussions, it is that they all have clear and reasonable boundaries. If a teacher tries to squeeze a discussion out of just saying "What do you think?" the answers could go anywhere, and rarely will they go somewhere productive. But at the same time, if the teacher makes the boundaries so prohibitive that there is only one path, he or she may as well just be honest and give it as a lecture.

The right level of boundaries means that students can still take the conversation multiple ways, but they are limited from going down unproductive routes. The way to do this is to be very careful about how you craft your prompts, mandatory responses, and other forms of framing. For example, in a question about Thomas Jefferson, here are three possible discussion prompts. One is too hands-off for anything but an exploratory discussion, one is too narrow and should just be a lecture, and the third is just right.

Too Broad

"What do you think of Thomas Jefferson?"

This prompt is too broad because it could go in any direction, from his affair with Sally Hemmings to his performance as president. This question will get the students thinking about their own thoughts, but who knows where they will go with them.

Too Narrow

"What was Thomas Jefferson's motivation for writing the Declaration of Independence?"

This prompt is too narrow if you are fishing for a specific answer. At that point, just tell the students what you want them to know about his motivation.

Just Right

"The role of the Church of England in British politics definitely influenced Thomas Jefferson, but can you think of any reasons beyond that for why he was such a huge proponent for the separation of church and state?"

This prompt is just right, because it gets out the information you want to present and then gives students a limited range in which to explore their own thoughts and make their own connections.

Use Movement

Even with well-crafted prompts and mandatory responses, students have a tendency to turn off during discussions, especially if they are otherwise tired or distracted. This predisposition to inducing daydreaming makes discussions a perfect place to incorporate movement in your lesson. If the students are up and moving it makes it very difficult for them to fall prey to the distracting thoughts in their heads.

One way to do this is to have students get out of their seats and move to different parts of the room to express their answer to a question. In English you could have the names of characters from a book on the walls and have students move under the names to answer various questions (like who is the guiltiest or the most likable); in math you could give multiple choice questions and have the four corners of the room represent a, b, c, and d; and in art you could have various work on the walls and have students move to discuss each piece.

Exit Slip

The most important thing to keep in mind about discussions is that they work best for things like exploration and collaboration, not instruction. As long as you think about that while figuring out your discussion objectives, making questions, and guiding the discussion, there is a good chance that you will end up with something as invigorating (though in its own unique way) as what you remember from college.

GROUP WORK

While the lecture is often the most-maligned member of the family of teaching tools, group work is easily the favorite son. Spend longer than fifteen minutes in the halls of an education school or a teaching conference and you are guaranteed to hear someone trumpeting the many advantages of group work. And they would be right.

When done right, group work can be a symphony of student learning. Group work not only helps build social skills, it also is a great environment for students to work with and process the information, refine their ideas by debating with their peers, and pick up important information they may have missed during class from their group members. In many ways, group work can bring together the advantages of all the other types of instruction into one exercise—that is, if it is done right.

That last part—if it is done right—is the problem with group work. Though it does come with lots of advantages, it is also incredibly difficult to do well. It isn't enough to just throw students into a group, give them a task, and let them go. Truly successful group work often requires a precision that few teachers manage to do right. To make sure you are one of those teachers, keep these three simple suggestions in mind whenever you do group work.

Define Roles and Responsibilities
(and Try to Match These with Talents and Capabilities)

Having a purpose is one of the most powerful motivating forces on the planet. People routinely push themselves to the limit, endanger their well-being, and even die for purposes they believe in. When people face monumental purposes, like medical residencies or climbing mountains, they often find they are able to push themselves harder and for longer hours than they ever dreamed possible. Some studies have even found that people with jobs, hobbies, pets, or some other reason to keep going live significantly longer. Clearly the power of having a purpose is profound, and because of this it is useful to give students a purpose as often as possible.

There are many ways to give purpose in the classroom. You can do it by explaining why the class is covering certain material, attaching extrinsic rewards (like grades, candy, or class dollars) to certain behaviors, or just making students feel good about their work (along with the many other techniques discussed in chapter 10). But one of the best ways to give purpose is to assign students roles when they work together.

Having student roles can do wonders for the students' sense of purpose, because it moves them from being "random group member 3" to being "the scribe" or "the group leader." This change in title may not seem like much, but all of a sudden the students have a position that if not done by them, won't be done at all. On the other hand, if they don't do something as "random group member 3," the others in the group can pick up the slack.

Having a purpose does more than just provide motivation, though; it also helps smooth over another common issue with group work: students rarely work together in a seamless fashion. It is not uncommon for students in a group setting to bicker with each other, or for the bulk of the work to fall upon a few students. By providing roles and responsibilities within the group, teachers are often able to limit the in-fighting and uneven distribution of work, because there is far less guesswork about where each student fits into the equation. This adds both accountability and peer pressure, because not only does the student know his or her particular job, the teacher and the other students know, too, and if the student doesn't follow through everyone knows. And not wanting to disappoint that many people can be a strong incentive to work smoothly.

Idle Hands Do the Devil's Work

Think about the amount of temptation present during group work. The teacher is generally engaged with another group on the other side of the room, the students are actually allowed to talk (and with each other!), and groups sitting in circles have lookouts on all sides who can warn the others when the teacher's attention shifts toward them.

With such opportunities for troublemaking present, it's not surprising that many teachers struggle with keeping students on task during group exercises. But what is the teacher supposed to do in a situation like this where the students seemingly have all the cards? The answer: give them a lot of work.

If the students have so much work that everyone needs to be focused for them to have a chance of finishing, the urge to talk is often instantly overshadowed by the need to get everything done. Because of this it is almost always a good idea to give students a little too much work during group activities. Try to plan group activities so that the students have a couple more problems than you think they can handle or a couple less minutes than you think it will take. This time crunch will often lead to a pressure upon the students that is far more powerful than if you were standing directly over them. It will give them a deadline pressure, and anyone who has completed something seconds before it is due knows exactly what a potent motivator that can be.

Make It Clear That Each Student's Contribution Matters and Is a Significant Part of the Evaluation

Even with a purpose and a time crunch, students still sometimes need a little added motivation to stay on task during group exercises. To help with that it often works to attach grades (or some other extrinsic motivator) to group work done in class. By incorporating grades you provide extra value to the assignment beyond learning (which isn't always the first, second, or even third priority of students) that helps them stay focused.

It usually doesn't take many points to act as a strong motivator of students in a group setting. Generally for an average-size group project, students will respond well if you assign as many points as you would for a small homework assignment. If your group work is a bit more involved, try to keep the number of points similar to the number of points you would assign for it if the project was done as homework instead. (Students often base how hard they should work on something on how many average homework grades it equals.)

Also, when you tell students their group work will be a graded assignment, let them know exactly what you are looking for in order to receive full credit. If you want them to be creative, work well as a team, or have equal speaking parts for everyone in the group, make sure you say so! Let them know if it is graded on effort or the outcome. Even if these seem like givens to you, for students they might not be, and if you are clear then they have no excuse not to give you exactly what you want.

At first the idea of using grades during group work in class can seem a little unsettling because there is nothing tangible to hold and evaluate. But after trying it, you may be surprised at how easy it is to grade student performance in groups. Even for a new teacher, it isn't hard to tell what A, B, and C group effort looks like, and then you just grade accordingly. Even more amazing is how little complaining students will give for what is essentially a purely subjective grade. They too know exactly what A, B, and C effort look like, and in most classes they will make sure it is in the A range if they know a grade is attached to it.

Exit Slip

When doing group work, even once you've taken care of all the major details like making sure everyone has a purpose, enough work, and added incentive, the little details can still contribute a significant amount to the success or demise of the assignment. These are the biggest of the little details to keep an eye on:

- The size of the group. Generally speaking the optimal number of students in a group is three or four. When you only have two there isn't necessarily the same level of collaboration, and when the number of students gets above four there are often too many cooks in the kitchen and someone will get left out. This is not to say that it should always be three or four, but in most situations that seems to work best.

- The students in the group. Students don't normally pick groups based on whom they would work well with. Instead they pick their friends, and this tendency is one strong reason for you to prepick groups (especially for bigger projects where the students working efficiently will be particularly important) or randomly select them (numbered cards or popsicle sticks are great for quick and random groupings) the majority of the time.

- The day. Some days students are just more distracted than on others. You can't always predict the level of student distraction, but other times, like before breaks or big school events, you can. On days when student distraction will likely be high, you may want to steer clear of group work and the freedom that comes with it, in favor of more structured styles of teaching.

CHEAT SHEETS

A teacher's life is filled to the brim with questions. Should I reprimand the talking student? Should I walk around during the group exercise or step back? Should I raise or lower my voice to get the students' attention? Hardly a moment goes by where teachers aren't forced to make a choice of some sort. The good news about these constant questions is that most of the time the answer will be apparent or won't be a particularly big deal either way. When it comes to a decision about marking a student late or allowing a student to use the bathroom, you just follow your precedents and the rules already in place. And whether you decide to walk around or not walk around during a group exercise, even if you don't make the best choice, it probably won't make much of a long-term impact upon your class and your reputation.

But occasionally a question comes along whose answer is both unclear and significantly important for the health of your classroom, and for new teachers making these choices can be genuinely terrifying. It is also very easy to make the wrong choice in these situations because terror is so effective at scrambling your decision-making ability. That is where this unit steps in. This unit is devoted to providing ready-made answers to those tough situations, so when they arise you won't respond with an "Uh . . ."; you will respond with the right action.

HOW TO RESPOND TO A QUESTION YOU DON'T HAVE AN ANSWER FOR

S tudents ask teachers questions for a multitude of reasons. Some are looking for help, while others are trying to get out of work. Some want to question authority, while others are looking to an authority figure for advice. Some may want attention, clarification, evaluation, or favors, or they might just want to find out if you watched *The Office* the night before. Whatever the reason, questions from students are a constant part of a teacher's day. Whether during class, lunch, planning periods, or even stepping out to a local coffee shop, there is hardly a five-minute stretch in the school day where a teacher doesn't have to field a student question.

One day I decided to record the student questions for the day to get an idea of how many questions I encountered on a daily basis. Here is what I got:

- "Can I have an extension on the paper? I made a lot of the changes you asked for, but I didn't have time to fix the grammar."

- "Should I run track or play baseball?"

- "My printer didn't work and the computer lab is closed. What should I do?"

- "I am having a hard time getting started on my story. Do you have any suggestions on how to start?"

And these were just the questions before my first period—before my day had technically even started. Sadly, the flood of questions soon overwhelmed me and I quickly lost count, but even by that point it was clear that a day's worth of questions could fill up a good chunk of a spiral notebook.

Even more challenging for many new teachers than the quantity of student questions is the fact that very few classroom questions have simple answers. The main reason answers are so tricky to come by is that the two sides involved are not equal. Teachers and students generally have drastically different mindsets, goals, life experiences, and levels of power. To span this gulf, coming up with an effective answer to even the simplest question can require a complex cocktail of decisions. For example, if you are asked for an extension on a paper, you will likely have to instantly weigh the following factors:

- Whether an extension could be given for the assignment

- How long before the assignment due date the student asked for the extension

- Whether the student was genuine or trying to take advantage

- If you say no, what the reasoning will be

- If you say yes, what date should it be pushed back to

- Whether to use this as a teachable moment (give them a speech or not)

This subtle complexity of student questions makes them a possible vulnerable spot for teachers, and more than a few students have figured this out. Because of this, it is not uncommon for students to confront teachers with questions that are more about probing for weaknesses and setting up excuses for later than for clearing up legitimate spots of confusion. For example, students may ask vague questions about assignments that aren't due for a long time just so they can come back later and say "You said . . . " when they haven't finished the assignment.

The dangers of questions, honest or not, are especially pronounced for new teachers because they haven't heard the majority of the questions before. Veteran teachers don't necessarily have an easy time answering every question, but they can lean upon their prior experiences. They have seen most situations and have precedents to guide them. New teachers don't have this experience, so every new question requires them to venture into the dangerous world of thinking on their feet (often with an audience, no less). But fear not—student questions may be random, but your responses to them don't need to be if you follow some of these rules to help you through.

Don't Be Afraid to Call a Time-Out

One day a student from my honors class approached me with a request to justify an essay grade. This request seemed harmless enough, so I acquiesced and took the paper to remind myself of my reasoning. As I flipped through it, I noticed that at first glance the grade did seem overly harsh. I didn't mention this internal debate out loud, but my face and hesitancy betrayed my conflict. The student, recognizing this as an opportunity, began to press her points harder and harder while also growing increasingly firm in her assertion of injustice.

At the same time, possibly because I had lost confidence in my correctness, I began to fumble over my words. Each time she pressed and I failed to parry her accusations, I felt a little bit smaller and she grew a bit more aggressive. Finally, feeling cornered, I curtly snatched the paper and responded that I would "take the paper back and give it another look." I then cut off the conversation and left, feeling quite foolish.

Even though this situation was a profoundly painful one, a valuable lesson was born out of it. The urge to retreat may have risen from a feeling of helplessness, but deferring the dispute provided an opportunity for me to reclaim control. By the end of the conversation the student was firmly in command and this change of roles, besides being greatly unsettling, caused my brain to freeze up. Once I was alone and no longer forced to talk unscripted, I was finally free to think again. This respite also gave me the time to reevaluate the paper (I determined upon closer inspection that my original grade was fair), compile a comprehensive list of reasons to justify my grade, and plan my approach to the next meeting with the student. When I finally returned the paper to the student, she was not happy with my conclusion that her grade wouldn't change, but after she heard my well-thought-out reasons there were no more arguments from her.

New teachers rarely think of it, but calling a time-out is always an option with a student, parent, or administrator. Time-outs are useful in a variety of situations, too. Not only do they give teachers a way to escape unwelcome situations, they also are useful for sensitive moments, when confronted with major decisions, or on any other occasion where some extra time could make all the difference. Time-outs also have the ability to please both parties in some situations. For example, when you call a time-out when dealing with a student you may be thrilled to escape, but by agreeing to take a closer look you can also validate their concerns by pledging time to look into them.

Stay Firm (at Least for the Moment)

If you are telling a student something and aren't sure about the words as they exit your mouth, it's all the more essential that you sound certain. Many problems with students begin because the teacher lets uncertainty show.

Students often get pigeonholed as unperceptive, and in some ways this may be fair, but it certainly is not true when it comes to recognizing uncertainty. Even small children often seem to have great talent for sniffing out indecision. This makes sense, too, because children's lives are mainly controlled by others (teachers, parents, coaches, etc.). In order get his or her way, a child's only choice may be to find and press upon the soft spots in the rules and decisions surrounding the child.

Whatever the reason, students vigilantly watch for holes in the teacher's plan and will advocate hard for themselves when they see an opportunity to get what they want. Teachers can avoid a lot of grief and unpleasant student interactions if they come across as confident in their actions, even if they aren't (especially if they aren't). If the students don't sense that they have a chance of winning the teacher over, they generally won't bother to try.

You Can Always Go Back and Change

Even though you don't want to waver in front of a student, it is perfectly acceptable to go off, waver on your own as much as you need to, and later revise what you said. No one, not even students, expects a teacher to be perfect, so admitting occasional mistakes doesn't put a teacher at much risk of losing credibly.

You can lessen the effect of admitting a mistake further by borrowing a page from the book of politics and framing it in your own way. You can say you rethought it, wanted to give the student the benefit of the doubt, decided a new direction was needed, or "mistakes were made" (OK, maybe not that last one). Admitting a mistake to a student should always be done carefully, which is why it is worth staying firm at first and assessing and addressing it later. But if mistakes are handled with the greatest care, they can be powerful teaching tools and do no damage whatsoever to your reputation.

Turn It Back on Them

As a teacher you will occasionally face questions that you wouldn't be able to answer with an hour and an iPhone. For these questions it may appear you have only two options: Either admit not knowing the answer (which is fine at times and can make you seem relatable—see chapter 3 for more details) or make up an answer (which generally doesn't end up well). But there is a third option that often is the best route of all when executed well: besides admitting defeat or venturing an answer, you also have the option to not answer and instead turn the question back upon the student. By turning it back on the student, you can take the pressure off yourself and turn it back on the student without looking like you froze on answering the question. Here are a couple of ways you could phrase this:

- "I don't know, but that's a great question. How about you look into it and share your findings with the class tomorrow."

- "Great question—What do you think?"

- "Great question! [to the whole class] What does the rest of the class think?"

Think about Your Responses to Common Questions

So far all the techniques discussed for dealing with questions have been reactive, on-the-spot tips. But new teachers can prepare for student questions in a similar fashion to preparing for a job interview. Both interview and student questions generally come in a couple of categories. Some will be things you've never dreamed of, but others can be predicted with a little thought. A good interviewee knows it's not possible to prepare for random questions, so he or she focuses attention beforehand on the questions that he or she knows will probably come.

A good chunk of the questions teachers will be asked are predictable, too. And though you don't know the exact form they will take, preparing answers ahead of time for inevitable questions will take some pressure off and allow you to save your brainpower for the truly unexpected questions. Some common questions you *will* get are on this list. (Some of these aren't phrased as questions, but they are asking a question, all the same.)

- "Why are we doing/reading this?"

- "Why did I get such a low grade?"

- "I have a version on my computer, but it isn't printed. What should I do?"

- "I'm sorry I didn't do my homework. I was gone all weekend at a camp, family vacation, conference [something else that sounds official]. Can I have an extension?"

- "I'm having a hard time with the assignment. I don't think I can do it."

- "I forgot my book/binder/materials for class. Should I go get it?"

- "Can't we do [something fun] instead of [the lesson you have planned]?"

Exit Slip

When you go forward and deal with student questions, it is important to know that even with all of the tips above, you will still make some mistakes in your answers. Because of the sheer quantity, variation, and intricacies of student questions, you will give imperfect answers—a lot of them. These imperfections will come in many shapes and sizes, ranging from not answering as well as you could have to being blatantly wrong. But whatever the level, it is important to know that imperfect answers are normal and human, all teachers make them, and in most situations the students won't even notice (let alone hold it against you). After giving an answer that has some variety of mistake in it, the two most important things to do are to not freak out or let your embarrassment stop you from fixing it. If you stay cool and address it in a composed manner, your class will likely see your errors as simple slip-ups instead of an indication of bigger issues.

A STUDENT CHEATS

A lot of student faults get aired out in teachers' lounges. Bad attitudes, lacking effort, and generally confusing behaviors on the part of the students are all popular topics for teachers who congregate in the lounge. But one topic never discussed is student cheating, or even student dishonesty. There are only a couple of reasons for why cheating wouldn't make the cut for discussion when the airing out all other student faults is so commonplace: (a) there is little to no student cheating, so there is no reason to talk about it; or (b) teachers are more embarrassed by cheating than by the other mistakes students make.

Out of these two options, the answer probably has more to do with teachers being a bit more embarrassed about cheating than their classes being devoid of cheating. Although it is generally rare, student cheating is an unhappy reality that most teachers encounter at least a handful of times per year (if they are watching for it). It is also one of the most profoundly hurtful things a student can do to most teachers. Students could glare, call the a teacher an assortment of malicious names, or even spit on them, and for many teachers it still wouldn't produce a sting as long lasting as the knowledge that a student cheated in their class.

Why cheating causes such pain is that it is not only dishonest, it is premeditated dishonesty. For most teachers, forgiving students for faults like talking, not doing homework, saying rude or inappropriate things, or even lying on a smaller scale is generally fairly easy because they are a by-product of not thinking. Serious cheating is the complete opposite of this; it only comes when a student makes a very conscious decision to cheat—and that can be hard to get over.

Another unfortunate fact about cheating is it's probably more likely to surface in a new teacher's class because many students think "new teacher" is a synonym for "sucker." And in some ways they may be right; new teachers have so much to focus on already that their senses for recognizing cheating may be significantly dulled. To help make sure this doesn't become you, here are a few tricks for the overworked new teacher to watch for and deal with cheating using minimal effort.

Strike against Cheating Before It Starts

A lot of cheating can be cut out of your class if you simply make sure that the students understand what constitutes cheating and know that you are looking out for it. Both of these may seem like givens to you, but to students they may not be. So make sure they are clear.

Make It Clear What Cheating Is

The definition of cheating seems obvious at first: It is any time when you break rules to gain an advantage. But inside the classroom, what constitutes cheating can become a bit more blurred. For example, in some classes homework is meant to be done in groups, while other teachers would consider working together as cheating. In English, book reports require students to compile what other people have said, while in an essay this would be considered plagiarism. There is also great variety concerning what is allowed on each assignment or assessment—they can be group or individual, open or closed notes, and allow differing levels of outside help or sources.

This is not to say all or even most cheating comes from misunderstanding on the part of students, but being clear on what constitutes cheating takes away any chance for misunderstanding. More importantly, it also takes away one of the most common excuses students use when they are caught: "I didn't know that was cheating." If the line between cheating and honesty is clearly drawn ahead of time, both at the beginning of the year concerning general cheating and on individual assignments where there could be possible confusion, that excuse has no legs to stand upon. Finally, outlining what is cheating ahead of time also sends the message to students that you will be watching for it, and when students know you are looking they may grow a little trigger-shy when it comes to trying to pull something off.

Read Them the Riot Act

If you were to ask most normal people about the profile of the average cheater, they would likely describe the troubled student with bad grades who doesn't appear to care about school. But in reality, this type of student is actually one of the least likely to cheat. Instead, the vast majority of major cheaters (at least for anything above copying homework) tend to come from the ranks of "good students" whose grades fall somewhere in the top half of the class. And when you take a step back, this makes sense, too.

Cheating often takes a lot of footwork and planning (sometimes more than just studying would have). Unmotivated students probably wouldn't be willing to put in the effort to pull it off, nor would they care enough about class to even attempt it. But motivated students looking for a little added grade bump have a much stronger motive to contemplate cheating. Think about it like steroids and baseball: There are very few mid-level high-school baseball players willing to undergo the risks and effort associated with pro- curing, injecting, and hiding steroids, when the benefits probably won't get them to professional baseball anyway. On the other hand, the Major Leagues, filled with the best athletes in the world, are jammed with players willing to endure the risk, effort, and possible national vilification associated with steroids to receive the little boost they provide.

Because cheaters often come from the ranks of good students, scaring students out of cheating before they do it can be a very effective strategy. To do this, start by reminding students that "cheating is the number one sin in school." Then list off the horrible consequences that come with cheating (in- cluding zeroes, suspensions, expulsions, and serious blots on their permanent record). Finally, conclude with an in-depth explanation of why cheating is so frowned upon and how it stands as a personal affront to teachers. In general, though this speech probably won't stop every potential cheater, it may scare quite a few students who are on the fence back off onto the honest side again.

How to Deal with Cheating After It Happens

Proactively taking on cheating will hopefully lower the occurrences of it, but it probably won't completely eliminate the problem. Because of this it is important to have a plan for when cheating happens. Here are a few pieces of advice for designing that plan.

Don't Be Lenient When It Comes to Cheating

Around the middle of October, it became very clear that one of my students wasn't playing me straight. This realization shocked me because the student in question was outwardly one of the sweetest kids imaginable. His combination of soft-spokenness, constant questions after class, and a nervous but boisterous smile made him a sentimental favorite of mine. He also worked hard and despite his ESL status and limited history with English he had a decent grade in the class.

It was probably this positive opinion of him that made me not think twice when he turned in an essay late and said it was because he didn't understand the directions. It also probably played a role in my decision that he should get a retake, not a zero, on the vocabulary quiz that I caught him using a pocket English dictionary on (once again he blamed the directions). But by the time, a few weeks later, when he turned in a revision on a paper that clearly wasn't his, my faith had run dry.

Unsure of how to handle a cheating student, I pulled the student aside and told him of my worries. At first he flatly denied any wrongdoing, but then when it was clear I wasn't going to budge, he finally admitted that his tutor may have become a bit too familiar with the paper. He then profusely apologized and pleaded not to be labeled as one of those kids. In the end, despite his grocery list of previous fishy situations, I decided not to throw added consequences on top of a zero for the revision grade (which wasn't a very big penalty), besides warning the student that even the slightest whiff of deceit would mean serious trouble.

Unhappily, his great escape did nothing to deter the student. In fact, it only made him bolder with his cheating and only a few weeks later I received another paper that, despite a few carefully inserted mistakes, clearly wasn't the student's writing. This time I threw the book at him, and the resulting suspension and zero lowered his grade from a B to a D. The shock of this precipitous drop finally did the trick, and the rest of the year the student never (at least to my knowledge) attempted to cheat again.

When looking back at this situation, one of the most striking features was how the compassion on my part concerning the student's early attempts at cheating ended up not being compassionate at all. When the student learned the teacher was hesitant to severely punish him, the lack of consequences only fueled his cheating. That is why if you find yourself with a cheating student, don't feel bad about giving him or her a tough punishment. You need to make it clear that cheating of any variety, even when accidental, is not acceptable and will receive no mercy. This is not to say that you should be unreasonable, uncompassionate, or searching for someone to take advantage of, but you need to be very careful about not being taken advantage of, too.

How to Ferret Out Cheaters: To Dig for Information or Lay It on the Table

Teachers and administrators often use two techniques with suspected cheaters. Both are aimed at producing a confession, which, if you can get it, makes dealing with dishonest students significantly easier. The first technique is something called "The Flood," which is where teachers with a lot of evidence backing up their suspicions lay down all their reasons for suspected cheating in rapid succession. Behind it lies the hope that when faced with an avalanche of evidence, the student will understand resistance is futile and quickly confess.

The Flood is a good approach for teachers with a lot of evidence who are generally assured of the student's guilt. But if a teacher just has suspicions but not enough evidence to be sure, it is often better to use something called "The Poker Approach." In this method, the teacher starts by letting the student know that there is something irregular about his or her paper. The teacher then points to specific suspicious areas and ask the student to explain them, all while keep an ear out for incriminating responses. The power of this Poker Approach comes from the fact that the student doesn't know what information the teacher already has. Being forced to sit in such an unnerving situation often makes students more likely to slip up and give important information or outright admit to the wrongdoing. The Poker Approach is also lower risk for the teacher, because since the teacher hasn't accused the student of cheating yet, the teacher can always back out to reexamine the case.

Get Administration Involved

Many new teachers are reserved about getting administration involved in anything because they don't want to appear inept or unable to take care of their own business. And overall this is not a bad approach to have; as a new teacher, you certainly want to be discerning about which problems you outsource to those beyond your classroom. But student cheating on any sort of scale is generally not the time to keep it all in-house. Administration wants to know details like that, and getting them involved opens you up to their experience and expertise. So as soon as cheating rears its ugly head, make an e-mail to someone above you one of your first orders of action.

Exit Slip

It has to be mentioned that you must be incredibly careful with accusing students of cheating. While having students cheat is one of the most painful things for a teacher to experience, being wrongfully accused of cheating is equally painful for students. If a student is wrongly accused, it often takes a whole lot to win him or her over to your camp again. This doesn't mean that you should shy away from accusing students when warranted; it just means that, like most things in the classroom, you should put some thought into it.

WHEN BAD THINGS HAPPEN
IN GOOD CLASSROOMS

A s a new teacher, you will probably have a lot of moments in the classroom that prompt you to ask afterward, "Did that really happen?" Usually these moments will be positive, odd, or just generally unexpected, but on rare occasions they may also derive their shock value from how quickly the normally positive classroom was transformed into a very negative place (whether due to violence, theft, serious disrespect, or other major problems). These significantly bad situations can be some of the hardest things for a new teacher to respond to, because often it seems hardly possible that the students, despite their talent for being a pain at times, are truly capable of doing something really bad. To help make sure that you aren't caught off guard during these situations, here are the most common bad things that can happen in class and what you can do to resolve them.

Violence

A little over a month into school I saw something that I never expected to see in the classroom: physical confrontation. This confrontation happened on the first major test of the year as I reminded the class that their cell phones are supposed to remain turned off and placed on the desks during tests, so as to avoid cheating via text messages and stored information. (This is a school policy, but it does work well to limit cheating.)

As I finished my little speech the entire scene unfolded directly in front of me. One of my students got up to blow his nose, and as he headed back to his desk he passed the desk of another student who was much higher in social standing. As an ill-advised attempt at humor, the student walking by picked up the seated student's phone and trotted back to his desk with a nonchalant gait.

I noticed this minor act of larceny around the same time that the seated student did. Before I could say anything, the seated student stood up and without hesitation swiftly and forcefully kneed the upper thigh of the other student, whose grin turned into a look of shock. This was followed by a moment of profound silence that was only broken by the words "What do you think you are doing?" in a voice so stern that it shocked me. In fact, it took a few seconds before I even realized that I was the one who'd said it.

After I said this both students flashed back to their seats and I stared at the class, and specifically the guilty student, in disbelief. Then I let loose a five-minute tirade about respect and what is expected and acceptable in the classroom. The student who gave the blow had a terrified look at first, but when I began to single him out his face turned into a look of confusion and innocence. This only set me off more and the whole scene culminated with me turning to him and saying, "Don't give me that. You know what you did and it was totally unreasonable and uncalled for."

As soon as I was done with this speech, I was suddenly at a loss for words. It was a big test day and they were losing time that was needed for the test. So I turned the class's attention back to the test, went over the directions in a voice still laced with anger, and sent off an e-mail describing the scene to the head of the middle school, who later met with both students and levied appropriate punishments.

Looking back at the situation there was some good, some bad, and a lot of lessons in my response. One of the positives of the response was the level of outrage present. Physical violence is the last thing students should have to worry about, so they need to know that your full wrath will fall upon anyone who brings it into your classroom. It was also good that everything was dropped to deal with it; some things are more important than the lesson, and violence is definitely one of them.

But there were also a lot of other ways I could have gone about it better. By reprimanding the student in front an audience of peers, I didn't heed the warning given in chapter 15: that having an audience will inspire obstinacy and resistance in nearly every student. And this led the student, who was legitimately scared at first, to eventually feign innocence to get a laugh out of his peers. If, instead of chewing him out in front of the class, I had grabbed him by the ear (figuratively, of course) and taken him straight to the office where he would receive his reprimand in front of an audience of adults, there is a much better chance that his initial fear would have had significantly more lasting power.

I also should have expelled the student from my classroom instantly (generally to the office; administrators get paid for resolving those types of situations, so don't try to take care of it all yourself). As soon as a student gets physical, he or she has forfeited the right to be in the classroom for the day and should be sent directly out. If you keep the student in class, as I did, it sends a message that the behavior isn't that severe—and that is not the type of message you want to send.

Serious Verbal Disagreements

Not all confrontations get physical, but just because blows don't get thrown doesn't mean a situation isn't serious. So if you find two or more students in a seriously heated verbal disagreement, make sure to treat it with the level of gravity it deserves.

Generally, the first thing you need to do with bickering students is to break it up. Often the best, and safest, way to do this is to get loud instead of getting between them. When someone with the authority of a teacher speaks with enough force, even the most intense arguments tend to dissipate for the moment. Once the argument is cooled, pull the students aside and do damage control. If there is no speedy or easy solution and the tone was serious enough, walk them down to the office (don't just send them—leaving two bickering students alone in the hall is a bad idea). If the problem seems solved, you can let them back into the classroom, but only after a warning that behavior like that won't be tolerated again.

Stealing of Your Possessions/Tests/Papers

A security specialist would probably be appalled by the actions of the average teacher. It is not uncommon for teachers to leave copies of upcoming tests and quizzes, grade books, ungraded work, and valuable items such as laptops lying in unsecured locations (such as all swimming around on the top of their desk). Combine this nonchalant attitude surrounding important items with the fact that teachers are very bad about locking their doors (assuming they even have a room key), and it is actually surprising that important things don't go missing from classrooms more often.

For the most part classes are, despite all of their security gaps, generally very safe places, but this does not mean they are crime free. Though students willing to steal from teachers are few and far between, they do exist and it is best not to tempt them with easy opportunities. So instead of leaving important documents in a location where any student can grab them in five seconds, put them in your desk drawers or in a stack of folders, so that it would take added effort and time for anyone to find them. Also try to lock your room whenever you aren't in it, or at least turn off the lights (thus making it less inviting). By taking these precautions you will not fully protect yourself against theft, but you will limit the amount of spontaneous theft. And this is important because most theft doesn't come from large student conspiracies; instead, it happens when a predisposed student recognizes an opportunity to gain an advantage and runs with it.

If you find yourself in a position where something important comes up missing, it generally works out best if you assume the worst. What that means is that no matter what is missing you should proceed as if a student took it. To do this, first make an announcement to each of your classes that goes something like this:

> _____ has disappeared from my desk. If you have it and return it today, no punishment will be levied. But if it isn't returned and someone is caught with it, then _____ will happen.

One advantage of addressing the situation like this is that you never actually accuse the students of stealing. Doing this is important because if you did just misplace it, you haven't charged the student body with crimes it didn't commit. This approach also often works because it extends both an open and forgiving hand and a strong and menacing fist at the same time. This can be a very persuasive tactic because it paints a clear picture for why student thieves should be afraid, and then opens up a last opportunity for salvation.

Once the students are warned all you can really do is keep an eye and ear out and press on with the assumption that whatever you lost is gone. If it turns up afterward it is a blessing, and if it doesn't you were prepared.

Serious Disrespect

Saying "Students challenge teachers" is like saying "Water is wet" or "The earth circles the sun." It is a fundamental law of nature, and no matter what you do there is no changing it. But not all challenges are the same. Most fall under the umbrella of minor testing; these are things like talking a bit too much, interrupting with a joke, or getting a bit sloppy with their work. These are just part of the daily duty of being a teacher and don't require any unusual considerations.

On rare occasions though, these challenges will cross into the realm of true and serious disrespect. What separates a normal challenge from the truly disrespectful ones is the intent. Normal challenges are tests or prods to see where you stand; disrespectful ones come with malice and are meant to belittle or bring you down. And if right now that distinction seems a bit vague, have no worries—you will know the difference when you encounter it.

When dealing with disrespect there are a couple of possible routes to take. The first is that instead of acting hurt or angry (both of which you will probably be), you can often diffuse the situation by making a joke or being self-deprecating. For example, if a student accuses you of being boring while teaching grammar you could respond by saying, "Yeah, but it's better than not getting into college because your essay is full of comma errors." By taking what is a very serious situation and doing the opposite of what everyone expects, often it literally strikes the offending student dumb and you can continue with the lesson. If you take this approach, don't forget to pull the student aside afterward and when they are on their own give them an earful about how completely out of line they were.

The unanticipated response of humor can be a great diffuser of tough situations, but some situations just can't be turned into a laughing matter. When the student disrespect is so profound that not even a joke can be made, it is time to throw the student out of class. While throwing the student out, it is important that you stay oddly level-headed. There will be time for anger later, but for that moment you need to show that you are a composed leader who will not suffer foolish comments, nor get angry just because a student baited you. So instead of having a fit, suggest that the student leave and then go right back to business as usual. At a later time you can get mad, figure out why the student did it, and deal with him or her accordingly.

A Student Says Something Horrible

On exceptionally rare occasions students will say things that are shockingly horrible. Examples of the types of horrible things they could say include comments that are exceptionally derogatory toward staff or students; explicitly sexual in nature; or racist, homophobic, or otherwise prejudiced.

When faced with such comments, the first thing you must do is explain in front of whoever heard it (including the student) why such language will not be tolerated. This turns what was only negative before into a teachable moment. Then you need to get the student who said it and pull him or her aside, even if class is going on. Once you have the student alone, make it clear that comments like that won't only get the student in hot water during class, they could get the student in serious trouble with their parents, fellow students, and the school in general (many schools can even suspend or expel on the grounds of hateful speech). Then hand out whatever punishment seems to fit the crime and let the student go, after saying that you never expect to hear anything remotely like that ever again.

Class Gone Wild

You will probably have days where, for reasons well out of your control, an air of anarchy invades your classroom. On these days students will be unruly and unreasonable and despite all of your best tricks (including carefully placed body position, requests to quiet down, getting silent, getting angry, administering punishments, and shooting teacher look after teacher look around the room), their out-of-control behavior will continue undeterred.

If you find yourself with a wild class that just won't settle it can feel hopeless. It can feel like maybe you'd be better served by curling up into a ball and waiting for the storm to pass. But there are a few last tricks that can possibly get you out of this situation. So don't curl up into a ball quite yet—try these tricks first.

Go with It

As odd as it may sound, there is such a thing as a class going wild for the right reasons. What that means is the class is still engaged with the material and pseudo-listening to the teacher, but at the same time their impulse control seems broken and the students are having trouble containing their outbursts, questions, or actions.

If you find yourself with a class that is going wild for the right reasons, one of the best ways to deal with it is to just go with it. Instead of fighting against the current through constant reprimands and shushes, try to direct their rambunctiousness toward more productive areas. This will help you save your energy and sanity, and sometimes through channeling their energy you can actually end up with a lesson that is better and more dynamic than your original! Here are a couple of examples of how to do that:

- If you are trying to give a lecture on Charlemagne and the kids keep interrupting you, take them outside, tell them they are in Charlemagne's court, and continue.

- If you are giving a presentation on the circulatory system and they are wild, have some of the wildest students come up and act out how blood is pumped as you explain it.

- If you are going over the night's reading on *Huckleberry Finn* and they won't settle, have students draw pictures of all the important events on the board.

Slow It Down for a While

Even though there is sometimes a bright side to a rambunctious class, a lot of times positives are nowhere in sight and, frankly, you feel ready to kill them. For these moments when an insane class is pushing you ever closer to the brink just think one thing: silent, individual, in-class activities.

There is nothing quite like a silent worksheet or set of questions to take a class's energy level down a few notches. One thing that makes silent work so effective in calming down a class is that it takes away a lot of opportunities to act crazy. Making a witty or sarcastic comment about a worksheet just doesn't have the same effect as doing it about an out-loud comment. Students also can't have even the most discreet of conversations in silent classroom if they want to avoid getting yelled at by you.

The quiet focus needed to do a worksheet or set of questions is another one of the factors contributing to the power of silent work to change chaos to calm. This effect can be further amplified if you assign a point value to the work the students are doing. When students have a concrete reason like grades to give them more focus, they naturally calm down even further.

So the next time you find yourself with an uncontrollable class, just drop everything and do a quiet activity. If you don't know exactly what they can do, give them a five-minute "Band-Aid" activity (by quickly amending an activity from your lesson or pulling something out of the textbook) to buy time while you scramble to come up with a longer silent activity for them to do.

Exit Slip

After reprimanding or getting otherwise tough on students, it is common for new teachers to feel that they should apologize, even when their response was justified and the students' behavior was appalling. After all, the students are still kids, and punishing them requires a sternness that isn't natural for many young teachers.

When faced with this urge to apologize, try to resist it. Though it comes from the right place, such profuse apologies rarely add anything positive to the situation. There is nothing wrong with justly punishing students, and apologizing for taking the correct action can send mixed messages. This is not to say that you shouldn't explain your actions, talk through the situation with the students, or express sorrow for its getting to that point. But you should never be sorry for acting in the right way.

PRESSING THE RESET BUTTON
ON THE CLASSROOM

In education school I had a teacher who got on our class's bad side faster than any teacher I had ever seen. On the first day she opened her lesson by describing her middle-school-style disciplinary program for our college class and mandated that her students should arrive ten minutes earlier than scheduled because she didn't run on "Michigan Time" (which was the deeply ingrained practice at the University of Michigan of starting class ten minutes later to allow for passing time). This totalitarian approach combined with a general standoffishness and a couple of poorly executed lessons made her public enemy number one in the minds of the undergrads within a week.

For several weeks after, a feud brewed. Every day the class grew increasingly resistant to her policies, and she responded by trying to clamp down further. Soon both sides were reacting with open hostility and disgust to the demands of the other, and it seemed like the whole situation would likely end in Armageddon. But then one day everything changed. This day the teacher came into class with a softer and more approachable demeanor. Before the class started she sat there with eyes rapt in thought, and then a wave of resolve washed over her and she stood up firmly and said, "This isn't working."

She gave the class a few moments to take this in and then she continued, "I want this to work. What can we do to make that happen?" Suddenly it was like the roof opened and all the anger inside the room was sucked away. Very quickly, several hands shot up with suggestions. Over the next thirty minutes both the teacher and the students made a lot of suggestions. Many of the suggestions from both sides were brutally honest, but in the end an agreement was reached.

Even after the agreement that class never became a favorite of most students—but it did become far more workable. Many philosophical approaches remained that the class quarreled with the instructor about, but the difference was that both sides saw each other as human beings, not the enemy. This moment also allowed the class to begin learning what lessons they could from the instructor, though there is no doubt that her best lesson was when she said simply, "This isn't working."

This experience illustrates how almost no classroom is beyond saving. This class contained more hostility than any I have ever seen, and yet with a simple declaration of the obvious it was granted a second chance. This does not mean the dramatic "This isn't working" moment is always the right route, but whether a class needs an overhaul or just a tune-up, there are always options to improve the teaching environment.

Level with the Class

Based on the success of the technique above, it might be understandable to think that leveling with students about the issues plaguing the class is the best way to set everything straight. And there are certainly situations where it is quite effective. But overall, such theatrics should be reserved only for the moments that truly call for them. The undergrad instructor may have had success with this approach, but much of the success came from the fact that the class was lost, and both she and the students knew it. If it hadn't been painfully obvious to everyone involved that the class was a train wreck that couldn't have gotten any worse, such a dramatic step might not have worked nearly as well.

The major reason to be sparing with leveling with your class is it carries a lot of risk. The power behind this technique comes from an open or implied admission of guilt on the part of the teacher, which will hopefully be followed by admissions of guilt from the students. Anyone who has been in a relationship for long enough probably knows this game. Once both sides admit and examine their faults, the opportunity to discuss compromises, ways to improve, and possible concessions generally swings open wide.

But confessing wrongdoing (especially about how you have run the entire class) in front of the students is a dangerous proposition. If the students don't feel you have run everything poorly, the admission "This isn't working" may only introduce the idea that you aren't doing your job. It is also quite probable that unless the students feel as you do, this approach will likely fall flat because it will lack the critical mass of emotions needed.

If you do find yourself in a situation where the train has gone completely off the rails, leveling with the students might work for you. But if you do go this route, there are a few lessons you should take from the undergrad teacher of mine. First, her moment wasn't too scripted or too off the cuff. She had clearly prepared some things to say, but when the students took the conversation into different areas she wasn't afraid to go with the moment. This combination of preparation and fluidity helped the class to respect the work she'd put in while feeling like they were equals in the conversation. Also, she didn't try to manufacture extra emotion, because she knew there was enough already. Trying to infuse extra emotion into this sort of situation could make the entire attempt come across as disingenuous, and that could make a bad situation worse. Finally, the teacher, while leveling with us and admitting faults, always kept up her teacher demeanor. This meant that even though the students were an integral part of rebuilding the class, there was never any doubt about whose class they were fixing.

Make the Change, Not a Scene

More than likely your class does not need a complete overhaul, but there is a good possibility that there are some things that need to be tuned up. One of the best and most straightforward ways to do this is to come up with new policies, and then just make the changes. When you tell the class about these changes you don't even necessarily need to admit to faults, put on a big show, or even explain your logic. All you have to do is tell them what the new policies are, give your reasoning if the situation calls for it (or they ask), and move on. If your changes are modest and the message behind them clear, there is little chance the students will protest or need added explanation. Instead, they will very likely go where you shepherd them and not give it a second thought.

Remind Them Who Is Boss

In most packs the position of leader is a tenuous one. With the great leveler of time weighing upon the top dog with each passing day, members of the pack often feel they need to test even the most established leaders to see if they've still got it. So they challenge them constantly, in small ways at first, and then with bigger and bigger gestures.

With a new teacher, the students often act in similar ways, which means even if you've established solid control over the classroom the students will inevitably slide a little bit from time to time. Manifestations of this slide commonly include some sort of lessening of effort, an increase in sloppy mistakes and excuses, or an escalation of rule breaking. When these "new" types of problems start arising with the class, there is a good chance the students are testing to see whether you've still got it. And at that point you need to do what every pack leader does when challenged—remind them of who is boss.

One of the best ways to remind students of your firm leadership is to simply get a little tough with your speech or actions. There are numerous ways to do this. If student effort is slipping, you could sternly reprimand the class for their level of effort or grade a smaller assignment with more attention to detail than normal. If students have been strolling in late too often, you could mark a large swath tardy and make sure they understand why. If students are becoming more careless, you could nitpick the little details to force their hand. Generally speaking, these little reassertions don't need to be a big deal, and most of the time they should show more bark than bite. And if they are done effectively, there is a good chance that afterward the students will straighten out for a while once they are reminded of the order of things.

Give the Class More Say

An old trick in business is for the boss to come up with a way to improve a business, and then to make sure the changes are embraced there is a "brainstorming session" with the people at the company whom the changes will affect. On the surface, this session appears to be about the exchange of ideas, but underneath it is carefully framed to push everyone in the direction of the boss's idea. The logic behind such a charade is that having people come up with an idea that already exists transfers ownership of the idea to everyone. At that point it is no longer just the boss's idea, it's the peoples' idea, which is important because people are much more likely to support a decision that they feel a part of.

Though a lot of us likely aren't comfortable with the puppetry present in this consulting trick, the lesson buried within it is a good one: When people (a.k.a. students) are part of the process they are more willing to support the final product. This does not mean that you should fill your classroom with stacked choices and rigged ballots, though. Instead, if you want to get your students to take more of a vested interest in the class you should give them some real say. There are lots of ways to do this. You can give the students projects where they have the choice between a diverse set of options, or you can allow them to have some say in how the material is introduced or reviewed. In most of these situations, students won't be fooled into thinking the classroom is theirs, but they will gain some small ownership. And even this sliver of ownership can lead to their working really hard to show you that they made the right choice.

Don't Make Too Many Changes Too Fast

An occasional correction to a class is generally a good thing, but constant changes usually result in a class that is significantly worse than if you didn't try to fix it in the first place. The problem with too many changes is that people don't usually stomach change well. Though rare, yet thoughtful, alterations are worth the initial stomachache, constant changes will simply leave the students disoriented and slightly nauseated. It will also establish your reputation as somebody who isn't sure what you want, and that is a reputation that is worth avoiding if you can.

In terms of how often to shake things up, try to limit major changes (not including minor prods) to a maximum of once every couple of months. With such a limited number of potentially useful changes, also try to really think out any modifications to class before implementing them, so your risk of needing to go back and alter the alterations is as small as possible.

Exit Slip

This chapter was introduced as your options for resetting a class that has gone off the rails, but many of these techniques would also be very useful for classes that are on track as well. In the same way that there is always a way to save a struggling class, there are also always ways to improve any class. So don't be afraid to use some of these techniques to perform a little readjustment on a class that is already going well, because looking for ways to get better is what good teachers do.

THE TASKS

Only a small fraction of your workload as a teacher actually involves standing up and teaching the kids. The rest of the time is eaten up by grading, planning, going to meeting after meeting, fighting with the copy machine, communicating with parents, and a thousand other minor tasks.

Most of these tasks don't need much explanation (like copy machines or meetings—just try not to freak out at both) or have already been covered (like lesson planning or grading), but there are a few important tasks of teaching that still need to be addressed. And make sure that you don't skirt these other tasks just because they are sideshows to the main event of teaching. The little things matter, and often your treatment of them can be what tips the scales in favor of a good year or not.

DEALING WITH PARENTS

P arents are often like ghosts in the classroom. You might not see them or speak to them, but that doesn't mean they aren't there following you every step of the way. And when they come out they can be downright scary.

After this point, the ghost metaphor breaks down in regard to parents, but in a lot of ways it is perfect for introducing their role in the class because so many new teachers forget that they even exist until one pops up and scares them half to death. And just because teachers aren't thinking about the parents, doesn't mean the parents aren't thinking about the teachers. In a lot of schools parents are as much a part of the classroom as the board, the books, and the students, so it is good to get to know them.

There is an entire spectrum of parents out there—from wonderfully supportive to completely uninvolved to those who levy intense pressure to the outright crazy—and young teachers are generally good at bringing out both the best and the worst in them. The reason young teachers are often such potent catalysts for the good side of parents is that they are generally fresh and enthusiastic, and this can lead to more student excitement and interest than average in their class. Most parents love this kind of excitement, and they are usually good about recognizing the new teacher as the person to thank.

Unfortunately, new teachers also have a talent for bringing out the worst in parents. One reason for this is that veteran teachers often know tricks to keep parents happy and have a lot more knowledge concerning how to protect themselves from parental trouble. New teachers are also a lot more likely to make major and minor mistakes (which could incite parents), and a lot of parents from the negative side of the spectrum feel far more comfortable with trying to pressure or take on young, impressionable teachers than ones who are established and savvy.

Considering the importance of the often invisible parents to the classroom, here is some information about the average parent and some tips for turning them from possible liabilities into one of your strongest assets.

How to Get Parents on Your Side

The average teacher probably spends more time with most of their students than the students' parents do. These parents also likely have to hear about you, your class, and the effect it is having upon their child on a daily basis—all while (thanks to time the child spends at various practices, with friends, or hiding up in his or her room) they barely get to see their own child.

Most parents probably won't hold this time imbalance against you, but there is a good chance it will breed some curiosity in them about whom their child spends so much time with. This interest can be further fed by the limited information parents often have about their child's teachers. Most of the time the only clues parents get concerning who you are come from the types of assignments you send home and the occasional out-of-context information they get from overhearing their kid talk about school.

With so much interest and so little information generally present concerning you, there is one surefire way to get parents on your side: just let them know what is going on in your classroom from time to time.

Letting parents know more about class doesn't mean you need to keep parents constantly updated on every little detail. In fact, not communicating every up or down with a student helps the student learn valuable lessons about taking care of their own affairs. (P.S. This is a great excuse if parents ever ask why you didn't let them know about a student struggling. Just tell them you want to teach students how to take care of themselves.) But by letting the parents in on a little bit of what happens in class, you can very quickly gain their support and love. Here are some simple things you can do to communicate with parents:

- Send a letter or e-mail home at the start of school addressing the parents.

- Have the students do assignments on occasion that involve parental/guardian interaction.

- Maintain a website with updated and clear information about the class.

- Drop a two-line e-mail at some point in the first half of the year updating the parents on something about their child.

- Send out a parental newsletter from time to time (with e-mail group lists this is a lot easier than it sounds).

Communication Rule Number One: Let Parents Know If Anything Changes

When it comes to communication, the one thing you must do if you want to have any chance at a good relationship with parents is to let them know if their child's performance changes in any significant way. Whether the change is good or bad, keeping parents in the loop for major shifts is always a good idea.

In terms of positive changes, informing parents about improvement is one of the most potent goodwill-building tools available to teachers. It is absolutely amazing how happy (and happy with you) a simple "Your child did very well on . . ." call will make parents. Part of why this type of call makes parents so happy is that it is a such a rarity; parents may be used to "bad calls" or "You can help us by . . ." calls from school, but very few are accustomed to getting calls about positive things. This novelty, combined with the fact that such calls commend not only the child but the parenting, is what turns random good calls into such powerful generators of goodwill. These calls also provide an extra reward to the student for improvement, and help reinforce the point that improvement will lead to accolades from both school and home.

Sending good reports home is a great trick for gaining parental support, but notifying parents when student performance slides is even more essential for building strong relationships with parents. The reason that being the bearer of bad news can help a relationship is that such bad news always leaks out eventually. Whether it is from sorting through their child's things, from the mouth of the child themselves, or on the report card, parents will find out eventually if a child is struggling. And when they find out it is far better if you are the one telling them.

Being the one who tells parents about the student's struggles frames you as an active teammate in helping their child. You are on their team and you are trying to help. But if you don't contact parents when their student struggles, and they find out from other sources, then suddenly you run the very real risk of being painted as the jerk who not only is failing their child, but didn't even have the decency to let them know about it. Also, if parents don't find out about a poor grade until the report card arrives, that means the parents can't do anything to help their child improve his or her grades; and few things can upset a parent more (or anyone else for that matter) than a feeling of helplessness combined with a sense of injustice.

Don't Be Afraid of Breaking the Bad News

As a brand-new teacher, I was terrified about notifying parents about students who were struggling in my class. I can still remember the first parents I had to tell about their child failing. At the time, I assumed that these parents would blame me for the poor grades and I would have to vigorously defend every decision I'd ever made in the classroom. But the second the parents walked in, I knew these fears were unfounded. They knew their child, and it was clearly not the first time their student had struggled. They were also far more interested in helping their child improve than in shooting the messenger.

Since that point I've come to look forward, in a strange sort of way, to speaking with the parents of struggling students. Generally they are very positive and offer some tremendous help and insight. As the foremost authority on their child, they are usually able to offer valuable strategies for helping their kid, while also providing some solidarity that struggles with the student are not isolated to just me.

The 5 Percent

With the first writing assignment of the year came my first unpleasant experience with a parent in the 5 percent. *The 5 percent* is a term used by an educational psychologist named Michael Thompson for those rare parents who make life difficult for a teacher. He calls these parents the 5 percent because the vast majority of parents are supportive, friendly, and willing to defer to the teacher's decisions. But about 5 percent of the parents will inevitably pick at small faults, attempt to micromanage, or take offense at every little detail of the classroom. These parents are unavoidable and can plague even the most talented and together educators, so learning how to manage them is essential.

My problem with a member of the 5 percent club started with an innocent enough request. She e-mailed to ask if I would talk to her daughter about an assignment that the daughter got a low grade on (at least low in her eyes—it was a B), so the experience wouldn't dampen her daughter's enthusiasm for English. This request was reasonable enough; I spoke with the student, sent a courtesy e-mail to the mom that confirmed I had met with the student and detailed what we covered, and then considered the matter finished.

But to my surprise the matter was far from finished. Instead of satisfying the mom, the e-mail ignited a blazing hot protective fire within her. Within moments another e-mail popped into my inbox, which not only refuted each point made in my e-mail but also attacked several of my classroom policies with a scathing mix of implied incompetence and passive aggression. As I looked at the e-mail I couldn't help but be confused about what had transpired. Before seeing the e-mail I was proud of how timely and thoroughly I handled the situation, and yet in response I received an assault on my class, my knowledge, and me as a person.

Composing myself, I wrote another e-mail that delicately refuted each of her points with a positive and forward-looking tone. After another few moments a short response came from the parent that apologetically and sincerely thanked me for all my work. Once again I thought I was done—and once again I was wrong.

About a week later the parent e-mailed again and requested to meet with me for "a few minutes." Though there isn't enough time to go into the full details of the whole meeting, I can assure you that the topics discussed, the tone of the meeting, and the outright hostility present made our previous e-mail exchange seem downright cordial. The first half of the meeting consisted of the mother going through a list of concerns about my class (her concerns were written in a notebook and organized with Post-its). Included in these concerns were questions about why there was no rough draft to the original assignment, whether I had taught all the material I graded on, and if my directions were clear enough to understand. She also occasionally mixed in comments about other mistakes I'd made (like days when my website was not up to date and vague parts of my lessons) and asked probing questions about my approach to vocabulary, outside reading, extra credit, grading, and even some school policies that I had no say over (like the size of her daughter's class and why we read the books we do). Then she concluded with a score of suggestions on how I could "make the classroom better for her daughter."

While all of this went on, my mind burned with a red-hot, indignant anger. There is something supremely offensive about having your class criticized. When your classroom is under attack, it is impossible not to think about all the planning, grading, and analyzing that goes into every minute of the school day. It takes so much time, energy, and yes, love, to create a class that in the end it begins to feel like your child. And there is no greater slap than when someone harshly criticizes your offspring.

When my chance to speak finally came, I struggled with how to address the situation. Should I come on strong and try to get her to back down? Should I be conciliatory and play the peacemaker? Should I appear injured in the hope that it would humanize me? After a moment's hesitation I made my choice, and I began a vigorous defense of my policies in which I quickly catalogued rebuttals to each point she made. Unfortunately, at first, my words betrayed my anger, which only caused the mother to grow more defensive and accusatory.

Realizing my strong-armed approach wasn't going to work, I took a deep breath and justified myself again, this time in control of my emotions. I once again went through my logic, but as I scaled back my anger and frustration the mother relaxed, too. The rest of the conversation went as well as could be expected. We were both still upset, but after the initial flare-up of emotions we talked reasonably about how to proceed in the future and eventually parted on decent terms.

This conversation was a brutal experience, but from it I learned a significant amount about how to deal with an unreasonable or upset parent. Here are three of the biggest tips I learned.

Leave Emotions Out of It

Emotions beget emotions; this is just a natural rule and it certainly is true when it comes to dealing with parents. If you are ever smacked with parental emotions and you respond by getting emotional too, the conversation stands little chance of succeeding. Besides, parents are dealing with their child, which gives them the right to be irrational. You, however, are a professional, which means it is time to check your ego at the door. This is not to say that you should sit there and take abuse or not defend yourself, but in my situation it was only when I scaled back my emotions that I was actually able to steer the conversation in the right path. The same will likely be true for you.

You Already Have Common Ground

No matter how badly the conversation with the parent is going, there is always at least one thing tying you together: You both want the student to succeed. You may have dramatically different views on how to accomplish this and the parents might be dead wrong, but at least your end goal is mutual. So when faced with unreasonable parents, try your best to continue to remind them that you are on the same team. This reminder often helps parents relax slightly, and it forms a good starting point from which both sides can work toward a resolution.

Listen to the Parents and Value Their Comments

Parents want to be valued just like everyone else. In fact, since they have a teenager in the house they likely have a stronger than average need to be valued. This means you should listen to what parents have to say, and no matter how crazy it seems, try to show them that you value their thoughts. If they are convinced that you are listening, they will often open up to your suggestions—which may seem equally outlandish to them. And from this foundation of agreement it will be far easier to move forward.

Other Parent Tips

- Call, don't e-mail. Calling always seems like more work, but in reality crafting an e-mail for parents (where you want to have perfect grammar, the right tone, and present your message) usually takes a lot more time.

- E-mail if you think a saved copy of the conversation will be necessary. Some parents tend to "forget" about your helpful calls and meetings. With those types having the e-mail time stamp can serve as a useful reminder.

- Turning parents over to the administration is always an option. Crazy parents are part of the reason administrators drive nicer cars than you, so if things are getting totally out of hand don't be afraid to suggest that "we get someone else involved."

- Save student work for parent-teacher conferences so you have something tangible to talk about. It is a whole lot easier to fill ten minutes about a student if you have a centerpiece to talk about.

Exit Slip

This chapter mainly focuses on ways to make sure parents don't become a pain in your neck. But parents can be so much more than just not a pain in your neck—they can be the best friend you could ask for. Good recommendations from parents often have the ability to help you catch the eye of administration and some parents aren't shy about donating time and money if the help is needed. They also act as great informants about the students, and their insights can be invaluable. So do what you can to cultivate the relationships with parents and they will no doubt make it worth the trouble.

CHAPTER TWENTY-EIGHT
TEACHING TO EVERYONE

When I outlined this chapter I had a simple vision: I wanted to create profiles of the five most common types of learning disorders to help young teachers deal with the LD (learning differences) students in their class. The thinking behind this approach was to make these common impediments recognizable by putting a face upon them, while also advising teachers on how to bring them back into the fray. So I picked up some famous books on the subject and interviewed all of the student support staff (who deal with LD students daily) at my school to inquire about what I should include in my "five students."

And what I got was of very little good—or at least I thought so at first. One support staff member after another struggled to give me specific answers and instead most of their responses ventured into areas that seemed overly vague. After exhausting this resource I next turned to books on the subject, but they also seemed vague, just in a more organized way. Finally, after a week of not getting answers from people or print, I gave up, moved on to other chapters, and told myself I would finish this one later.

But as I worked on other chapters I couldn't help but wonder why all the resources around me had been so vague and generally useless. How could these authors and student service specialists not know more about something that they spend their lives doing? And then it hit me—the problem had nothing to do with a lack of understanding on their part and had everything to do with a gap in my own understanding. Specifically, my problem was that I focused too much on the specifics. I wanted to know exact things. I wanted to know exactly what an ADHD student looks like, how one should behave around a student who fits in somewhere on the autistic spectrum, and the best way to help a dyslexic student read. But in the world of learning differences such specifics don't exist. ADHD students come in a variety of forms, how to behave around an autistic student depends on the kid, and dyslexic students can't all be helped exactly the same way.

The reason I bring up this story is that many new teachers approach students with learning differences the same way that I did. They see them as "the autistic kid" or "the student with ADHD" instead of how they probably should look at them—as "John," "Katie," or "Alex." It is important for teachers to remember that the diagnosis a student has is just one small piece of their story (like what sports he plays or who her parents are). It helps make up who the student is, and for that reason it shouldn't be ignored, but it doesn't define the student. And as soon as teachers realize this, they generally have a lot more success in connecting with them and teaching them.

Everyone Has Learning Differences

Though some may not be labeled in the *Diagnostic and Statistic Manual of Mental Disorders, fourth edition* (DSM-IV), everyone has issues when it comes to learning. As Mel Levine, one of the leading voices concerning LD students, says in his book *Keeping a Head in School*, "Nobody's brain is perfect. Some people can't learn to whistle. Others have trouble remembering names." What he means by this is that everyone has learning differences. We all learn in unique ways and with a different cocktail of strengths and weaknesses. No one is completely above or below average in everything, and that means if teachers try hard enough they can find things to celebrate and things to improve in all students regardless of the different ways they learn.

What to Do to Make Sure You Teach to Everyone

This rest of this chapter now has a slightly different focus from my original idea of trying to paint pictures of the common students with learning disorders. It still has five suggestions, but instead of trying to guess what the students in your class might be like, the tips now revolve around how to teach to every single student, regardless of how they learn. So whether you have a large population of diagnosed LD kids or not, here are some suggestions on how to teach to everyone in your class.

Teach to the Different Learners

Depending on the source, the number of different types of learners falls somewhere between three and eight. But regardless of who's talking, three types of learners generally always receive mention: auditory learners, visual learners, and kinesthetic learners. And if as a teacher you can focus on making sure to reach out to these three, you will generally be in pretty good shape.

For those who aren't familiar with the learning types, the idea is that we all learn in slightly different ways. Some people learn better if they hear something (auditory learners), others learn better when they see the information (visual learners), and still others can retain information better if they engage their muscles while learning (kinesthetic learners). Within these groups continuums exist as well; some students might learn effectively in all three ways or in just two out of three. One student may be great at visual learning but have almost no auditory retention whatsoever. Or a student may only really learn effectively by hearing or doing something.

There is no set way to teach to these different learners—instead, just try to keep them in mind when creating your lesson. Here are some examples of how to do this:

- When lecturing (which is generally auditory), have visual (like notes on the board) or kinesthetic (like having them take notes) components, if at all possible.

- For a discussion, try to include something besides just talking (which is also auditory). To do this, you could have students jot down important points, include visual prompts, or move around the room and stand in corners based on their viewpoint.

- Don't have students answer questions in the same way. Questions can be answered through writing, talking, drawing, acting, and numerous other ways.

Assess Different Strengths

It is important for teachers to realize that what a student produces doesn't always match what he or she knows. The student who writes the best essay in class about Theodore Roosevelt doesn't necessarily know the most about him. And the student who gets the lowest grade in the class on a trigonometry test doesn't necessarily know the least about it. As teachers, we try to create assessments to measure students' knowledge. Most types of standard assessments (tests, quizzes, papers, projects) have some success with that, but there are other factors that can impact any type of assessment besides the student's level of knowledge. Maybe the student knows it but gets nervous during tests and freezes up, maybe the student knows a lot about Theodore Roosevelt but also is a poor writer, or maybe the student understands the basic idea of something but through forgetting one simple step everything gets messed up.

This imperfect nature of assessments means that they inevitably aren't going to be 100 percent accurate, but that is not to say they are all bad, either. Teachers need to know whether students are learning and their lessons are working; students need to know that if they aren't learning the teacher will eventually find out, and they need to learn how to deal with a world that will judge them at times. And assessments are good at meeting all of these objectives.

What this means is that assessments, despite their imperfections, belong in most classrooms, and instead of trying to cut them out teachers should strive to make their assessments as fair and accurate as possible. To do that they should follow the suggestions already made in the book (like making sure the directions and expectations are clear and that their students are ready for them) and do one very important thing: use a variety of assessments that require different types of strengths.

Every different type of assessment generally requires two things to achieve success: (1) knowledge of the material covered in class and (2) semi-unrelated side strengths. For example, when writing an essay students need to know not only about the topic of the paper, but they also need to know how to format an essay, write fluidly, use correct grammar, and incorporate numerous other rules about writing essays (like how you generally shouldn't use first or second person), even if the teacher has never mentioned these things before.

When making a video, suddenly many of the side strengths so essential to essay writing are no longer applicable; at this point, students don't need to worry about grammar, essay format, or whether they can use first or second person. But as one set of necessary skills disappears, it is replaced by a whole new set of requirements (like knowledge about shooting and editing videos, how to frame a shot, how to act, and how to influence an audience). By mixing up the types of assessments you give (like having a paper, test, and video as the major assessments for a quarter) you can give nearly every student a chance to do an assessment that plays on their strengths and that they can feel good about, while also making sure that most students come across an assessment or two that lies outside of their comfort zone and pushes them. Having multiple types of assessments also helps you rest assured that a student's high or low grade doesn't have more to do with their side strengths concerning the type of assessment than with their level of knowledge.

Be Nice

Students with significant learning impediments are often more fragile than the average kid. By the time they reach your classroom they've probably been told too many times by classmates, teachers, or their parents that they are dumb, lazy, or hopeless. And even if they haven't been told these things directly, the looks they are given and the reaction to their work can be more than enough to make these messages clear.

Students in this situation often have what is a very normal reaction for anyone who has to face something painful: They build walls to absorb the impact. And these walls, just like the learning differences that lead to them, can take a lot of forms. Students may get lazy so no one can call them dumb (for if they don't try, they won't be dumb); they may act badly or oddly to draw attention away from their faults, or they may withdraw into themselves so they don't have to deal with things. Or they may behave totally normally on the surface but have numerous walls underneath.

When it comes to dealing with these students, the best way to get them to lower most of these walls is usually simple: be nice to them and point out their strengths. For the most part, these walls are there as a response to hurtful comments or thoughts from others, and if the students get the sense that you will not add to the deluge of negativity they may slowly grow willing to lower some walls in your presence. (This does not mean you can't give constructive criticism, though. It just means you should be careful about how you do it and stay as positive as possible.) And once the walls lower, students generally blossom in various ways. They may feel more comfortable about giving their best effort, come out of their shells, embrace their strengths, or let their work (not their odd or poor behavior) speak for them.

Learn More about the Students

At the beginning of the year, you will probably get one of three things:

- A list of students with diagnosed learning issues

- A list of students with diagnosed learning issues and some variety of recommendations concerning them (like Individualized Education Plans [IEPs], behavior plans, and the like)

- Nothing

Whichever of these three you receive, it is generally a smart idea to add to the often unsatisfactory information you are given concerning the students. The first step toward doing this usually involves taking a trip to the support staff in your school to inquire about the students with learning differences in your classes. What makes this trip, regardless of time crunch, so worthwhile is these support staff will likely have worked with your students for years and they are generally a gold mine of valuable information and useful skills. Even if you already have a long list of accommodations and suggestions for helping students, you will likely get significantly more personalized and well-thought-out suggestions in person. And if you just have a name or nothing at all, then finding out more should be a no-brainer.

Beyond talking with support staff, you should also make sure to learn as much as you can about the various learning differences that your students may struggle with. Though students' learning differences don't define who they are, they certainly do impact them. The more information you have about potential ways to help those students succeed in your classroom the better. Here are some good ways to get this added information:

- Talking with colleagues

- Talking with the parents

- Going to conferences about learning disorders and the brain in general

- Reading (when looking into things to read try anything by Mel Levine, especially *The Myth of Laziness*, which is considered by many in the field to be a landmark work)

Keep the Lines of Communication Open

For many of the same reasons that LD students have significant walls, they also are not always the best communicators. And that makes it all the more important to try to communicate with them. Not only will attempting communication with them reinforce the message that you care, there is also the chance that it will eventually lead to some major insights about what works for them in the classroom. But this isn't always easy, so here are some tips on how to approach communicating with them:

- Simply ask how they are doing every once and a while. The cumulative power of fifty small greetings over a year can be astounding.

- Ask them about nonschool things occasionally. By branching conversation out to their life outside of school, you can demonstrate that you are interested in them as people and possibly get some hints about alternative routes to reach out to them.

- Ask about their thoughts after giving a lesson or assignment. Avoid direct statements like "Did that work for you?" because these often don't lead to truthful answers (depending on their feelings about you, they likely will or won't want to disappoint you). Instead, ask what they thought about it or what the pluses and minuses were.

- Keep at it. LD students are often both scared and bothered by teachers because previous teachers may have been the ones pointing out their deficiencies. But if you stay persistent and positive, you can usually get past these feelings.

Exit Slip

In your class you will likely be asked to make accommodations for some students, and if you aren't asked to, you should do it anyhow. When students have learning differences, they often aren't on a level playing field, and expecting them play the same game can be a truly cruel practice. But how can you change their requirements, while still preparing them for a world that will expect results regardless of their issues?

The answer I've come up with to this incredibly tough question is to apply accommodations to the process, but not to the results. What this means is that I will allow a longer time to take tests or to write papers, allow increased levels of collaboration and aid, and possibly change up some of the steps, but at the end I will grade their test or paper like anyone else's. The advantage of this approach is that it addresses their issues, while also still holding them accountable in a way similar to how the world will later on.

THE TRAPS

There are a lot of reasons that the first year of teaching is a roller coaster of emotions. To name a few, you are overworked, you make a lot of mistakes, and you have to deal with forces of nature (students) far more unpredictable than earthquakes or tornadoes. And if this isn't bad enough, there will also be problems that you didn't see coming, and when they do come you will likely be left blindsided, disoriented, and wondering what happened.

Sometimes the most seemingly unremarkable things (giving a student a B, telling the class they need to work harder, or showing a *Harry Potter* clip in class) can suddenly unleash an unseen firestorm that would have seemed laughably incomprehensible beforehand. Luckily, major problems of this variety don't happen too often, and many of the most common ones can be avoided with a little forethought. To help you dodge common new teacher pitfalls, this unit exposes some of the standard traps and explains how you can avoid them.

CHAPTER TWENTY-NINE
JUST SAY NO: THE PITCHES

During the first week of school one of my mentor teachers came into my room, smiled a sly smile, and said he had a gift for me. Unsure of what to expect, I smiled back, said he shouldn't have, and secretly hoped for something to rescue me from the stack of papers already dominating my desk. The mentor reached into his pocket and clasped a small object. He asked me to put out my hand, and once my palm lay open he dropped a small shiny button onto it.

Needless to say, I was slightly disappointed by the small silver button. With all the buildup, I expected something more interesting than an ordinary button. But this is where I was mistaken—the message on the button was exactly what I needed at that moment. On it was written the word *no* in a variety of languages.

At first I was confused by the button and shot an inquisitive glance at my mentor, who seemed to be enjoying my perplexity. He paused with a smile and then explained himself. "There are going to be a lot of people in the next few weeks who are going to want something from you," he began. "But the fact is that if you agree to do everything people ask you to do, it will probably burn you out. It is very important, both for your students and for yourself, that you have a life and that you stay fresh. So please, pick very carefully what extras you add to your teaching load and don't be afraid to just say no." With that he wished me a good day and left me to ponder the button of no's.

Over the next few weeks I quickly found out how right he was. In that span I was approached by staff about getting involved with the cross-country team, the literary magazine, the after-school program, and the admissions process. Various students asked me to help oversee other groups, including the anime club, roller-hockey team, and a weight-lifting class. I wish I could say that I took my mentor teacher's advice, thought deeply about how much I could handle, and then chose accordingly, but like many new teachers I was able to be lured, pressured, or bought into almost every extracurricular that came my way. This is what I learned.

Why It Is Hard to Say No

One reason it is so hard for new teachers to say no is that they are at one of the most fragile points in their lives. They are new to a very public and difficult job, and this leads to high-profile mistakes—a lot of them. At the same time, teachers are trying to endear themselves to staff, students, and administration, and in some cases fighting to come back the next year. This combination of pressure and mistakes makes any opportunity to build connections to members of the school community almost impossible to decline. So new teachers often jump on board with anything and everything asked of them.

Why You Should Think about Saying No More Often

New teachers mean one thing for a lot of occupants of the school: hole-pluggers. These teachers don't know it yet, but they are the shining ray of hope for many in the school community who have interests that currently sit understaffed. Veteran teachers already have their established routines and interests, and they rarely get lured into new areas of the school community. But new teachers are a blank page, and like a new story they can go in a thousand different directions if given the right nudge.

Combine this potential with the fact that new teachers rarely have a lot of money and are usually desperate to make friends in the school, and it starts to become clear why *you* will give so much hope to all those with pet projects within the school. This is also why you will likely be asked to do ten different things before you leave the building on the first day of classes.

Despite the obvious advantages of building bridges and possibly even getting a little extra cash, saying no should always be on the table when you are asked to add something extra to your plate. As a new teacher you will probably have very little time to spare even before adding extracurriculars, and if you add too many you will have no (or negative) time left. This time crunch is due to the fact that teachers, like medical residents or beginning lawyers, are generally asked to do more in their first year than they will ever have to do again. During this baptism by fire, new teachers are not only asked to do everything the rest of the staff is required to (and at a much slower pace because they are unaccustomed to the demands), but they also have to design significantly more material than their peers, perform specific new-teacher tasks like attending mentor meetings or typing and turning in lesson plans, and they can never stop learning if they want to have any chance at success. After all this, any sort of time floating around for extracurriculars can be pretty limited.

Teaching is also an outlandishly draining job, which means it is necessary for teachers to consistently recharge their batteries. When you don't take downtime because of too many activities, you run the risk of hurting your performance in the classroom and your quality of life outside of it. This is because overextended and exhausted teachers generally struggle to keep up things like enthusiasm, creativity, reflexes, and joy—all of which are traditional strengths for new teachers.

The final issue with getting overextended is that biting off too much can actually damage your teaching because it can force you to make unpleasant choices. If you have to plan lessons, grade papers, figure out a workout schedule for the track team, and edit papers for the literary magazine, something will inevitably suffer. Unless you are superhuman, you will likely be too tired and uninspired to give each task the attention it deserves—which means the only choice you will have left is how much you will let each of your responsibilities suffer.

These reasons and maintaining your general sanity are just a few of the many reasons you should always consider saying no. Because if your performance suffers due to overload, it doesn't really matter if you got into the activities originally with the best intentions. At that point you are more likely to burn out or burn bridges than to build connections or a strong teaching background.

Why New Teachers Should Get Involved in Something

Now that extracurriculars have been thoroughly painted as the enemy, this piece of advice probably seems more than a little bit contradictory—but all young teachers should get involved in some school activities outside their classroom doors. Though it is true that having excessive commitments will likely lead to some major headaches, the many positives that come from having a reasonable amount of extracurriculars far outweigh the negatives of a little extra work. The key is finding a balance.

The strongest argument for why all new teachers should do some variety of extracurricular is that it allows you and the students to see each other in a totally new light. Students behave very differently in clubs and sports than they do in class, and as a coach or adviser, you will likely act somewhat differently, too. This shift in behavior and tone allows the normally walled-off sides of teacher and student to get small peeks into the more human qualities of the other, and this can lead to a whole new understanding or appreciation of the opposite parties.

As a coach or adviser, you will discover surprising talents and sides to kids you'd written off, and you will learn more about their hopes, fears, interests, and backgrounds than you ever could in the classroom. On the student side, they will get to see their instructor in a more relaxing setting where certain emotions and actions receive freer reign than they can during the school day. This setting also allows you to build more personal relationships with the students because of the added time, and specifically the added one-on-one time.

Extracurriculars come with a host of other advantages as well. They do make you look motivated to administration (in a very visible fashion), often there are financial rewards, and they can be downright fun if you get into them. There is also something to be said for giving back, especially to extracurriculars you were involved with in school. A lot of sports teams, clubs, and other student activities helped shape who many of us are, and even if helping provide that same opportunity to your students today doesn't feel good (which it will), it has to be good karma.

Exit Slip

With so many positives, it is highly recommendable that all new teachers get involved in an extracurricular or two. But please remember not to overdo it, or all these positives can quickly evaporate, leaving only a pile of negatives instead. You should also be especially careful about not allowing yourself to be pressured. Go only with the activities you feel comfortable with or want to do. If you are able to do that, and say no to the rest, you will be one step closer to making your first year a great one.

THE URGE TO BE GROOVY

D uring my first semester of teaching, I faced a silent killer of lessons that plagues many new teachers. In retrospect, this trap had been damaging my lessons from student teaching onward, but like many new teachers I didn't even know the problem existed for a long time. In fact, it wasn't until a series of unfortunate vocabulary lessons over the first two months of the school year that the problem and the damage caused by it suddenly became clear.

The Problem

The unfortunate lessons in question consisted of eight chapters' worth of vocabulary lessons that fell flat and eight vocabulary quizzes on which the students underperformed. No matter what I did, the weekly vocabulary words didn't seem to stick with students. By the end of the eighth lesson, I was at my wit's end. The seemingly small task of creating vocabulary lessons had developed into one of my biggest struggles, and with each failed lesson worries about how to approach the next lesson ate up more and more of my time.

As I prepared for the ninth lesson, I tried to figure out what had been going wrong. If anything, my vocabulary lessons appeared on the surface to be can't-miss. They were some of the most entertaining, interesting, and fun lessons of the year, and the students appeared to be both engaged and enjoying themselves. Yet week after week, the excitement and connection so strong during class did not translate over into understanding of the words. And then it hit me. I was making the same mistake that I'd often been chided for during student teaching: I was trying to make my lessons "too groovy."

"The urge to be groovy" was a term coined by my student teaching mentor to describe a syndrome that he claimed affects nearly all new teachers. His theory was that an upbringing filled with teacher movies like *Dangerous Minds*, *Stand and Deliver*, and of course *Dead Poets Society*, combined with scores of uninspired teachers in their own schooling, has created a generation of new teachers who "want to do things differently." So they grab onto these movies and the few "fun" lessons they recall from school, and decide that what the students need more than anything else is to be dazzled on a daily basis. Then they try to fill their classroom with one exciting, inspiring, and life-changing lesson after another.

Why Getting Too Groovy Can Hurt a Lesson

A groovy approach like tearing the pages out of a dull textbook (à la Robin Williams) is wonderful fantasy and works well for film, but this doesn't mean it always garners the same success in real life. The main problem with overly groovy lessons (and what makes them overly groovy) is they often have the wrong objectives. In a normal lesson the main goal of the lesson, regardless of the topic, is generally to help students understand and retain the knowledge as well as possible. But when teachers focus on blowing their students' minds constantly, the objectives can subtly shift, and before they realize it, their lesson becomes more about entertaining and amazing the students than helping them learn.

My vocabulary lessons were a perfect example of this silent shift toward being too groovy because the main objective of each lesson wasn't (despite my claim to the contrary) to help the students learn the words; instead, it was to make the usually tedious task of learning vocabulary more palatable. While designing each lesson I tried to take the Mary Poppins approach of providing a spoonful of sugar to help the medicine-flavored vocabulary go down. To do this, I included at least one exciting twist designed to engage and entertain the students in each lesson. One time I had the students draw a picture of each word. Another time they created group stories by passing the paper to a neighbor after each sentence. Another time they acted out the words. Throughout all of these "groovy" activities only two things stayed constant—the students found the lessons fun and the results on the corresponding quizzes were lower than I wanted.

There are several reasons why overly groovy lessons often fail. The first is that if you get distracted by entertainment, student learning doesn't receive the attention it deserves. When it came to the vocabulary lessons I wasn't focused on maintaining a good learning pace because I wanted to go at an entertaining pace. And at times I didn't include enough repetition or use the word in context because those activities (despite their proven positive impact upon learning) didn't fit with the games I had in mind.

The second reason that too much grooviness can actually impede learning is because it becomes a distraction for the students. Think of it like a shell game. The students get so busy watching all the pageantry that they forget about the important part: where is the pea? Or in the case of the vocabulary lessons, what is the meaning of *sanctimonious*? And afterward, students may forever remember the fun of the lesson, but if they don't remember the words, what is the point?

How to Avoid Getting Overly Groovy

All of the negatives that can come with groovy lessons do not mean that teachers shouldn't strive for inspirational, exciting, and engaging lessons. On the contrary, it is important to inspire, create, and explore—that is why most of us go into the profession and your students will love you for it. The danger doesn't lie in putting passion, fun, or exploration into lessons; instead, it lies in forgetting that you are there to teach, not to entertain.

To avoid falling into the overly groovy trap, just make sure everything you do is aimed at improving student learning, not at improving the time they are having in your class. These two goals are not mutually exclusive; sometimes the best way for students to learn is for them to have a great time. But other times it might not be the best way for them to learn. And there is nothing wrong with having a straightforward, simple lesson every once and a while—sometimes the most seemingly pedestrian lessons provide the best platforms for learning.

Exit Slip

Fun has just as much a place in the classroom as the desks and the board. And as long as you keep student learning first, you can and should add as much enjoyment as possible. There are infinite ways to effectively bring fun into the classroom, but here are a few of the most useful:

- You could have students act, dress up, hold mock interviews (this works for any subject; you can interview everything from gravity to Genghis Khan), and otherwise incorporate theater.

- Students love to draw, create artistic projects or representations, and put an artistic twist on nearly everything. (I once had students design their own grammar books. The amount of effort they put into designing the books has never been equaled by another grammar assignment.)

- Have the students bring in food on occasion. As was mentioned before, food is powerful stuff.

- Take time to savor and revel in the enjoyable moments during class. It is perfectly all right to take a minute away from the lesson plan to laugh and have unscripted fun for a few moments.

CHAPTER THIRTY-ONE
FRIENDLY FIRE

Besides maybe dogs versus cats, does any rivalry feel more natural than students versus teachers? According to popular culture, students and teachers are the perfect adversaries. Like oil and water, they form two distinct factions—one representing the old guard and another representing the changing world—and their only connection comes through common friction with the other side.

And there is certainly a little kernel of truth to this representation of the relationship between students and teachers. They are often in very different places, have very different goals, and certainly don't see eye to eye on everything. But despite the multitude of differences lying between them, the two sides often aren't nearly as polarized as advertised. In fact, not only are teachers and students rarely sworn enemies, most of the time they develop close bonds and fondness for each other. This is especially true with young teachers, who often arrive with a far better understanding of modern students and a great desire to be accepted by them. Students, too, also generally have a higher-than-average interest in gaining the approval of young teachers because they are usually the "coolest" among the stable of teachers.

Building strong relationships with students as a young teacher is often a very powerful and positive thing (with many advantages described later), but it has its downsides, too. The biggest problem with growing close to students is that it is very easy for both sides to begin subtly viewing each other as friends of a sort—not as teacher and student. And though being friends is rarely a bad thing in this world, when students become buddies instead of pupils a whole host of significant downsides generally follows.

Friends Are Less Willing to Listen to Your Suggestions

When a student feels like a teacher is a friend, it might be logical to think that the student would grow more open to the teacher's suggestions—but in many cases, the exact opposite happens. Instead of growing more willing to listen, students can become more closed off to criticisms from teachers they view as friends, and sometimes they will even be downright obstinate in their refusals of them.

This somewhat counterintuitive twist happens for the same reason that it can be harder to get everything from ski lessons to fashion advice from your friends—people generally want their friends to focus on their good side, not to criticize them or point out their flaws. Friends are supposed to stroke egos, take your side, and tell half truths, and this isn't always your role as a teacher. And while sometimes you will try to build a student up or hold a student back from a painful truth (you would never tell a student that his or her writing is just awful, even if it is), you are also required to provide a lot of constructive criticism. If your students view you as a friend, it can be very difficult for them to take it or take it seriously.

This resistance to criticism can extend to comments during class as well. If a student sees you as a friend, then your suggestions "Be quiet" or "Get on task" may not be as scary as they once were. At this point, they are no longer firm orders from an authority but minor appeals from a friend, and those are much easier to disregard.

Students May Manipulate a Teacher's Need to Be Liked

What teacher doesn't have at least a slight desire to be known as the "favorite teacher," the "fun teacher," or at least the "accepted teacher"? Teachers spend a huge chunk of their week with students, and it is only natural to want people you spend so much time with to like you. But unfortunately, a lot of students are aware (consciously or unconsciously) of this common teacher desire to be liked, and they can use these longings for acceptance and friendship against you in several surprisingly sophisticated ways. These are a couple of the most common.

They Play Up the Positives

Sometimes students play up the positives and say everything any teacher would want to hear—not because they are being friendly, but because they want something. They mention how cool the teacher is, how much fun the teacher is, or that the teacher is among their favorites in an effort to gain leniency, easy grading, less work, or to positively reinforce (that's right—students do it to us, too) a fun or easy assignment.

Of course, not all such comments are born of manipulation—in fact, most probably aren't—but ulterior motives can be tucked among such sweet praises. With that in mind, try taking all such compliments with a grain of salt, and try your best to treat students and classes exactly the same, regardless of the compliments they shower upon you (though feel free to enjoy them!). Sometimes this means you will have to fight the feeling of guilt that inevitably comes when you give a student who claims you are their favorite a bad grade. And don't worry about your status as a favorite teacher dying away if you aren't always fun or easy. If you truly are a student's favorite, a tough, but fair assessment or assignment shouldn't damage that status, and if it does, that is a small price to pay for doing the right thing.

They Name-Call

The other way students manipulate a teacher's natural desire to be liked is by taking the opposite approach from playing up the positives—they name-call. When it comes to name-calling, students know most types of names are off limits for teachers, but they also generally understand that pretty harsh messages can be sent through more subtle means. So instead of calling you a jerk, students will sometimes do whatever they can to make sure it is painfully obvious to you how distinctively uncool you are being at the moment. Common ways they do this include scowls, cold shoulders, heavy sighs or "ughs," or active ignoring.

On the surface, these actions are polar opposites of playing up the positives, but underneath, the goal is essentially the same. These students are still using "teacher coolness" to get try to get what they want, but this time the reinforcement has moved from positive to negative. By taking the you-are-so-uncool route, they are trying to make you feel guilty about being a tough grader or a disciplinarian, and thus hopefully pressure you into easier grading, looser rules, or some other form of leniency.

How to Approach Either

When faced with scowling or pandering, the best approach is to just have a thick skin and try not to take it personally. Remember, momentary student reactions of the positive or negative variety generally don't mean much for the long term. It is not uncommon for a student who proclaims you the favorite one day to turn on you the second you hand out a B. It also is not uncommon for a student who is scowling, sulking, or disgruntled about something to walk into the next class with a big smile and pleasantly say hello. So try your best not to bite on every mood swing of the students. Instead, stay focused on the long term, and in the end, the students will likely have more positives and fewer negatives to say about you.

Student Friendships Are Generally Not Appropriate

Students and teachers can never have a truly equal friendship. It just isn't possible. A lot of different obstacles stand in the way of this friendship—varying ages, perspectives, and stages of life all make it difficult—but the biggest reason that teachers and students can't be friends, no matter how the teacher approaches it, is that the power dynamic between them is unequal. No matter what the grade level, school, or situation, the teacher will always hold power over the student, and that will inevitably skew the relationship.

This uneven power distribution has a lot of ramifications for most types of interactions. It means the teacher's words will almost always carry the greater weight in any conversation, the teacher's ability to convert students to their beliefs will usually be profound, and the possibility of students fully understanding their perspective will be almost nil. These reasons and many more make pursuing a true friendship with students both impossible and inappropriate.

What Level of Friendship Is Appropriate?

The level of friendliness to have with students is one of the finest lines new teachers have to walk. There are certainly a lot of issues that come from becoming too friendly with students, but just as much damage can be done by staying too distant. It is critically important that students do like you, are close to you, perceive you as friendly, and feel that you like them. If students feel close to and liked by a teacher (as was discussed in chapter 4), it almost always leads directly to more consistency, generally better work, and a whole host of other positives.

To make sure that you strike a good balance in terms of your friendliness with students, it often works to think about it as having one hand open and extended and one hand shut and withdrawn. With the hand that is open you welcome and reach out to students, while simultaneously you use the closed hand to keep some distance and hold some choice things from them. By maintaining this balance of reaching out and holding back, teachers are often able to make students feel close, yet somehow separate; liked, but with limits; and that their teachers are friendly, but not friends.

In order to work on cultivating your own fine line, try including some of the following in your open and closed hand.

With the Open Hand, You Can Reach Out by . . .

- Listening closely and valuing what students say (and make sure that they recognize you doing this). This doesn't take too much instruction; just quietly listen when they talk and respond to it afterward.

- Telling them little appropriate stories from time to time that let students know a little bit about you. When you do this, just make sure not to give away too many important personal details (more on this in a moment).

- Asking them questions about what they think and enjoy both in and out of school.

- Focusing on student strengths on a regular basis. If you've gone three or four weeks without a positive comment, make sure you commend them on the things they are doing well.

- Coming across so that it is clear that you care about them, their thoughts and feelings, and whether they are successful in the future.

In the Closed Hand, You Can Keep Some Distance by . . .

- Withholding most personal details. Having a somewhat mysterious personal life is a good thing for a young teacher. Try holding back any information on where you go out, information about a significant other or friends, and anything about your life beyond generalities (things like that you enjoy hockey or playing the bass).

- Not divulging personal beliefs. Teachers have a very real ability to sway the personal and political opinions of their students with their own. So keep them out of the classroom if you don't want to enter a dubious moral area.

- Staying unemotional (at times). Being a little stoic in class can be a good thing. This is not to say that you shouldn't be happy, sad, or upset at times, but being selective with when you show your emotions can separate you ever so slightly from the students.

- Avoiding touching. As a general rule, new teachers, especially males, should avoid touching their students in any way. This puts up a good divider, while also taking away any chance that the touching could be misconstrued. If you are looking for a good way of turning down a hug or any other contact (which can be tough because you don't want to hurt the student's feelings), just say you think you are getting sick and give a little fist bump (or something of that variety). After a couple of weeks of your "getting sick," the students will recognize what is going on and requests for hugs will likely disappear.

Exit Slip

In the end, the blanket statement of saying that you shouldn't be friends with students is a bit of an oversimplification. In your relationship with students you do want many of the elements of friendship to exist; you want students to feel liked, unconditionally supported, like they can come to you with any issues, and that you have a stake in their future success. But at the same time other attributes of friendship, like the lack of boundaries, unwillingness to criticize, and the complete openness to say and do what you please (on either side) should be left out. So get out your tightrope shoes, and if you are able to hold this fine balance you will be a long way toward developing strong, long-term, and appropriate relationships with your students.

Unit Ten
THE TRICKS

In your first year of teaching, completing all of the required duties takes an astronomical amount of time and energy. But there is a silver lining—you will never have to work that hard again. As a second-year teacher, you will still have a lot of work, but free time will be a bit easier to come by and the load pressing down on you won't seem quite as heavy. When you are a third-year teacher, the clouds of overwork often part, and you suddenly find yourself with a life again.

The odd thing about the diminished workload from your first to your third year is that your actual workload probably hasn't dropped at all. Maybe by your third year you will have a bank of lessons and activities to work from, but these deductions from your weekly work are often offset by new duties picked up along the way. And even if new duties aren't added, it still generally doesn't explain the massive difference in time required to do their job between first- and third-year teachers.

Instead, the explanation has something to do with an idea presented at the beginning of the book: working smarter, not harder. By their third year, teachers have generally become so practiced at the tasks required and have garnered so many tricks for cutting down time that they can literally cut their work in half. And though this book can't do anything about giving you practice, it can pass along the time-saving tricks that come along with it. So far, many tricks for working smarter have already been passed along, but there are a few important ones that still need to be discussed before the book can end. Here they are, and may they help you reclaim some hours of your life.

THE ADVANTAGES OF
BEING A NEW TEACHER

I t is generally assumed that when a new teacher comes into a school, he or she is probably going to have more trouble and be less effective than the veterans. But this does not mean new teachers are dead weight or purely "an investment." Like most things in life, being young and inexperienced has its share of disadvantages, but it also comes with several distinct advantages. These advantages may not completely negate all of the mistakes you will make, but if embraced and developed they can go a long way toward painting you as a teacher who works, instead of a work in progress.

Face It, You Are Cool

OK, maybe you weren't always very cool and to this day that isn't exactly how you would characterize yourself. But to the students, no matter how you define yourself, there is a very good chance you will seem cool. Here's why: To most teenagers, people in their twenties are like mythic heroes. They are close in age to the teenagers, but they have powers those teenagers could never dream of (like going out late, dating whomever they want, and legal access to a whole host of societal vices). Combine that with the increased sense of confidence, self, and rationality that generally comes with age (at least compared to teenagers) and a general lessening of awkwardness, and the result is someone who appears pretty cool.

This means that despite all of the anxieties likely floating around your head as a young teacher, the students probably see you as cool the second you walk in the door. Ironically, the fastest way to destroy this image is to strive to be the cool teacher. When teachers pursue coolness by trying to talk with the students like they are one of the gang, make a lot of forced hip references, or do some other variety of pandering, the students will just as likely see through it as anyone else. And that isn't good for maintaining your street cred.

The best way to hold onto your coolness is to just own your standing with the students regardless of how cool their view of you is. In the same way that coolness flees from those trying to be cool, it generally flocks to people who accept where they fit in the world (having confidence in yourself is probably the most essential trait for being cool). So just be yourself and be all right with where you stand in the world of the school, and there is a good chance that the students will find you at least a little cool.

The reason it is worth using ink to address the seemingly trivial topic of coolness is that being cool does carry certain advantages. The type of effort and engagement the cool young teacher can inspire is nothing short of amazing at times. During my first year, I saw students spend countless hours on small projects for extra credit, do additional work that was never assigned, and even write more than fifty pages (more than once) on assignments that required just five pages—for teachers they found cool. If a student finds a teacher cool, he or she also often becomes more likely to readily forgive the teacher's mistakes, listen closely to the teacher, and assign extra weight to the teacher's words (and the information behind them).

With these advantages, being cool is definitely a good thing. But just like your mom or dad probably told you, being cool is not the only thing. Being cool can add a little dash of something extra, but there are lots of teachers not seen as cool by the students who are terrific educators. And there are lots of cool teachers who aren't effective at all. So whether your students happen to find you cool or not, your job is to not worry about it (which is harder than it seems). Coolness is nice, but it won't make or break a teacher—and besides, your coolness will probably be maximized if you don't think about it.

You Are a Liaison with the Younger Generation

Generally speaking, the longer you are in the classroom the more knowledge you will gain about your subject area, how to run the classroom, the psychology of the students, and teaching as a whole. But there is one type of knowledge that actually diminishes with every day you spend as a teacher: your understanding of student life outside of school.

When you walk into the school as a new teacher, you are as close in age and perspective to the students as you will ever be, and in many ways that instantly makes you the leading authority concerning student interests in music, movies, trends, and life in general. And even though this knowledge mainly concerns trivial matters (like knowing about the latest iPhone apps or who Lady Gaga is) it can make a significant positive impact on your class if used right.

Again, at this point it has to be mentioned that this does not mean you should try to pretend you are one of the kids or throw out one "modern" reference after another; you are a long way removed from being their age and trying too hard to connect to their outside interests will likely come across as desperate or odd. But that doesn't mean you should shy away from involving the outside interests of students in the classroom, either; it just means you should pick your moments. A couple of teen culture twists in the classroom will be fun and engage them, while constant ones will be strange.

One of the best spots to include references to outside student life is in the assignments you give. A couple of examples of how to do this are having students draw a fake Facebook page of a historical figure, a character from a novel, or a mathematical equation (complete with statuses, friends, news feeds, and profile pictures) or having them make movies to post on YouTube. Just by framing a normal character profile as a Facebook profile, changing a normal classroom video to a YouTube video, or adding some other little modern variation to another assignment you can often catch the attention of some students who might not be otherwise interested or at least create a buzz that will likely lead to better overall results.

You Have a Fresh Perspective

One of the biggest strengths that new teachers possess is their perspective. Every new teacher who comes into a school brings a fresh set of eyes with which to gaze upon the school, and the value of this should never be underestimated. Fresh perspectives are a billion-dollar business, and among other things they are the reason editors exist and businesses consultants can often command large sums of money for stating the obvious.

As a general rule, we humans are the worst at seeing things right underneath our noses. No matter how talented or self-aware the faculty or leadership at a school is, they will still have difficulty recognizing all of the opportunities and flaws present within their schools. This is where you step in. With your fresh perspective, you can instantly offer value to any school by pointing out the obvious, or at least the things obvious to you that everyone else seems to overlook.

The best way to capitalize on your fresh eyes is to look for opportunities in the school. Are there areas where cross-curricular cooperation would improve the curriculum? Is there a need for a new club or sports team? Is there a way to make your curriculum more multimedia? By finding and making the most of these "obvious" opportunities that exist at every school, a new teacher can make some serious contributions right away that can go a long way toward winning the support of the administration, parents, and students.

With your new perspective, you will probably also be more conscious of the flaws that established people in the school overlook. You can do a lot of good and win a lot of goodwill by finding and improving these flaws, but with flaws you need to tread a little lighter. A couple of suggestions for improvement are generally welcomed by any school and can go a long way toward building your reputation as an innovative thinker. But rocking the boat too much can lead to everything from minor hurt feelings and defensiveness to outright hostility. As was discussed in chapter 26, human beings just aren't programmed to react well to too many big changes at once. So as a first-year teacher, go ahead and push for a few choice changes, but after that let sleeping dogs lie (at least for the moment). Recommend a new book, not a completely new library. The opportunity for a new library will come, but only if you go about making the changes by degrees.

Students Are More Willing to Believe You

In the eyes of students, all teachers are probably fairly dubious sources, but young teachers generally come across as the most trustworthy members of the faculty. The reason for this is ironically the same reason that students are more willing to talk back or show young teachers disrespect at times—because the teacher looks nothing like their parents. Though young teachers do fit the description of an authority figure on paper, they often have faces that point more to their recent experience of being young and clueless like the students than to their level of authority, and that can make them automatically more trustworthy to the average student.

This added trustworthiness comes with several advantages: It makes it easier for students to talk to and confide in new teachers, and it adds extra weight to most of their advice. But no advantage of the added trustworthiness is more significant than the increased ability it bestows upon new teachers to level with their students. When you level with your students, the idea is to try to motivate them by letting them know how the real world works and how what they are doing now will help them when they are out there. Here is an example of how that might go:

> You need to have an interesting opening to your essays because in the real world you will, at some point, need to interest someone in your writing who is not required to read it. Whether this is a college application essay [bringing college up is very effective because even middle schoolers are often already quite concerned with college], a cover letter for a job, or a love note, I don't know. But that moment is what we are practicing for now, and that is why your introduction needs to be compelling.

In general, students hear this type of "it will help you in the long run" speech all the time from teachers, parents, coaches, and other adults in their life, and for the most part they are very talented at dismissing it. But when it comes from a trustworthy new teacher, students often grow far more open to the message of these speeches. This approach is especially effective when you have work that the students are or probably will be resistant toward, and it also works really well in one-on-one conversations with students who are in trouble or aren't meeting your expectations.

Your Mistakes Are More Readily Forgiven by Everyone

Students may call you on them, administration may come to speak with you concerning them, and parents may gossip about them, but unless you really mess up, new teachers are generally forgiven for most of the mistakes they make. This doesn't mean that, as a new teacher, you have a license to be sloppy, but no one with any rationality expects you to be perfect. So, make the best of this situation! Try new things, take risks, go outside the box, and don't be afraid to experiment. Also, don't freak out when something doesn't work out. If ever there was a time to take risks and occasionally mess up, it's when you have a get-out-of-jail-free card. Again, this doesn't mean getting lazy or loose or going crazy with something is probably going to end well, but while you are young take some risks and your teaching in the future will be better for it.

Exit Slip

The advantages that come with being young or new all have incredibly limited shelf lives. Sooner than you would expect, your status as the new teacher will fade away and your perspective, believability, and the amount of free passes will often fade right along with it. So make good use of these advantages while you can, because before you know it you will simply be Mr./Mrs. _____, for better and worse, instead of the new guy/girl.

THE ROLE OF EMOTION
IN THE CLASSROOM

E motion in the classroom is sometimes seen as a sign that a teacher is overworked, underskilled, or generally struggling. And in some situations this is certainly true, but that does not mean that emotion on the part of the teacher is always a bad thing. Humans are emotional creatures (especially new teachers, for whom every day can be a roller coaster of emotions), and as teachers we are dealing with exceptionally emotional creatures (teenagers). With so much emotion floating around, there is no reason not to channel some emotion into your classroom from time to time, so long as you do it with care. When used intelligently, emotion is a powerful tool, and it is one that teenagers can easily understand and relate to.

Anger

One of the strangest pieces of teaching advice I ever received came from my mentor during student teaching. After a particularly tough week, he told me that sometime early the following week I should get angry with my class. Unsure of such an unorthodox suggestion, I protested that I wasn't sure anger worked or whether you could choose when you got angry. At this he smiled, and to my surprise he began to tell me about his new puppy.

"My puppy," he began, "is in the process of being housebroken. And inevitably he will wander off the housebreaking pad and do something he shouldn't, because he is a puppy. When he does this, I need to get him, scold him, and place him back on the pad. It is the only way to truly train him. That is what I want you to do: The class is your puppy and they have wandered off the pad. Now I want you to put the puppy back onto the pad."

With my instructions in hand I proceeded to get mad at the class the next week, and though it didn't make a massive difference, it did affect the class a little. For the next few days the class remained slightly quieter and treated me with moderately more respect. And even though the effect on the class was not great, it did show me how anger may have some place in the classroom after all.

Now that I've had more experience with getting angry at classes (some planned and some not), I recognize what a powerful tool anger can be in the classroom—but beware, you should not throw fits in front of your students whenever you please. Anger is not a cure-all and should be used incredibly sparingly. In fact, during most circumstances anger will probably be ineffective or have downright negative effects on a class, so you need to pick your moments.

An example of a time when anger wasn't helpful also comes from my student teaching, though it was a few months later when using anger felt more comfortable. On this day some of my students were baiting me through quiet (but not too quiet) chatting and antics. Finally, about halfway through the lesson my patience had worn thin and after an especially long bout of talking I raised my voice and growled at the class "Be quiet!" While I did this, I tried to keep my face stern and neutral, but I'm quite sure my exasperation and annoyance danced across my face. The student response to this was mixed; some looked genuinely remorseful, but most of the loudest students had victory painted all over their faces—and moments later the bad behavior from them was back and worse than ever in the hope for an encore.

The problem with my anger in this situation, and the reason it wasn't effective at putting the "puppy back onto the pad," was that it wasn't on my terms. The ringleaders of the behavior wanted to see me mad, and I didn't disappoint. I danced just liked they hoped, and in the end my anger brought nothing but even worse behavior. This is why, as a general rule, the last time you want to get angry at a class is when the students hope for it. If students are baiting you in the hope of a response, you should punish them, but don't do it with anger.

Instead of getting mad at the obvious times, the best time to use anger is as the rare exclamation point when the students aren't necessarily expecting it. Try saving your anger from more obvious times for the moments when the students aren't baiting you—like when they've been consistently late with homework or aren't putting in the work that they should during a group project. In these moments they probably aren't expecting any major emotions, and that surprise attack gives your anger the ability to unsettle most students, including those students who wish to see you mad.

When you do get mad, it is essential that you make sure you don't overdo it. Overdoing it will terrify the students or make them laugh—neither of which you want. Instead, you want your anger to be stern, authoritative, and controlled (and only to use a moderately louder voice). You want to make clear through your anger that your intentions are serious and the students can and should do better. Often this effect can be magnified if combined with the threat or implementation of some negative consequence like a seating chart, a quiz, or some other punishment. The hope is that by doing this you will make the students look inside themselves and realize that they haven't treated you or each other right.

Then once your point is made you want to back off. Anger works as a quick counterpoint to your normal demeanor, but if you dwell on it too long students will likely stop looking inward and they will begin to reflect the anger back at you. Generally, when you show anger toward the whole class, you want to use language that doesn't blame individuals or groups of students (such as "The homework is coming in late far too often"), so as to avoid individual students becoming defensive and leading the charge against you.

Few books out there advocate getting angry at a class, but it does work in a classroom if it is controlled, tempered, and infrequent. Remember, growing angry with the class must be a rare occurrence (generally less than once a month), as it derives its power from the fact that it works as a contrast to a teacher's normal conduct. As soon as anger becomes common, it no longer is a contrast; it is part of the teacher's personality, and thus loses its original power. At this point you are just the angry teacher, and that reputation comes with few positives. But if used rarely and used right, anger can be the perfect tool to put the puppy back onto the pad.

Joy

Another emotion that should be in all teachers' repertoire is joy. As a teacher you will encounter some intense frustrations and disappointments, but there is also much daily joy to be had in the profession. And there are a lot of advantages to making sure you don't forget that.

One way joy can significantly improve teaching is that happiness and fun (like enthusiasm) are contagious. In fact, pretty much all emotions on the part of the teacher are highly contagious. It is amazing how just being in the proximity of a tired teacher can make students tired, how working around an impatient teacher can make students impatient, and how spending even a few minutes with a happy teacher can lift the students' spirits. So if you want a warm feeling of happiness to drift over the room and settle upon the students, try your best to not worry and be happy.

Showing your joy in the classroom is also very important because people generally respond positively to those who enjoy their professions. Think about going to a concert, sporting event, or comedy show; if the audience recognizes that the performers are enjoying themselves and not just earning a paycheck they feel as if they are a part of something special. This same principle extends well beyond show business, too. I was once on jury duty (which has to be at the top of the most disgruntled audiences you can play to), and the man in charge of the jury pool obviously enjoyed his job (and not in a sadistic way). He had energy, cracked a few jokes, and never lost his genuine smile, and after about ten minutes of listening to him speaking, the jurors were transformed from being irritated about being there to being far more open to being part of the process. And all that was needed for this monumental shift in perspective was someone openly enjoying his job for a couple of minutes.

The exact advantages of joy are hard to nail down or quantify, but they are there, so be happy in your class as much as you can. To do this, make jokes, keep a smile going, laugh at students (even silently) when they say or do something ridiculous, and never forget that a classroom is best when it's happy. Also, try to steer clear of the politics, the failures, the gossip, the number of times students tell you their printer broke, and the other negatives present on any given day. For if you make a conscious decision to focus on all of the joys that can be found within the classroom walls, and celebrate them as much as you can, there is a good chance your life both in school and out will become a lot happier.

Calm

One of the telltale signs of new teachers is they look, sound, or act frazzled. That is to say, they often behave in that flat, wide-eyed, sleep-deprived manner that is normally reserved for parents of infants and med-school residents during their twenty-four-hour rotations. And there is certainly a good reason for that; this book has already discussed several times the extreme pressure and demands put upon young teachers in their first few years, and it is only natural to get a little fried by that.

But despite all of the work and stress, it is important for teachers to channel as much calm as they can while in front of the students. The reason for this relates back to something discussed in chapter 3, about respect. Students are looking for a leader in the classroom, and calm is essential to the students' viewing you as a strong leader. Calm also makes the students feel more comfortable (remember, they are often barometers of the teacher's feelings), and it makes you look like you have everything together, which will help in building their respect. So whenever things are getting crazy or you are feeling rattled, take a deep breath and do your best to settle down—because your calming down is often the first domino needed for getting everything back on track.

Contrast Your Emotions

Think about the best concert you've ever been to. Did the band get up on stage and play as fast as they could for hours or did they slip in a few slow songs? Did they play with all of their energy for every second or did they vary the energy throughout the show? The odds are that despite how good a purely high energy show sounds on paper, the best concert you've been to probably had moments of fast, high energy and slower, lower energy—and there is a good reason for this beyond giving you time to get concessions.

The concert probably had fast and slow, intense and relaxed, and innovative and comfortable parts because the secret to tugging at the emotional strings of your audience is contrast. Contrast is why even the most full-throttle Arnold Schwarzenegger movie and the most passionate Danielle Steel novel have down moments (no pun intended, get your mind out of the gutter). If you don't have the downs, the audience can't fully appreciate the ups. And if you don't have sad moments, then the happy moments don't pack the same punch.

This power of contrast is not just effective with books, music, and action movies, either; it can also be of great use in our classrooms. When bringing emotions into the classroom, strive not to typecast yourself with the overuse of any one particular emotion. If you are always angry, the students will soon see the anger not as a sign of underperformance or misbehavior, but as an inherent flaw. And this effect goes the other way, too. If you bubble over with happiness about every little thing, then when you truly come across something worth being happy about, your emotion won't carry the same power.

In your class you instead want to vary your emotions from day to day, exercise to exercise, and moment to moment. Here are a few tips for doing that:

- Don't always guilt-trip or reprimand students, even if they constantly mess up. Find some positives to contrast their negatives with.

- Save your highest praise for work that actually warrants it, so those students who've done something amazing know that your exuberance comes from being actually impressed and it's not a canned response.

- Save your top level of energy for the moments when it is important to get the students excited. If you treat every activity like it is the most fun thing in the world, your enthusiasm will probably lose some of its novelty and power.

- Have some "down" moments during class where the students work quietly, reflect, or process the material. These moments help them process information and recharge their batteries so they can bring all the excitement needed to the next activity that calls for it.

Exit Slip

When it comes to the classroom, there is a large distinction between using your emotions and letting your emotions use you. If it is under your control, emotion is a powerful and useful tool that can do everything from getting students to settle down to look inside themselves, but when you are controlled by emotion little good usually comes out of the situation. This means that as a young teacher, at many moments you have to ignore the surging emotions coursing through your veins, and try to act despite or even against them—which is no easy task. And though you will likely falter at this on occasion (for you are human), if you keep striving to let your emotions work for you instead of vice versa, then very likely emotions will become one of your strongest overall allies in the classroom.

THE USE OF TECHNOLOGY

The education community, largely because of the fiery passion of its members, has a tendency to run a little wild with new trends. Every few years, from some corner of the education world, an idea, technique, or approach will pop up that gets anointed by a few influential voices as the savior of education. Then, seemingly overnight, schools across the country scramble to incorporate it into their curriculum so they too can be counted among the saved.

Right now the clear "chosen one" for saving education is technology. Go to any conference or pick up any educational journal and you will find significantly more discussion of technology than any other subject. This interest in technology has also found its way into most school offices, and the result is that whatever school you end up at will likely fall within into one of two categories: (1) it has a strong technological focus or (2) it has a strong desire to have a technological focus.

If you show up at a school that falls within either of these categories, there is great advantage to being a teacher who can use technology effectively in the classroom. At a school with a tech focus, the administrators, teachers, and parents will see you as someone in line with the school's methods and goals if you have technology skill and interest. At a school that wants to be more tech-focused, there is an even bigger advantage to being technologically savvy because you will represent a potential solution to the school's problem (and giving yourself added value is always a good thing).

Teaching with technology comes with a host of advantages for the classroom, too. When used effectively, technology can improve both your teaching and assessment of students, and it is capable of generating excitement and engagement like few other things. It can also connect the classroom to the greater world, make learning more interactive, and create new dialogues—and often it is just more fun.

Considering all of the upsides that come with technological knowledge, one of the best investments you can make for your teaching is to learn a bit about it. Generally speaking, taking even a couple of hours to familiarize yourself with the use of technology in schools will put your knowledge further ahead than 90 percent of your fellow teachers and make you seem pretty tech-wise to the average observer. To help you get started down this path, here are some basics for how to use technology in the classroom.

Use It for Production

When most people think of technology in schools their brains probably turn first to watching videos, giving PowerPoint presentations, playing interactive games, and various other ways of using media to show information. But though technology is very good for showing information, if you stop there you will miss out on another side of technology that can lend a great deal to the classroom—using it for production.

Using technology for production means that instead of just watching technology you use it to create something new. Technology is an amazing tool for producing all types of things, from movies to books to presentations. Creating professional-grade products is now within reach of the common classroom via simple programs that are free or cheap and quite simple to use. Technology is also really good at producing a sizable audience for things that had no audience before (to put this into perspective, a dog skateboarding can get more than ten million views on YouTube).

Despite the power of technology to bring both production and an audience to the classroom, many teachers are very hesitant to take this route. One possible reason for the hesitation is that though using technology for production is in reality often quite user-friendly, it can seem exceptionally intimidating. Incorporating PowerPoint or video clips into the classroom is one thing—those media are comfortable, most teachers probably have some experience with them, and they don't seem too complicated or technical. But producing a book or a movie on your own? For many teachers this can easily seem out of reach.

For my part, at the start of my teaching career, I fell into the category of teachers who are intimidated by all technology not part of the Microsoft Office package. To change this I sought out voices that could teach me more about combining technology and education; this eventually led me to the story of High Tech High, which is now a series of schools in the San Diego area that have had great success with incorporating technology into the classroom. What made High Tech High such a good resource for me was they don't use technology as a gimmick to garner attention and grant money, nor do they constantly stream video after video into the classroom. Instead they focus on using technology to create and produce tangible final products, and in that pursuit they've perfected several high-tech projects that are within the reach of the common classroom. Here are a few of the most effective.

Films (and Specifically Documentaries)

For many students, shooting a film seems a lot closer to pleasure than business. They get to goof around, let their creativity run wild, play with editing features, and even make a bloopers reel. Because films often seem more like play, many students are willing to put significantly more effort into them than they would for most other assignments. And this doesn't just apply to traditionally "good" students either. Students who couldn't be convinced by a million dollars to study or write for more than a couple of hours may not blink an eye at spending that amount of time producing a video for class.

Beyond inspiring commitment, student videos are often very good at teaching and reinforcing information. If a student does a video on the solar system, he or she will have to write a script, rehearse it, maybe go through multiple takes to get the right one, edit it, and watch it afterward. In every single one of these steps, the student will encounter all the information covered in the video, and by the end that knowledge will be so firmly entrenched that no amount of video game playing can dislodge it.

When doing a video, this high level of learning and motivation is not a given, though. Video projects generally need a strong structure (through clear guidelines on length, style, expectations, and quality) or the final result can quickly go from a ten-minute film full of wonderful learning to five minutes of students standing around and giggling incomprehensibly followed by a five-minute blooper reel of them standing around and giggling incomprehensibly. The problem with letting students do whatever they want is that when given that sort of freedom they will generally just charge ahead and shoot a random video with little preparation. On some smaller assignments, this tendency to not plan isn't always a big deal, but for something as involved as a video this type of approach almost always leads to pieces of junk. So before letting the students shoot, it is essential that you give them clear structure and expectations, and if you do they will generally thank you with amazing films.

Before having the students produce a video it is also really important that you teach them a little bit about film production. This doesn't mean you need to turn your class into film school, but you should teach them a few basics that they may not know:

- You should create a script beforehand.

- It is important to think about transitions between scenes and the order of scenes.

- You should have stage directions in your script, or at least think about the staging.

- You can include music or effects with simple computer programs.

These ideas aren't rocket science and many students will intuitively do all of them, but others won't. By taking just five or ten minutes to explain these basics, you will significantly minimize the chances of getting a movie that is missing one or more of these simple, yet crucial, elements. And the further you go beyond these basics in your discussion of movie making before the students create the video (especially if you show lots of examples), the more polished the final products will likely become.

Once you've laid out clear guidelines and taught the students a few basics, there are almost no situations where films can't work. Often video projects can get pigeonholed as being reserved for English class, but there is so much more to do with film than just shoot modern versions of *Romeo and Juliet* or *Beowulf* (though that is fun). Documentary movies can be made about nearly any subject, and many times students enjoy making nonfiction films more than fictional ones. When having them shoot documentaries, just make sure they know that nonfiction doesn't mean it can't be creative. Little is worse than a series of dry student films that are essentially monotone class presentations put on video—though that being said, little is better and more engaging than a well-thought-out and creative student film of any variety.

Publishing

When it comes to publishing student work, what the students write is just the tip of the iceberg. After the work is written, you will still have to contact and work with an outside company, it will cost money, and there is editing, art work, and layout design that need to be done as well. For many teachers the pile of work that comes with publishing makes it seem totally out of reach, especially considering the fact that getting students to write a regular paper can often be a formidable task. So they smile at the idea, say that *would* be fun, and don't give it another thought.

If you fall into this group, it is time to think about it again. Thanks to modern technology, publishing is not nearly as difficult as it once was (or may seem). In terms of contacting an outside company to publish the work, there are numerous websites, including Lulu.com and Blurb.com, that are both incredibly convenient and affordable. These sites just take a couple of minutes and an Internet connection to sign up for and their entire span of services is generally really cheap. They also make all of the editing, formatting, and artistic design easy through a series of very user-friendly steps.

Publishing offers an added bonus that can make the entire process significantly smoother: motivation. For most students, there is little exciting about writing a normal research paper, and generally a lot of them will have to be pulled through it every step of the way because frankly they don't care. But when that research paper turns into a book, complete with pictures and their name in the author spot, suddenly the whole process can seem that much more appealing. Having a tangible book to show friends and family (and also possibly even put up for sale!) cannot be underrated as a motivating factor for a lot of kids—and just like with movies, it will often inspire them to work harder than you or they ever thought was possible.

With all of its advantages, substituting a real published book for research papers or normal projects can bring a spark to a lot of curriculums. In fact, the only major downside that often persists is the money aspect, but there are ways around that. You could have students write books in teams where the cost is dispersed among all the members, you could get money from department budgets, you could recruit community or business partners to help pay for it, or you could actually sell the books to other schools, organizations, or even on Amazon.com (and this is what High Tech High does).

So think about publishing again. You will be happy you did!

Google It

Do something for a second. Try to name something that you couldn't find results for on Google. Turtles playing Frisbee? They have T-shirts, doctored photos, and greeting cards. Can people eat grass? There is a whole message board debating the merits and stories of people from poverty-stricken regions baking bread from grass. When it comes to googling for information, the question isn't whether you will find information on a certain subject; that's a given, and nearly every topic will have thousands of entries. Instead, the question is whether the information you find will be useful or not.

This profusion of information on every topic imaginable means that googling for ideas and activities when creating your lessons is generally a good idea. And even though many of the posts you find will be worthless, there are also some very useful ideas, websites, information, and activities to be found for nearly every subject. I've found everything from engaging online quizzes about fragments and run-on sentences to a random generator that insults you with a new insult from a Shakespeare play every time you tap the "Insult me" button. Online gems like these are not only wonderful for filling gaps and adding a bit of extra spice, they also make you appear to be technical when all the knowledge it takes is knowing how to search Google and set up a projector.

Personal Communication

It is easy to take the communication age for granted. If you are a young teacher, you probably don't remember much about what life was like before the Internet and cell phones. But if you need a history lesson about it, all you need to do is look in most of our schools. Despite the fact that teachers can use technology to connect their classes to the broader world, few do. Instead, the classes stay the same as they have always been, where the only communication happening is in person between the teacher and the students (and the occasional students texting with a friend under their desk).

There are a lot of technological ways you can get new voices into your classroom beyond yours and your students'.

E-mail

Professionals are almost always willing to take some time out of their day to talk with students. It is great marketing and makes them feel good about themselves. So whether you teach science or civics, try to start an e-mail exchange with someone in your field. Maybe you could e-mail workers at NASA's jet propulsion laboratory, a local politician, or a working journalist. The odds are you won't have to send out too many e-mails before you get a bite.

Skype

Even a few years ago video chatting seemed completely futuristic, but thanks to Skype it is outlandishly easy. All you have to do is buy a cheap camera (which you can often charge to the school), sign up, and create a user name. That's it. Then when you e-mail professionals you can ask if they have Skype, and if they do you've laid the foundation for a video conversation. Also, shoot for the moon when you pick someone to talk to. There are strong reasons for why everyone from successful authors to high-up politicians would want to take a couple of minutes out of their day to speak to a school class.

Blogs

Later this chapter will discuss students' having their own blogs, but there is also a lot students can gain from reading carefully screened blogs of others. If you are a civics teacher, you could have students look at respectful blogs from across the political spectrum, and if you are a music teacher, there are number of very interesting music blogs. When it comes to blogs, almost everything exists, and with just a little searching you may find something appropriate for your class.

How to . . .

Three of the most common suggestions for increasing technology in the classroom are to use PowerPoint, set up a teacher website, and have the students write in blogs or wikis. And though the incorporation of these three suggestions can certainly add a lot to class, their effectiveness can only be maximized if they are used right. To make sure you are getting the most out of these basic classroom technologies, here are some guidelines to help you along.

Give a PowerPoint Presentation

PowerPoint is probably the most widely used and most widely misused technology. Almost every teacher uses a PowerPoint at some point, yet few use it right. The major PowerPoint problem is that a lot of teachers tend to put up their PowerPoint and read off it like a teleprompter. They turn their back on the students or hunch over a computer and read the words straight off the screen. When teachers do this, they ironically often end up with presentations that are halting, uninteresting, and considerably less dynamic than if they'd just delivered them without the "aid" of the PowerPoint.

To use PowerPoint right, use it as a reference or supplement, not as a focal point. This means you can refer to it, but should never read from it. A perfect PowerPoint presentation will generally have the core information on the screen, and instead of reading off the information you explain and elaborate on it. It is also very important that you only take momentary glances at the screen or computer. To have full effect as a speaker you need to make sure you are connecting with your audience, not with the screen at the front of the room.

Remembering your audience is only the first step toward truly great PowerPoint presentations, though. Here are some other little things you can do to boost your PowerPoints:

- Keep the amount of information per slide minimal. This makes it easier for the students to process and for you to stay organized. To ensure this, never drop your font to anything smaller than eighteen point.

- Don't turn the lights out all the way. The second all the lights go down, half the eyes in the room will shut as if by magic.

- You can download all sorts of additional slide designs for free online.

- Utilize the PowerPoint functions. Check out the template features (especially on PowerPoint 2007 and above), use the animation features to make a point or catch attention, or even embed pictures or audio clips. These seemingly frivolous features can be invaluable for helping to grab or retain student attention, and they just generally make it more fun.

Set Up a Website

These days it seems like most schools require their teachers to keep up a basic website with homework and announcements. And if your school doesn't require this, it is not a bad idea to do so anyway (to do this set up a Google page or any other variety of free website shell). Websites help make parents happy (through increased communication), allow students who are out sick to stay current, and take any shred of validity from the excuse "I didn't know what the homework was."

In general, websites are wonderful goodwill-creating tools, but there is one thing that can cause them quickly to become a serious source of contention between you and the students, parents, and administrators: not keeping the website updated. The problem with not updating your website is that once you create a website, parents and students begin to rely on it for information. Then if one day the information isn't there, they suddenly won't know if any homework is due. This can lead to some serious freak-outs (and parents don't like freak-outs). A nonupdated site is also a very tangible example of you making a mistake. Though for teachers (and especially new teachers) mistakes are part of the job, few mistakes are as concrete and easy for everyone to see as an out-of-date website. And when you combine an angry parent and an obvious paper trail the result often isn't very good for you.

Use a Blog/Wiki

Blogs and wikis are the bright and shiny newcomers on the education scene, and for those unfamiliar with exactly what they are and where you find them, here is a crash course: Blogs are where students have their own personal page that also generally has an area for posted comments from others. There are infinite hosts (or sites) for blogs, but Blogger is the one that I've found to be the most user-friendly. Wikis are where the class creates a web page that can have information added to it by any member of the class. Like blogs, there are numerous sites that allow you to do this, but the most widely used by educators seem to be PBworks and Wikispaces (which will give you a free spot without any advertising if you let them know you are a teacher).

The major advantage of either of these technologies is that they allow a level of collaboration and interaction that is very difficult to do with paper alone. When everyone puts their thoughts online, suddenly the whole class is open to read and react to each other's thoughts whenever they want. But these advantages aren't guaranteed just because students use a blog or wiki. In many classes with blogs and wikis, even though students can look at the postings of other students, most still don't. For various reasons (with common ones including a lack of interest, effort, or time) these students treat their online sites as a new venue to write in the same old fashion and make no effort at connecting to the ideas of others.

Because of this tendency for students to not take full advantage of all the opportunities provided by wikis and blogs, if you decide to include them in the classroom it is often a good idea to require students to post *and* interact (especially early on). The posting part of this is easy, but getting them to interact is significantly harder. Here are some possible ways to get them to interact:

- Having assignments where students must make comments on the blogs or wikis of others that will be graded on thoughtfulness and connection to the original post

- Framing debates online where two or more sides argue via their blogs

- Assigning group or class wikis where students will receive both personal grades (for their contributions) and group grades (for the overall quality)

Exit Slip

Like many of the saviors of education before it, there are many good reasons for the buzz surrounding technology. But technology (also like most of these saviors) is only one piece of the puzzle. It is a great tool to help take education forward, but it is not the final answer. Just because a teacher uses a PowerPoint or SMART Board does not mean his or her lecture is better than one without. And just because a student writes an answer on a wiki or a blog does not mean he or she learned more from the assignment.

The truth is that what schools need more than a SMART Board in every class is a smart teacher in every class. All of the gadgets and cool software in the world won't help if the teacher doesn't know how to use them. In fact, a lot of technology actually detracts from learning if used improperly or at the wrong time (think about the poorly done PowerPoint lecture). So don't just charge ahead and use technology on every possible occasion. Use it when it makes sense, and make sure to do it right. If you do, everyone will likely see you as a tech wizard.

BECOMING AN ORGANIZATIONAL CHAMPION

I t's time to come clean. Though I constantly badger my students to use their planners, from middle school through college I never had a planner of any type. Part of the reason behind my avoidance of planners was pure obstinacy: everyone said that I should use one, so I didn't. But the main reason was I didn't really feel like I needed one. In general, my system of mentally sorting and filing information worked well enough that planners seemed unnecessary.

When I came to teaching I brought my mental system of organization to the classroom with me. I was aware that the life of a teacher probably meant a lot more to manage in my head, but I figured my brain was up to the challenge. And for a couple of days it was—but then I forgot something. The next day I forgot several more things. Soon it became very clear that my new position in the classroom required me to change more than just my title. Other changes needed to be made, starting with a comprehensive overhaul of my mental system of organization.

Despite my historically strong memory, to this day I constantly forget things at school when I don't write them down. The best reason I can find for this newfound absentmindedness is the fact that a school pulls teachers one hundred different ways at once. On an average day, a teacher may have to juggle student requests for missing work, a parent e-mail that needs a response, a member of the support staff asking for a student assessment, a change in baseball practice time, students asking for help after school, remembering that one period didn't get as far as another, administering student retakes during lunch, and making sure to remember about their advisee's performance of *The Nutcracker* they promised to attend. With so many balls in the air (not to mention the memory space required for remembering lessons) even a top-flight juggler would have trouble catching every one without help. To make sure you don't drop too many of these balls, try the following suggestions for staying organized and bolstering your memory in the frenetic atmosphere of a school.

Establish a Set Time for Doing Routine Tasks

Stupid little details like inputting attendance, keeping their school website current, or updating grades are the types of things most often forgotten by teachers. What makes small tasks like these so forgettable is they are the most mundane and bureaucratic. There is little to no pleasure, interest, or sense of accomplishment that can be derived from putting attendance into the computer, and with such little positive reinforcement present, the brain will often go out of its way to skip over these tasks in favor of more stimulating activities.

Even if inputting attendance or updating the website are not your school-related equivalent of watching paint dry, there will likely be some duties which fit that description. But whether you like them or not, these tasks generally need to get done in a timely manner, and if you are sloppy or negligent with them it can bring a lot of unnecessary trouble for you. There is almost always going to be an administrator, a parent, or even a student who chooses to focus on your minor oversights instead of your many successes, and with these individuals the best defense is to stay consistent with the little details so as not to give them ammunition to use against you.

But how are you supposed to get consistent with tasks that your brain seems determined to overlook? The answer is to take these forgettable and mundane tasks and establish times during the day, week, or month (depending on the tasks) reserved for doing those things that you drag your feet on. For example, you could always update the website on Sunday nights after dinner or put in attendance at 3:00 P.M. every day. Without a set time like this, it is far too easy to continually push these duties back until you have pushed yourself right into trouble. When a time is set, you may dread it when it approaches each week, but you probably won't forget about it.

Do Things the Moment You Think of Them

Here is a scene that unfolds a lot for the average new teacher: You are sitting in your room grading a seemingly never-ending stack of papers. Suddenly a neuron flashes across your brain that reminds you that you agreed to e-mail a student's parent about her most recent paper grade. This sudden thought also causes you to breathe a sigh of relief when you realize how close you came to forgetting such an important task, and you resolve to send an e-mail before the end of the planning period. Then you go back to grading and promptly forget about the e-mail all over again.

This scenario sounds like a joke, but situations just like it lead new teachers into situations that aren't very funny every day. The problem with saying you will do something later as a teacher is that schools have a thousand and one ways to distract from even the most pressing tasks. Sometimes the distraction comes in the form of an e-mail from a department head, an urgent student question, or a sudden realization that copies still need to be made for the next class. Whatever diversions fate sets on your path that day, the only way to ensure you don't get sidetracked is to do any important (or even unimportant) tasks the second they are presented or the second you think of them. If you aren't able to do them right at that moment, create some sort of reminder and do them as soon as possible. For only through taking on tasks as quickly as possible can you stand much of a fighting chance against the general distractions of life that are patiently waiting to lead you astray.

Write It Down

Regardless of how many routines they create or how prompt they are at doing things as they come up, teachers usually still have an exceptionally large amount on their plate at any given time. Because of the sheer quantity and varied nature of the tasks asked of the average teacher, it is essential for teachers to figure out some sort of system to keep everything they need to do organized.

One of the best ways to do this is to constantly carry around a little notebook, planner, or even scrap paper to record all thoughts that shouldn't be forgotten. Though in this age of electronic gadgets the idea of using actual paper may seem slightly primitive, it generally seems to work better than any of the more technologically advanced options. The reason is that though these items are great for organizing, they can be hard to take out in every situation or for every passing thought. On the other hand, it only takes a couple of seconds to scrawl a reminder across a little piece of paper.

Once you've figured out where you will put your list, use it for everything that is even slightly important. When you forget to pick up homework, write it down. When you promise to observe another teacher, write it down. When you think of a way to make a lesson better for the next class, write it down. Whenever you say you will do something, wish you could do something, or know you have to do something, write it down. In the end, there is no better way to avoid absentmindedness than to have a comprehensive list of all important thoughts that you can pull out on a moment's notice.

Storage

A good goal to have as a new teacher is to try to store every single piece of information you can. Every lesson plan, vocabulary quiz, lab report, or good idea you have in your possession is a possible lesson plan, vocabulary quiz, lab report, or good idea that you don't have to create at a later date. So save everything you do, shamelessly steal whatever lesson plans and materials you can from fellow teachers, and constantly keep your eyes peeled everywhere you go for good lesson ideas.

Once you begin gathering materials, make sure to store them in a sensible way. It doesn't matter how good the materials you collect are if you can't find any of them down the line. Here are a couple of suggestions for a simple, yet effective storage system.

Get a File Cabinet and Computer Folder Purely for Lesson Plans and Materials

If you have one place on your computer and one place in your room for all school materials, the odds are much more likely that everything will end up there. So at the beginning of the year make a computer folder labeled "Teaching Year 1" (or whatever year you are in) and designate a drawer in your class for school materials. Then as the year progresses just toss all the materials you've used (whether digital or physical) in the proper folder.

During the school year, it probably isn't worth worrying too much about organizing this folder of materials. The average school day has enough challenges without having to worry about organizing lessons and materials you're not currently using. So once a lesson is over or you collect materials from a colleague, throw them in your folder and move on. (Not worrying about organization at the moment also makes it more likely you will follow through on putting papers in the right folder because it isn't much extra work.) Then at the end of the year, when things have quieted down, you can take a couple of hours to sort and organize the materials for the following year.

Organize Your Digital Materials by Topic, Not by Date or Lesson Number

A lot of teachers organize their lessons by date or number. They label their lessons as "Lesson 2/23" or "Trigonometry Lesson 7," only to find out that when they come back months or years later in the search for lesson ideas such names are essentially useless. Months after the fact, no teacher is going to remember what types of activities are included in their lesson from 12/7/09 or "Lesson 3."

In order to make your titles more useful at later dates try giving your lessons and activities titles that will serve as good reminders in the future. For example, if you have a lesson on 10/24 during the Frankenstein unit that also discusses vocabulary, call it "10.24Frank/VocabLesson." That way a year or ten years from now you won't have to open the file to know what useful things may be hiding in it.

The Best Back-Up Is a Physical Copy of Everything

At the end of the year make physical copies of everything on your computer. Do this even if you have a portable hard drive and you've saved the files on your e-mail. If a material only exists in digital form it always runs the risk of crashing, being corrupted, or disappearing. But a physical file, though certainly more clunky, isn't going anywhere unless the school burns down.

A Few Last Little Memory Tricks

- Keep students regularly updated with grades and they will remind you if you need to make any grade changes.

- If a student does have a grade dispute or points out a grading error, have the student circle it on a grade printout and hand it back to you. Without the grade printout, forgetting to make a little grade change is way too easy. But if there is a sheet cluttering up your desk, it makes forgetting about it that much harder.

- If you read an e-mail that demands a reply but you don't have time to respond at the moment, mark it as unread or as a draft. The bold print of (seemingly) unread e-mails and red writing of drafts scream for attention and act as perfect reminders about important e-mails.

Exit Slip

The unit on tricks ends with organization because staying organized is the undisputed champion of saving time in the classroom. In a place where you have hundreds of students, hundreds of papers to grade, hundreds of minor tasks, hundreds of requests, and infinite possibilities about what is coming next, organization is the only way to ensure your head doesn't implode, even if your memory is normally pretty good. So take some time to get and stay organized and your brain will thank you.

A FINAL WORD

This book provides a lot of suggestions, and following them should put you on the path to becoming a good teacher. But when it comes to becoming a great teacher, unfortunately this book can't be of nearly as much help. This is because no amount of pointers from *any* book can make you a truly great teacher. Instead, greatness is something that you must strive for on your own and in your own way. And though there aren't any clear directions or maps toward greatness, there is one similarity shared by seemingly all great teachers that may help point the way: those who become great generally have a constant and unwavering drive to become better teachers.

This drive to improve is so essential because teaching is like wading through a strong current. As long as you work hard and push forward you will likely gain more and more ground, but as soon as you stop moving and lose that forward momentum it becomes very difficult to hold your ground and not get swept back. The classroom, like a current, never stops moving and evolving. Every moment, every class, and every year brings a new set of challenges, and if you don't move, evolve, and occasionally push against it, even the strongest teachers with the strongest lessons can get left behind.

So treat every lesson not as a final piece that is over once it has been delivered, but as a starting point; search relentlessly for the next good piece of advice (from books, conferences, and colleagues); and look at each period and project as a case study on how to improve your class for the next time. Through consistent reflection on the right and wrong turns of each day, teachers can get better and better and better, with no ceiling in sight. And that is how you wake up one morning and realize that you are great.

ABOUT THE AUTHOR

Matthew Johnson is someone like you. Not too long ago he too exchanged the comfortable world of college for the harsh chore of job searching and the overwhelming task of orchestrating and conducting five classes a day, five days a week.

His experiences, and the lessons learned from them, are fresh and have not been filtered through the sands of time. Not too long ago he felt his heart try to push out of his chest cavity before the first parent-teacher conference. He recently had his first experience with managing a classroom stuffed with teenagers whose bodies were telling them to zone out, blurt out, or act out. Only a couple years back he had to decide for the first time what his grading scale would be; whether a discussion, lecture, or group work would be a better use of class time; and what the details of his bathroom and late policies should be.

During his training and the two short years of his career Matthew has already experienced a variety of schools, taught most of grades 7–12, and striven to be a part of every little corner of school life. Right now he currently works, writes, and surfs (when the swell is right) in California.

He also survived his first year of teaching and is ready to help you survive too.

CPSIA information can be obtained at www.ICGtesting.com
Printed in the USA
BVOW03s1837130916

462008BV00001B/9/P